In loving memory of Sylvia Tappin and Sir John Harvey-Jones

THE NEW SECRETS OF CEOs

200
global chief executives
on leading

Steve Tappin & Andrew Cave

NICHOLAS BREALEY
PUBLISHING

This revised paperback edition first published by
Nicholas Brealey Publishing in 2010

3–5 Spafield Street
Clerkenwell, London
EC1R 4QB, UK
Tel: +44 (0)20 7239 0360
Fax: +44 (0)20 7239 0370

20 Park Plaza, Suite 1115A
Boston
MA 02116, USA
Tel: (888) BREALEY
Fax: (617) 523 3708

www.nicholasbrealey.com
www.theSecretsofCEOs.com

The Secrets of CEOs first published in 2008

Library of Congress Cataloging-in-Publication Data

Tappin, Steve.
  The new secrets of CEOs : 200 global chief executives on leading / Steve
Tappin & Andrew Cave. -- Rev. paperback ed.
    p. cm.
  Includes bibliographical references and index.
  ISBN 978-1-85788-543-9
 1. Chief executive officers. 2. Leadership 3. Executive ability. 4.
Executives. I. Cave, Andrew. II. Title.
  HD38.2.T367 2010
  658.4'092--dc22

                                                                    2010009796

ISBN 978-1-85788-543-9

British Library Cataloguing in Publication Data
A catalogue record for this book is available from the
British Library.

FSC
Mixed Sources
Product group from well-managed
forests and other controlled sources

Cert no. SGS - COC - 2061
www.fsc.org
© 1996 Forest Stewardship Council

Printed in the UK by Clays Ltd
on Forest Stewardship Council certified paper.

CONTENTS

FOREWORD

by Sir Richard Branson

I must admit I'm not a great reader of business books. To be honest, when we started Virgin almost 40 years ago now we totally ignored the established business theories and strategies and struck out determined to do things differently. There weren't any business books where actual CEOs, from a range of different organizations, shared real experiences and lessons learnt with people just starting out. I wish there had been – perhaps I might have saved myself a few headaches along the way!

Let's face it, the world is constantly changing – no big surprise there – but the sheer pace of that change can be staggering, confusing, and downright terrifying at times. Steve and Andy have identified the new facts of life that most businesses are hit by on a daily basis, especially hard globalization, sustainability, and the war for talent. The developments on the internet, particularly when it comes to reaching out to your customers with new and interactive content, fascinate and totally baffle me. I hadn't gotten my head around Web 2.0 when someone in my team told me not to worry about it, that was yesterday and today we're looking at Web 3.0!

Hard globalization is a reality for Virgin. I have always had the dream that Virgin would one day become one of the world's most respected brands. As we expand outside of the UK across America, India, Australia, Asia, and the Middle East, I feel that dream is getting closer to becoming a reality. But hard globalization brings with it very specific challenges and *The New Secrets of CEOs* highlights many of these. All businesses need to be aware of their global footprint.

One of the most impressive developments within businesses today is the belief that to truly become a successful, thriving company (whether that be a firm of 10 or a global organization employing 50,000 people) you have to place corporate responsibility and sustainability at the heart of your business. As recently as ten years ago this was unheard of. Every large business had a charitable foundation, but this was seen very much as a "nice to do" rather than a core strategy within your organization. Customers expect the companies they are purchasing from to act in an ethical, sustainable way. As business leaders it is crucial we repay that trust by going the extra mile to ensure best practice at all times. On a global level, the behavior of people, industries, and enterprises has immediate and often long-term effects on our world. If mankind makes a mistake, it can be catastrophic.

I believe that it is up to companies like Virgin to lead the way with a holistic approach to business. It was this belief that led me a few years ago to pledge Virgin Group's profits from our transportation businesses over the next ten years (approximately $3 billion) to clean energy initiatives. I hope that through the strides forward that our airline and transport companies across the world continue to initiate, trial, and invest in – successes such as our most recent biofuel trails on Virgin Atlantic and Virgin Trains – other airlines and transport businesses will also follow suit. When all businesses put sustainability at the heart of what they do, we will see a radically positive change in the impact we have on our planet. I believe that day is not too far away.

I was heartened to read Part III of this book. For a long time I have been drawn to the Gaia theory, a hypothesis formulated by James Lovelock almost 40 years ago, which states that the Earth is a living entity, like a single cell. This way of thinking can apply to business too. I have never been a fan of command and control and believe that the authors' model of a cell-like organization could be a really powerful way of running a business in the future. I have always believed that one of my strengths has been my ability to trust the people around me 100 percent and to be able to truly delegate responsibility to the managers of our businesses. You cannot expect those who you rely on to run your companies every day to really put their neck out and go that extra mile if you do not give them a sense of ownership. Let them make mistakes, support them through the bad and the good times, and instill in them a sense that your business is their business – and most importantly, mean it.

Your people are everything – without them you don't have a business! This book touches on this very point throughout, whether it is delegation, ensuring you encourage creativity and innovation, or simply letting your hair down with your staff and having some fun. I can hand on heart say I am only one of many entrepreneurs at Virgin. We employ like-minded people who love to innovate and challenge the norm. To quote my good friend Stephen Murphy, "We employ rock climbers, not people who need ladders." At Virgin it is this creativity and the ability to challenge the norm that mark us out from the rest and ensure we continue to grow. Employing the best people who will not only be loyal to your company but are also not afraid to challenge it when things become a bit staid is the best way to ensure you stay ahead of the curve.

At Virgin we not only know how to work hard, we know how to party hard! It was great to see that many of the other CEOs interviewed for this book remind us that working is meant to be fun. We spend most of our lives working: what a shame it would be if you're spending that time doing something you hate. Even when things get a bit rocky you can still learn from it. Had a bad day or week? Take the team out and have some fun. It's amazing how a little downtime gives you a new perspective on what you thought was an insurmountable problem.

Naturally, and more's the pity, it can't all be party, party, party – so check out Chapter 13 on building a career. I agree in the future the best thing is not to be limited by traditional corporate careers but to be clear on what you want from life and get as much varied experience as you can pack in. I still get some of my best and most memorable experiences from setting up and launching new businesses around the world – that's probably why I can't stop doing it! I was glad to see that the authors recommend this as a great way to learn. Read and enjoy...

I'll end as Steve and Andy do, by asking: Why not you?

THANK YOU

To Hugh Lloyd-Jukes, the third member of our fellowship, for his clarity of thought, relentless intellectual challenge, and driving execution, without which this wouldn't be the book it is.

To Thea Dettmann for setting up the original 150 meetings, patiently rescheduling most of them, and at the same time developing the book's graphics.

Thank you to Sarah McDonnell for her enthusiasm, patience, and sheer hard work which keep Xinfu running smoothly while we globalize.

A particular thank you to Dr. Alan Watkins for his critical contribution in helping frame Part III, pushing our thinking on personal leadership, and especially sharing his direct expertise on peak personal performance.

Thank you to Savio Chan and Jessica Tu for sharing their deep knowledge of China and Chinese business and for their introductions to some of the CEOs featured in this edition.

Thank you also to Steve's former colleagues at Heidrick & Struggles for their support and contribution to making this project happen. In particular, to Kevin Kelly, Steve Langton, David Peters, and Bernard Zen-Ruffinen. Also to Michelle Marin Chau, Nele Van Ginneken, Gaston Dolle, Alice Au, Aysegul Aydin, Sheng Lu, Steve Mullinjer, Christine Stimpel, Amy Qian, and Alicia Yi.

Andrew would like to thank Damian Reece, Head of Business, The Daily Telegraph, for his role in setting up the partnership that led to this book. Thanks to Ra Tickel and Martin Strydom for their encouragement and enthusiasm for the project, and to Matthew Bishop, Ed Trissel, Helen Dunne, and Claire Anderson.

We would both like to thank Nick Brealey for his challenge to make the book truly global and his diplomatic guidance. Thank you also to Sally Lansdell for helping us to find "one voice" and for developing and structuring the content without losing the essence of the book.

Thank you to our reviewers for giving so generously of their time to provide such detailed and thought-provoking feedback: Mark Armitage, Richard Baker, James Bilefield, Andrew Kakabadse, Kathleen Klasnic, John Neill, Dwight Poler, Veru Ramduny, Emma Reynolds, Tom Standage, and Frank Tang, and in particular Alan Watkins. Also the hundreds of people we've informally bounced ideas off over the last year or so.

Most of all, thank you to our families – Jo, Lauren, Hannah, and Jessie, and Paula, Roy, Margaret, Wendy, David, and Lisa – for their love and understanding.

Steve Tappin & Andrew Cave
London, March 2010

THE CEOs

Thank you to all the CEOs who gave up so many hours of their precious time to this project – and to their miracle-working assistants who managed to match our diaries.

Adams, Paul, CEO, British American Tobacco
Ambani, Mukesh, chairman, Reliance Industries
Amelio, Bill, president & CEO, Lenovo
Armitage, Mark, president US, The CarbonNeutral Company
Arora, Nikesh, president of global sales operations and business development, Google
Bailey, Sly, CEO, Trinity Mirror
Bajaj, Rahul, chairman, Bajaj Auto
Baker, Richard, chairman, Virgin Active
Banga, Vindi, president, foods, home and personal care, Unilever
Barry, Mike, head of corporate social responsibility, Marks & Spencer
Basing, Nick, former CEO, Paramount Restaurants
Beccalli-Falco, Ferdinando, CEO, GE International
Beeston, Kevin, former chairman, Serco
Bell, Chris, former CEO, Ladbrokes
Bell, Sir David, chairman, Financial Times
Berrien, James, president and publisher, Forbes Magazine Group
Bilefield, James, president, Condé Nast Digital International
Bing, Xiang, dean, Cheung Kong Graduate School of Business
Bolland, Marc, CEO, Marks & Spencer
Bond, Andy, CEO, Asda
Bond, Sir John, chairman, Vodafone
Breedon, Tim, CEO, Legal & General
Brikho, Samir, CEO, AMEC
Broughton, Martin, chairman, British Airways
Brown, Frank, dean, INSEAD
Browne, John, Baron Browne of Madingley, former CEO, BP, managing partner, Riverstone Holdings
Butler-Wheelhouse, Keith, former CEO, Smiths Group
Carayol, René, leadership expert
Carr, Neil, vice-president, Rohm & Haas
Carr, Roger, chairman, Centrica
Carroll, Cynthia, CEO, Anglo American
Carson, Neil, CEO, Johnson Matthey

Castell, Sir Bill, chairman, The Wellcome Trust
Chambers, John, chairman and CEO, Cisco Systems
Cheung, Stanley, managing director, Walt Disney China
Chuanzhi, Liu, chairman, Legend Holdings
Clare, Mark, CEO, Barratt Developments
Clarke, Tim, former CEO, Mitchells & Butlers
Clifford, Leigh, former CEO, Rio Tinto
Conde, Cris, CEO, Sungard
Connolly, John, global managing director, Deloitte Touche Tohmatsu
Coull, Ian, CEO, Segro
Cox, Phil, CEO, International Power
Crawshaw, Steven, former CEO, Bradford & Bingley
Crombie, Sandy, former CEO, Standard Life
Daniels, Eric, CEO, Lloyds Banking Group
Davies, Lord, UK Trade Minister
Davies, Sian, CEO, Henley Centre
Davis, Sir Crispin, former CEO, Reed Elsevier
Davis, Gareth, former CEO, Imperial Tobacco
Davis, Mick, CEO, Xstrata
Davis, Tony, president and CEO, Tiger Airways
Delay, Tom, CEO, Carbon Trust
Dell, Michael, chairman and CEO, Dell Computer
Diamond, Bob, president and chief executive of corporate and investment banking
    and wealth management, Barclays
DiPietro, Kenneth, senior vice-president, human resources, Lenovo
Dobson, Michael, CEO, Schroders
Drechsler, Paul, Chairman & CEO, Wates Group
Duddy, Terry, CEO, Home Retail Group
Dyke, Greg, former director-general, BBC
Dyson, Sir James, founder, Dyson
Elfrink, Wim, chief globalization officer, Cisco Systems
Emmens, Matt, CEO, Shire Pharmaceuticals
Evans, Chris, founder, Merlin Biosciences
Fahour, Ahmed, CEO, Australia Post
Fairhead, Rona, CEO, Financial Times
Fake, Caterina, co-founder, Flickr
Fawcett, Adrian, CEO, General Healthcare Group
Ferguson, Iain, former CEO, Tate & Lyle
Flynn, Doug, former CEO, Rentokil Initial
Fontenla-Novoa, Manny, chief executive, Thomas Cook
Forbes, Steve, CEO, Forbes
Fox, Simon, CEO, HMV Group
France, Brian, CEO, NASCAR
Frangos, Jean-Marc, senior vice-president of technology and innovation, BT Group
Froggatt, Tony, former CEO, Scottish & Newcastle
Gammell, Sir Bill, CEO, Cairn Energy

Garber, Mitch, former CEO, PartyGaming

Gardner, Sir Roy, chairman, Compass Group

Giampaolo, David, CEO, Pi Capital

Glocer, Tom, CEO, Thomson Reuters

Godrej, Adi, chairman, Godrej Group

Gooding, Val, former CEO, BUPA

Green, Harriet, CEO, Premier Farnell

Green, Philip, CEO, United Utilities

Halusa, Martin, CEO, Apax Partners

Harrison, Andy, incoming CEO, Whitbread, former CEO, easyJet

Harrison, Bob, CEO, Clinton Global Initiative

Hartman, Richard, CEO, Millennium & Copthorne Hotels

Haste, Andy, CEO, RSA (formerly Royal & Sun Alliance)

Havner, Ron, vice-chairman, CEO and president, Public Storage

Hennessy, Murray, former CEO, Avis Europe

Heseltine, Lord, chairman, Haymarket Media Group

Hester, Stephen, CEO, Royal Bank of Scotland

Hoberman, Brent, co-founder, Lastminute.com

Hogarth, Peter, founder, The Change Partnership

Holliday, Steve, CEO, National Grid

Hornby, Andy, CEO, Alliance Boots

Hornsby, Chip, former CEO, Wolseley

Hotard, Edgar, chairman, Monitor Group (China)

Howard, Stephen, CEO, Business in the Community

Hsu, Jacob, CEO, Symbio

Iyar, Subrah, CEO, WebEx

Jackson, Michael, former chairman, PartyGaming

Jiangnan, Liu, CEO, Alcatel-Lucent China

Jianzhou, Wang, chairman and CEO, China Mobile

Jiren, Liu, chairman and CEO, Neusoft

Johnson, Peter, former chairman and CEO, Inchcape

Judge, Barbara, chairman, UK Atomic Energy Authority

Jung, Andrea, CEO, Avon Products

Kakabadse, Andrew, professor of international management development, Cranfield University, School of Management

Kamath, KV, chairman, ICICI Bank

Kelly, Kevin, CEO, Heidrick & Struggles

Kemp, Harriet, former vice-president human resources excellence, ICI

Kent, Muhtar, president and CEO, The Coca-Cola Company

King, Martina, former managing director of country operations for Europe, Yahoo!

Laidlaw, Sam, CEO, Centrica

Laphen, Mike, CEO, Computer Sciences Corporation

Larcombe, Brian, former CEO, 3i

Leahy, Sir Terry, CEO, Tesco

Leighton, Allan, former chairman, Royal Mail

Leoni-Sceti, Elio, former CEO, EMI Music

Levene, Lord, chairman, Lloyd's

Levy, Gigi, CEO, 888 Holdings

Ma, Jack, CEO, Alibaba Group

Makin, Louise, CEO, BTG

Mallya, Vijay, chairman, Kingfisher Airlines and United Breweries

Manduca, Paul, senior independent director, Morrisons

Manwaring, Tony, CEO, Tomorrow's Company

Mayfield, Charlie, chairman, John Lewis Partnership

Mazumdar-Shaw, Kiran, chairman and managing director, Biocon

McCaig, Ian, CEO, Lastminute.com

McCall, Carolyn, CEO, Guardian Media Group, incoming CEO, easyJet

McDonald, Bob, CEO, Procter & Gamble

McGregor-Smith, Ruby, CEO, MITIE

Middleton, Julia, CEO, Common Purpose

Mills, Brad, former CEO, Lonmin

Minhong, Yu, chairman, New Oriental Education and Technology Group

Moore, Philip, former CEO, Friends Provident

Moraitis, Thras, head of group strategy and corporate affairs, Xstrata

Mordashov, Alexey, CEO, Severstal

Morton, Bruce, co-founder, Ask Gen Y and e3 unlimited

Moulton, Jon, founder, Better Capital

Murdoch, James, chairman and CEO, Europe and Asia, News Corporation

Murphy, Gerry, former CEO, Kingfisher

Murphy, Stephen, CEO, Virgin Group

Murray, Alan, former CEO, Hanson

Murthy, Narayana, chairman and chief mentor, Infosys

Nadar, Shiv, founder, HCL; chairman and chief strategy officer, HCL Technologies

Neill, John, CEO, Unipart Group

Nilekani, Nandan, co-chairman, Infosys Technologies

Norman, Archie, chairman, ITV

O'Donnell, Sir Christopher, former CEO, Smith & Nephew

Parker, Alan, outgoing CEO, Whitbread

Parker, Sir John, chairman, National Grid and Anglo American

Parker, Mark, CEO, Nike USA

Parekh, Deepak, chairman, HDFC

Patel, Ketan, founder partner, Greater Pacific Capital

Philipps, Charles, CEO, Amlin

Pindar, Paul, CEO, Capita

Pluthero, John, executive chairman of Europe, Asia and US and international, Cable & Wireless

Poler, Dwight, managing director, Bain Capital Europe

Polman, Paul, CEO, Unilever

Powell, Ian, chairman and senior partner, PricewaterhouseCoopers

Premji, Azim, chairman and CEO, Wipro

Pym, Richard, chairman, Halfords, Bradford & Bingley and Northern Rock (Asset Management)

Quintana, Bob, president and founder, RLQ Consulting Group
Rake, Sir Michael, chairman, BT and easyJet
Reece, Damian, head of business, Daily Telegraph
Reynolds, Emma, co-founder, Ask Gen Y and e3 unlimited
Richards, John, former CEO, Hammerson
Robbins, Anthony, CEO, Anthony Robbins Companies
Robert, Don, CEO, Experian
Roberts, John, chairman, Royal Bank of Canada: Europe
Robertson, Kate, UK group chairman, Euro RSCG Worldwide
Robinson, Sir Gerry, former CEO, Granada
Roney, Mike, CEO, Bunzl
Rose, Sir Stuart, chairman, Marks & Spencer
Rosedale, Philip, founder and chairman, Linden Lab
Rosenfeld, Irene, chairman and CEO, Kraft Foods
Rosling, Alan, executive director, Tata Sons
Rudd, Sir Nigel, chairman, BAA Group and Invensys
Ruimin, Zhang, chairman and CEO, Haier Group
Salem, Enrique, chief executive, Symantec
Salway, Francis, CEO, Land Securities
Sandler, Ron, chairman, Northern Rock and Phoenix Group Holdings
Satwalekar, Deepak, lead independent director, Infosys; CEO, HDFC Standard Life
Scheifele, Bernd, chairman, Heidelberg Cement
Schoenmaker, Theo, head of sustainability, Philips
Secher, Jan, CEO, Clariant
Shareef, Juhi, founder, Juhi Shareef & Associates
Sharman, Lord, chairman, Aviva
Shaw, Russ, director of innovation, Telefonica
Shivkumar, D, CEO, Nokia India
Shu, Qi, former senior vice-president, Hewlett-Packard, China
Sinclair, Charles, chairman, Associated British Foods
Singh, Kanwalinder, India and South Asia president, Qualcomm
Siwei, Cheng, former vice-chairman, Standing Committee of the National People's
     Congress
Smith, Angela, group people director, Virgin Management
Sorrell, Sir Martin, CEO, WPP
Spencer, Michael, CEO, ICAP
Standage, Tom, business editor, The Economist
Stitzer, Todd, CEO, Cadbury
Story, Ed, CEO, SOCO International
Studzinski, John, global head, Blackstone Advisory Partners
Sutcliffe, Jim, former CEO, Old Mutual
Svensson, Krister, founder, CMi
Tan Pheng Hock, CEO, Singapore Technologies Engineering
Tang, Frank, founder, Fountainvest
Taylor, Stephen, former CEO, BizzEnergy
Thompson, Dorothy, CEO, Drax

INTRODUCTION

The previous edition of this book was published in September 2008. It was the first time more than 150 top chief executives from across the western world and the emerging eastern super-powers, with over 1,000 years of CEO experience between them, explained in their own words:

❑ What it's really like to be a CEO – and the health warning that should come with the job.
❑ The secret to dealing successfully with the five hard facts of life that will be critical to business success in the coming decade.
❑ What motivates and drives some of the world's top CEOs and how they really lead their businesses in practice.
❑ How businesses and leaders need to evolve to win.
❑ The leadership experiences required to succeed in the new world of work.

This latest, updated edition includes more than two dozen new interviews with leading global CEOs on the specific and crucial topic of how both western and eastern business leaders should respond to the "reset" economy following the global financial crisis. It provides advice to chief executives on how to be better business leaders, as well as offering practical guidance for today's young and aspiring managers.

Our research

As well as several years of research, this book builds on more than 30 years of working as a personal confidant of some of the top

CEOs in the world on the CEO agenda, including business and personal leadership in Steve's case, and as a financial journalist specializing in profiling and interviewing the world's leading business executives in Andrew's.

We have interviewed CEOs who lead more than 200 companies with total revenues of well over $1.8 trillion – about the same as the economy of Italy. Their businesses range across the globe. In Europe they incorporate two-thirds of the FTSE100 index, including leading businesses such as Tesco, BT Group, and WPP Group. They include new corporate champions of India such as Tata, ICICI Bank, and Infosys; leading Chinese and Russian companies like Haier, Alibaba, and Severstal; and US corporate giants such as Google, Cisco Systems, General Electric, Dell, and News Corporation. Altogether they span a broad cross-section of corporate life, from industrial groups like BP, Xstrata, and BAE Systems to virtual worlds like Second Life.

WHAT DID WE FIND?

First, we need to issue a warning.

Being a CEO should be one of the best jobs in the world. It offers the chance to make a real difference. However, real life for most CEOs is tough and many are not enjoying it. Rather like Frodo Baggins in *The Lord of the Rings*, while they are heavily burdened by the responsibility and ultimate accountability of their role, they cling to their position and can't bring themselves to stop – something that the global financial crisis of 2007–09 brought sharply into focus. So where have our CEOs come from, what drives them, and how do they operate? We uncover the real lives of CEOs in Chapter 1.

The rest of the book is in three parts.

PART I: FACING UP TO THE FACTS OF LIFE

In this section, we assess how western and eastern leaders alike should address rapidly changing realities that are fundamental to understanding how to win as a CEO. We start with the world economic "reset" resulting from the global financial crisis and recession. While the term is widely used to reflect the changed global economy, CEOs are divided on what it truly means and how far-reaching the consequences will be. Chapter 2, Winning in the Reset, provides some answers.

Beyond the aftermath of the crisis, life for CEOs was already set to become much, much tougher, thanks to five important business realities that companies will encounter in the coming years. We unpack the following transformational changes in Chapter 3.

Profiting from "hard globalization"

Top CEOs believe that we are entering a period of fundamental change on a scale not seen for several hundred years. The world has moved beyond the two-way flow of western organizations heading east and top eastern companies entering western home markets. These opposing competitive flows are merging into a turbulent storm of full global competition for the first time: the start of what we call hard globalization. We share top leaders' views on the mindset, strategy, and tactics required to make the shift from a domestically focused international business to an integrated global company.

Decoding sustainability

The need to operate businesses in a sustainable fashion is now given at least lip service by most global companies, but there are broad disagreements on exactly what that means. Our interviews found that most business leaders remain confused, largely because the definition of sustainability continues to change. There is more to sustainability than being green and ethical, and social considerations are being taken much more seriously by an increasing number of leaders who believe that doing the "right thing" is also great business in the long term. We take you through what the best CEOs are doing and how to strike a balance between running a successful business and saving the planet, both environmentally and socially.

Surfing the third wave of the web

Most CEOs confess to not having a strong handle on the latest developments in technology – a major concern, given that the web and related technologies will be the preeminent platform for connecting the world in the next decade. Chief executives will have to ensure that their organization can properly exist in and navigate between real and virtual worlds, but most companies are not moving fast enough to profit from the social networking revolution of Web 2.0 and have not adopted an interactive way of doing business. To help, we uncover the secrets of leading web CEOs.

Riding the cycles of capitalism

The recession that followed the effective closure of western capital markets as a result of the US subprime mortgage crisis that infected the wider debt markets in 2007 is reckoned to be the biggest in the history of modern capitalism. Yet capitalism, as Karl Marx observed, is beset by regular cyclical crises. Even though the world economy has been reset, navigating severe downturns, as well as making the most of market booms, will remain a key skill for top executives. A great challenge is managing capital through such cycles, and our CEOs share their strategies.

Waging the first world war for talent

Alongside the battle for the customer, CEOs say that the most important battleground for competing global companies is that for talent. This decade will see the first world war for the globe's top 1 percent of talent. The key drivers are poor demographics in the West, shortages of skilled workers in the East, and the lack of global leaders. Chief executives claim to make recruiting and promoting exceptional talent a top priority, but many give it insufficient focus or time. The global reset has helped many CEOs recognize the important of talent in first surviving and then winning, and we expect many others to rethink this issue fundamentally. Chief executives will have to be much more heavily involved in development and new breeds of human resource professionals and external search partners will need to step up to the task.

Part II: Leading at the top today

Part I gives you the latest insights from CEOs into the critical trends shaping the world. In Part II it's time to understand the common secrets for success: What have the best CEOs learnt about how to lead?

During our research we identified the most highly regarded CEOs by talking to their peers and observers of their businesses and by conducting our own research into their performance. We thus identified the top quartile of CEOs running international businesses. When we studied this group, we found that there were five main leadership approaches that remained consistent among top CEOs in Europe, America, and Asia alike:

❑ **Commercial executors** have a driving focus on achieving the best results in their industry, combined with a relentless attention to detail in order to ensure that operational and strategic ambitions become a reality. Tesco chief executive Sir Terry Leahy is a prime example as a leading international retailer, while in the US the model is epitomized by Andrea Jung, CEO of Avon Products. We hear their philosophy at first hand in Chapter 4.

❑ **Financial value drivers** aggressively pursue shareholder value. They understand the metrics of their industry and are often highly skilled at identifying value-enhancing corporate transactions or realizing value from portfolio disposals. Mick Davis has led the creation and rapid growth of miner Xstrata, masterminding a set of acquisitions that have transformed it from a small collection of coal and mineral assets into one of the top ten UK companies by stock market capitalization. He is profiled in Chapter 5 alongside Irene Rosenfeld, chairman and CEO of Kraft Foods and another noted financial value driver.

❑ **Corporate entrepreneurs** have something to prove. They disrupt industries because they believe in a better way of doing things.

They excel at spotting breakthrough opportunities and making them reality; their vision for their companies is their life vision. In Chapter 6 we profile two of the best of the breed: Sir Martin Sorrell, chief executive of advertising group WPP, and Michael Spencer, CEO of money-broking giant ICAP.

❑ **Corporate ambassadors** have a worldwide vision that has a broader societal impact. This involves operating at a geopolitical level and delivering transactions that transform industries. Chapter 7 profiles Lord Browne, the former CEO of BP who is now forging a new career in private equity, and Sir John Parker, chairman of Anglo American and National Grid.

❑ Finally, **global missionaries** are on a personal mission to make a significant difference and a corporate mission to make their companies great. They are typically customer champions and they lead by inspiring people and energizing them to tap into their potential. Our examples in Chapter 8 are John Chambers, the evangelical chairman and CEO of Cisco Systems, and Zhang Ruimin, chief executive of Chinese conglomerate Haier.

We take you through each of the five types and profile the examples, detailing their upbringing, what motivates them, and how they really lead their businesses. We set the profiled leader in context with comments from other CEOs of their type and show how they typically measure success, the situations and industries in which they generally perform best, and their relative strengths and weaknesses.

This part of the book should help you understand how you lead and where the gaps and shortfalls may be in your own leadership approach, as well as which industries and situations are most appropriate for your skill set.

PART III: LEADING INTO THE FUTURE

Part III sets out how CEOs will lead in the future, taking account of the new facts of life from Part I and drawing on the experience and insight of the chief executives profiled in Part II.

Top CEOs believe that the current leadership model of many traditional western "command-and-control" businesses is destined to fail because the challenges we describe in Part I will be too overwhelming for the structure to survive. Our research found that top chief executives believe that they must organize their businesses more organically. In the next decade many successful companies will replace command and control with more fluid and fast-moving, cell-like organizations.

We describe how a chief executive provides business leadership at the nucleus of the cell by giving greater freedom to act to much more decentralized operations, while still policing performance. Our interviews found that most CEOs are better business leaders than personal leaders – they are generally comfortable with strategy and formulating operational plans, but are rarely good at lifting an organization, injecting pace or fresh energy. So in Chapter 9 we give examples of the new leadership qualities required to maintain the faster-moving, more entrepreneurial, and energetic businesses of the future.

Individual CEOs will not have all the answers and skills; even if they did, they would not have the personal bandwidth to follow up on every action required. Top chief executives will require a small team of confidants (between three and five people) at the center of the business. These extremely talented global players will have the skills and the appetite and values to sustain a world-class company. We give some guidance on how to pull together this new fellowship of the CEO and how to get it to work in practice.

What if you're not yet a leader but are determined to be one? In Chapter 10 today's rising stars advise you on the apprenticeship you'll need to follow to become a leader for tomorrow.

Finally, the last chapter revisits our CEO health warning. Chief executives offer specific advice on how to have a winning career and a successful life. We show how developments in the fields of elite sports, personal performance, and neuroscience can be applied to help leaders be and remain at their best.

THESECRETSOFCEOS.COM

We have set up www.theSecretsofCEOs.com, a website that reveals further secrets via CEO video interviews, webcasts, blogs, and community forums to help you continue your development as a leader. You'll also have an opportunity to register and join our community of tomorrow's leaders.

But first let's find out what it's really like to be a CEO.

1

THE REAL LIVES OF CEOs

Life at the top isn't all it's made out to be. That was one of the findings from our interviews with leaders of top global companies in the initial edition of this book, and since then the global financial crisis of 2007–09 has brought it even more sharply into focus. As business was elevated from the financial sections of the newspapers to front-page headlines, CEOs were thrust into the spotlight and put under unprecedented scrutiny.

For some leaders, such as former Royal Bank of Scotland chief executive Sir Fred Goodwin, former Northern Rock CEO Adam Applegarth, former Lloyds TSB chairman Sir Victor Blank, and former Lehman Brothers CEO Richard Fuld, the events of the crisis dealt reputational blows from which it will be difficult to recover.

Others outlasted that pressure period, but will find the going even tougher from now on as they remain under microscopic attention in economic conditions from which it will be tricky to extract growth. Many CEOs will not survive and, indeed, we predict a cull of a large number who can be classified more accurately as professional managers than genuine leaders.

Before we outline how CEOs need to develop to overcome the new and changing challenges they're facing, it's important to spend a while understanding something about the backgrounds they emerged from and what their lives are really like.

One might expect our corporate leaders to be people with naturally excellent personal qualities and carefully cultivated life and business experiences. However, in reality many of this decade's top CEOs have actually had to overcome hardship in their background and upbringing. While this has inspired them to achieve great things, in many cases they confided to us that the drive to do something significant has cost them in other areas and they have found it hard to enjoy life outside their career.

A number of CEOs lost a parent or sibling at an early age. The mother of former BP chairman Lord Browne survived Auschwitz during the Second World War, while the mother of Marks & Spencer chairman Sir Stuart Rose committed suicide when he was 26. The brother of WPP chief executive Sir Martin Sorrell died at birth.

Some CEOs have emerged from considerable poverty, most notably the charismatic Manny Fontenla-Novoa, chief executive of FTSE100 travel group Thomas Cook. A Spaniard from Galicia, at the age of 11 he arrived in the UK with his parents and four siblings after his father's hardware shop got into serious trouble. They were penniless and he was unable to understand a word of English. "We came over on the proverbial banana boat from La Coruña to Southampton. I was terribly seasick," he recalls. "It was a really sad time for my parents, really traumatic, and we all had several jobs. My father worked as a waiter and car park attendant, while my first job was at 12 in a food shop."

Fontenla-Novoa went to a London secondary modern school where he had a language to learn, new friends to make, and great teasing to suffer because his forenames were Jesus Manuel – something he remedied by switching to Manny. He had been in the top 1 percent of pupils in Spain and was about to enter a top school, but was placed in the lowest-streamed classes in London because he couldn't speak English. "I went from doing complex algorithms to being with people who just about knew how to add up or multiply," he says. "It was a bit of a backward step, but to be able to work when you're 12 and give your first pay packet to help your mum, that's a great thing." Remarkably, after joining Thomas Cook's printing department when he was 18, he worked his way up to the top job.

Another successful émigré is Enrique Salem, chief executive of Symantec, the US group best known for its Norton antivirus software. He is the only Colombian national running a Fortune 500 company. "You've just got to go for it," he says. "It's about being fearless. If you are always saying that bad things can happen, you're never going to take on anything meaningful or you're not

going to take any risks, and you just can't be that way. I had a lot
of energy growing up. We came to this country from Colombia
when I was four. It was risky. My parents left
their families behind. My dad took a new job   *Be willing to take some risks,*
in a foreign country. Who knew if it would   *take some chances*
work or not? For me one of the most impor-
tant things that I try to do is be willing to take some risks, take
some chances."

There are other rags-to-riches tales, especially in the fast-
developing economies of India and China. Infosys chairman
Narayana Murthy, for example, decided to do something significant and entrepreneurial with his life when, while hitchhiking
around Europe as a young man, he was mistakenly arrested and
thrown into a tiny cell in Bulgaria with no food or water for 72
hours. The company he later founded is now a multibillion-dollar
enterprise.

A different example of social mobility among CEOs is the rise to
Tesco chief executive of Sir Terry Leahy, the son of a caretaker who
grew up in a prefabricated house on a Liverpool council estate.

In a number of ways, therefore, some inspirational CEOs have
channeled their energies into making a difference after a degree of
trauma or adversity. But what do they actually do on a daily basis?

WHAT ARE THEIR LIVES REALLY LIKE?

The chief executives leading our biggest companies are still largely
twentieth-century leaders. About 60 percent of them can be more
accurately classed as professional managers than leaders. They're
running organizations with tens or hundreds of thousands of
employees all over the world, but have become overburdened with
processes, red tape, and day-to-day minutiae.

Today's chief executives are wrestling with their professional
lives. They don't have long to prove themselves to impatient stakeholders, and this task is made all the harder by huge confusion
about who they are actually running their companies for and what
to focus on most.

Our chief executives are grappling with leadership. About 50 percent admit that they find the job intensely lonely and don't know who to turn to for advice. A common response from those we interviewed was: "I can't talk to the chairman because in the end he's the one who is going to fire me. I can't talk to my finance director because ultimately I'm going to fire him, and I can't tell my wife because I never see her and when I do, that's the last thing she'll want to talk about."

Many top chief executives also find it difficult to have time for a fulfilling personal life. They spend years getting to the top and then give up virtually all their personal time to doing the job before they're either ousted with a payoff or, with luck, retire on a generous pension.

WHO ARE THEY DOING IT FOR?

One might think that it's clear enough who chief executives run their organizations for. After all, companies are owned by shareholders, who put up the capital for them to grow, whether organically or by acquisition. It is shareholders who can vote down a CEO's remuneration, as happened with GlaxoSmithKline chief executive Jean-Pierre Garnier. They can also, of course, liaise with the chairman and the senior independent director to force the CEO out.

However, our research found a surprising division of opinion on the issue of who the most important stakeholders of a public company really are. Some 38 percent of the CEOs we interviewed say that shareholders are their most important stakeholders, but 24 percent say that customers are more important, and 13 percent value their staff above all others. The remaining 25 percent see all stakeholders as ranked equally.

Gareth Davis, former chief executive of
Everything revolves around the Imperial Tobacco, is typical of the shareholder
shareholder lobby. "Everything revolves around the shareholder," he says. "We live for the shareholder." Another chief executive is even more voluble: "The most

important stakeholder has to be the shareholder, Everyone says businesses have to do something in philanthropy to solve the world's problems, but it is not our money. It belongs to the shareholders."

Mike Roney, chief executive of plastics group Bunzl, shares this view: "Certainly in the UK and the US, you have to say that the shareholder is the leading stakeholder. Without that, you are not in business." Clearly, chief executives need to take account of their shareholders. After all, not many survive for long if they ignore them.

However, some chief executives believe with equal conviction that other stakeholders are more important. In part this reflects the management style of particular CEOs, but it also depends on the industry in which they operate. Retail and banking chief executives, for example, are almost unanimous in saying that they put customers above even shareholders. Lord Davies, UK Trade Minister and former chairman of international banking group Standard Chartered, explains: "You have got to keep your customers. You have got to think about them and be very customer-centric. The reason why chief executives become chairman at so many banks is because of the importance of continuity in the relationships with customers. A non-executive cannot provide those sorts of important relationships with customers, governments, and regulators."

Peter Johnson, former chairman of international motor distribution group Inchcape, adds: "Ultimately the most important people are customers because if they don't like what you're doing, you have nothing." James Bilefield, former director at Skype and now president of Condé Nast Digital International, is another executive who is clear that customers have to come first. As he says, "It starts and ends with the customer, it has to be the customer. It's the customer, stupid. Technically and legally, you have to put the shareholders first, but to deliver for them you have to put delighting customers at the core of all that you do."

Then there are chief executives who say that they run their companies for their staff, before shareholders and customers. Such

CEOs tend to be in multinational industrial or commodity-based businesses. For example Alan Murray, former chief executive of building materials group Hanson, says, "Employees are very important. We have 1,800 sites worldwide. We cannot supervise all the people all the time, so we need people to understand the culture and what they can do and cannot do. We have to make sure that everyone understands the message and that everyone understands the message in the same way." Brad Mills, former chief executive of mining group Lonmin, also selects employees as his most important stakeholder, as does Chip Hornsby, former chief executive of international plumbers' merchants Wolseley.

The most sensible approach for an aspiring chief executive, however, is probably to try to embrace all three major stakeholder groups. Sandy Crombie, former chief executive of life insurance group Standard Life, believes that looking after the needs of shareholders, customers, and staff should be an "unbreakable circle" that helps each reinforce the other. Eric Daniels, chief executive of Lloyds Banking Group, agrees: "Ultimately if you neglect any of your stakeholders you will have a problem. If you are about building a long-term customer franchise, you cannot do it without your employees, your regulator, and your shareholders giving you the luxury of the time to do it in."

Andy Harrison, former chief executive of budget airline easyJet, is perhaps the most succinct at summing this up. "If you're not focused on your customers, nothing works," he says. "If you're not focused on your people it becomes very tough, and if you don't look after your shareholders that's very tough as well. You have to strike a balance. Choosing one is unsustainable."

BEING THE BOSS IS TOUGH

To be the final decision maker in a multibillion-dollar business with hundreds of thousands of employees and pensioners relying on you is an awesome responsibility. The stresses placed on CEOs almost require them to be superhuman and they are not always that well prepared for the role. As Graham Wallace, former Cable &

Wireless chief executive, says, "Often CEOs have excelled in a very different job and the skills that have made them successful are not necessarily the ones that will make them successful as a major company chief executive."

Many CEOs have particular weaknesses that they need help to address. Some find it difficult suddenly to be in charge of people who were previously their peers. Others consider that their position prevents them from forming close relationships with their teams, and some feel forced to resort to rather unlikely sources of support.

One FTSE100 financial services boss brings an actress into head office every month to train him how to act out the CEO role. He justifies this by explaining that he is an introvert and has to learn to perform for staff, the media, shareholders, and analysts. "I am a very shy individual," he reveals. "I would not naturally engage with people. It's just a management style I have developed over the years. We all put on a show. We are all actors and I have learnt to act. The actress comes in and coaches me in body language, presentation style, and public speaking. I am an introvert and introverts get drawn in. I don't need to have a high regard for friendships or closeness. I can retain my intellectual distance with people who work for me."

Similarly, the boss of a FTSE100 services company chooses to bring a singer into group headquarters for much the same reason. "It's very difficult for someone like me who's quite reserved because I have to talk to a lot of people outside the business and to stakeholders so it is very challenging," he says. "I work with a voice coach who is an actress. She says, for example, 'What emotion do you want to convey?' and I say that maybe I want to convey more emotion in a presentation. She teaches me to do it."

A very widespread problem for CEOs is a difficulty in engaging with their emotions. Leaders are meant to be dispassionate about difficult decisions, but Alan Watkins, who runs executive coaching consultancy Cardiac Coherence, believes that some take this to extremes. "Their tendency not to be attached to the emotional side of things gets to be exaggerated," he says, "and this blindness to human needs really reduces their leadership effectiveness.

Unfortunately, many chief executives are managing rather than leading." Watkins considers that chief executives are overworked and focused on driving out results while struggling with processes, so that they often achieve by perspiration, sheer willpower, and by shutting down their emotions. "Chief executives need to be motivated and more passionate," he says. "And to do that, they need to understand themselves better."

Chief executives need to understand themselves better

Another business coach recalls the case of a chief executive client who was particularly devoid of emotion. He recalls: "I asked him to think of a time in his life when he had felt really passionate about something and he sat in silence before eventually saying: 'No, I have never felt that.'" The coach asked him whether he had felt emotional when he scored a goal as a 9 year old and again an unflinching "No" was the response. Then the coach asked the CEO to decide the emotion that would most describe him. "All he could think of was being even-tempered," says the coach. "He worked so hard to keep his emotions in check that the strongest one he felt was being controlled."

While these examples are extreme, many CEOs do find they need support to cope with the huge pressures of the role. They get this support from a range of sources. Tony Froggatt, the former chief executive of brewer Scottish & Newcastle, leans heavily on his wife, who is a former human resources director at Whitbread and Australian services group Brambles. "I'm fortunate she is so understanding of the pressures," he says.

Other CEOs draw strength from the advice of their chairmen, and many turn to professional coaches: 39 percent of the FTSE100 chief executives we interviewed said they have used one. Andy Harrison articulates the reason: "It's very hard if your team become friends because you may have to fire them," he says. "You should get close enough to your team to talk about business issues but not get too close to them and risk losing a degree of objectivity." However, coaches are not universally praised. "If you look at coaches and mentors, they are generally people who have not actually run big businesses themselves, so how can they tell you how to do it?" asks Sir Martin Sorrell. "They're shrinks," agrees Richard

Pym, chairman of motoring retailer Halfords and banks Bradford & Bingley and Northern Rock (Asset Management). "Some of these coach people are just weird."

We'll unpack the different sources of sup-   The chief executive's job is solitary. port top CEOs draw on and what they're best   You really don't have a peer group. used for in Chapter 11. It's clear that, what-
ever support network they build, loneliness is part of the role. "If you are lonely, get a dog," says Mike Roney somewhat unsympathetically. "But the chief executive's job is solitary. You really don't have a peer group in the same way that you have when you're one of a number of executives working at a larger company. It's not like the times when you could meet up with your peer group and listen to someone say that your boss is an idiot." Ultimately, CEOs have to learn to be tough, resilient, and self-sufficient. For some this comes naturally; for others it needs to be learnt.

Despite support networks, the pressure does sometimes get too great and a few chief executives adopt some approaches we'd not like to see repeated. One is revealed by Shelley von Strunckel, the Californian who created the first astrological column in a UK broadsheet newspaper at the *Sunday Times* and has a sideline reading the fortunes of well-known executives from the worlds of business and entertainment. She uses an astrological chart of the heavens, sun, moon, and planets, based on an individual's place and date and time of birth, to examine a person's strengths and blind spots, and then looks at astrological trends to forecast what's going on around them. "Often chief executives are very focused on their strengths and are ignoring their weaknesses," she says. "I help them understand their weaknesses, based on their horoscope, so that instead of sidelining their weaknesses, they learn how to use them. Usually they come to see me because they are in crisis. People don't tend to seek support when everything is rolling along."

Von Strunckel claims to have predicted takeovers and stock market crashes. She even says that she forecast the credit crunch that began in 2007. And she recalls once working out from the stars that the head of a major Hollywood studio was going to be on television explaining a major fraud in the company. "Not only could I see a fraud going on, I saw how the fraud would appear," she claims. "I clearly saw him being interviewed on television. He kind of went pale when I said that. There had been a huge scandal and it had showed up in his chart. And he was, indeed, later on television. It turned out later that he knew about it, although he did not acknowledge that to me at the time."

Although it's not in the least comforting to think that some CEOs may be relying on astrologers to guide their business decisions, it shows the possible effects of the tremendous stress associated with the role.

Don't get personal

It's all very well to be driving for top performance and getting the support you need to achieve it, but work isn't everything. Is it possible to have a healthy personal life as the chief executive of a major public company?

Most CEOs find it extremely difficult. More than half of those we interviewed said that they have little time for family or personal interests and passions, such are the demands of being the boss. Others accept that getting anywhere near a balance requires compromise. Inevitably, this involves CEOs' spouses and families, and it sometimes begins from the moment of appointment.

"My wife knew what she was letting herself in for," admits Charles Philipps, chief executive of Lloyd's of London insurer Amlin. "Before we were married I had to go to some printers to sign off a document for a client. I was not expecting it to take long and thought that we could go out that evening afterwards, so she came to the printers with me. She was still there at 5 a.m. the next morning and she still married me."

Another boss, the chief executive of a power company, took the post despite protestations from his spouse. "Did I have a deal with my wife?" he asks. "Well, she said she did not want me to do this job and I kind of ignored it. She said, 'You've gone ahead' and I said, 'I didn't think you were serious, darling.' But she was half serious. She was asking if I had thought through all the consequences. Was I going to make sure I keep my family promises? How could I fulfill the promises I had made to my shareholders and not fulfill those I had made to her? It's a good question and I can't answer it. It's very difficult. Try going on holiday without your mobile phone. My wife says 'Your Blackberry is not coming', but there's no way I'm leaving it behind."

> Try going on holiday without your mobile phone

Both Peter Johnson at Inchcape and Ed Story, chief executive of oil exploration group SOCO International, made formal arrangements with their spouses. "My wife has put up with God knows what," admits Johnson. "I was on a plane all the time, I was just never there. I once went to Australia twice in a week. I was on a plane to Japan three times in one month. Every Sunday night I was heading to airports and every Saturday morning I was arriving back at 5 a.m. I made a deal with her and said I am going to stop when I am 60."

"Ours is an evolving deal," adds Story. "She says, 'When are you going to sell this? You always sell. What are you going to do when you sell? Are you going to stay here?' I say not very much. We're still negotiating it."

Maintaining a healthy work–life balance is much harder for chief executives of multinational companies who need to be constantly on the move. "My wife and I have lived in 19 houses since we married," says Leigh Clifford, the former chief executive of mining giant Rio Tinto. "I think chief executives try to kid themselves about how much time they have to spend on peripheral stuff. You have to be discerning with your time. You only get one dig at the crease. Your personal affairs can get into a bit of a mess. You don't tend to give them the time and attention they need."

Lord Davies believes that one of the most important differentiators between good and bad international chief executives is their ability to sleep on a plane, which has a knock-on effect on their family life. "If you're a bad traveler and run an international business, it's a nightmare," he says. "You're not sleeping and you're coming home wrecked. It's a job, for Christ's sake. When they put you in the box and it is over, you're not going to be judged on how much profit you made."

For Richard Baker, chairman of Virgin Active and former chief executive of Alliance Boots, it's all about personal discipline. "You

have to be quite disciplined and focused at a personal level with your family life," he says, "because if you're not careful, you'll arrive at a time where you're working nonstop. My wife says I'm terrible at dinner parties because I just recede. I spend my life talking and I like going to dinner where I can just sit and listen to someone else's conversation. One of the biggest issues is having time on your own."

Some CEOs manage to rationalize this lack of time for themselves and their families. "You have to have a life. My kids advise me: 'Dad, get a life,'" reveals Sandy Crombie. "I have a life. It is not the same life as everyone else's but it is my life. There are only 24 hours in a day and I sleep 7 of them. I have been married for 36 years. I don't tell myself to get a life because I have got one. It comes with the job."

Perhaps surprisingly, Crombie's lengthy marriage is not unusual. Only a handful of the CEOs we interviewed have been divorced, with the overwhelming majority of the rest married for more than 20 years. However, the job can bite deep into those marriages. Many CEOs end up compartmentalizing their work and home lives, living in company flats or traveling during the week and going home at weekends. "My family are used to not seeing me during the week," says Paul Adams, chief executive of British American Tobacco. "They see me at weekends but not all the time or every weekend. It's the life they've grown up with."

"I can't remember my boys growing up," states one CEO who has been married twice. "I can't remember them when they were young. People ask whether you make a choice between your family and your career. You definitely do. I don't think you can have both. You need to choose." And in fact Jon Moulton, managing partner of private equity group Better Capital, actually prefers investing in companies where the chief executive has been divorced once, arguing that they are better motivated to succeed. "I take a lot of interest in the chief executive's marital status," he confides. "One divorce is slightly better than none, because managers are motivated and challenged and sometimes they need to rebuild their wealth. Two is more worrying and three is a catastrophe. I don't generally make private investments when I see three divorces."

Sir Martin Sorrell, who went through a highly publicized divorce, believes that everyone is defined by the meeting in their lives of work, family, and society. "There are very few people who can get the intersection of those three circles perfectly balanced and I have not managed to do it," he admits. "Getting the balance right is very, very difficult. All the stuff I do outside the business is related to business."

> There are very few people who can get the intersection of work, family, and society perfectly balanced

It is therefore clear that a healthy work–life balance can be very difficult to achieve if you are running a major public company. Some of the most effective CEOs say that they only manage it by relying on their secretaries to send them home on time or by learning to be extremely disciplined. We'll come back to some of the disciplines used to achieve a fulfilling personal life in Part III.

THE GOOD NEWS

So you can see why we think being a CEO should come with a strong health warning: It's a grueling job and most chief executives don't have much of a personal life. However, there is good news: Some CEOs do manage to juggle home life and business and really enjoy the job. We'll take you through how they do that in Chapter 11. This is heartening, because the realities of doing business in the coming decade, such as companies increasingly becoming globally dispersed and the internet enabling faster information flows and swifter decision making, will make it even harder to be a chief executive.

If you do want to be a CEO or learn more about doing the job, the rest of this book will take you through the detail of the emerging global realities and how top CEOs cope with them. It will show you how some of the best of the current crop of CEOs got to where they are today and how they actually do their job, as well as offering suggestions on how best to lead in the coming decade.

PART I

FACING UP TO THE FACTS OF LIFE

2
WINNING IN THE RESET

"If we fail to change things will not be pretty. And if you think you're exempt, you're wrong."   *Jeff Kindler, chief executive, Pfizer*

"People did not, regretfully, suffer enough... the crisis passed so quickly I don't know how many of us have learnt the lessons... we must heed the crisis's wakeup call or we will face much graver consequences."
      Jack Ma, chief executive, Alibaba Group

If you carried out an internet search on the word "reset" a few years ago, you would have ended up with thousands of web pages on how to reboot your computer. Now it has rapidly become accepted terminology for signaling that, after the financial crisis of 2007–09, the corporate world has changed and must operate differently.

The names of the business leaders who have given currency to the word rather make the point. Take General Electric chief executive Jeff Immelt: "This economic crisis doesn't represent a cycle. It's an emotional, social, economic reset." Or Microsoft chief executive Steve Ballmer: "In my view, what we now have will be a fundamental economic reset. The economy is going to have to reestablish itself at a level of spending that reflects the real value of underlying assets before we can all start growing again at a healthy rate."

Then there's Jeff Kindler, chief executive of US pharmaceutical giant Pfizer. "The political environment in the US is so toxic and short term focused that we are not having the conversations we need to reset the economy," he told Britain's CBI conference in November 2009. "If we fail to change things will not be pretty. And if you think you're exempt, you're wrong."

But note how these leaders use "reset" to denote different things. The term describes a world where there are dramatically contrasting opportunities for economic growth in emerging and developing nations. It also presents a world of increased financial regulation and an environment of greater public distrust of business. In addition, it is employed in a clarion call for more ethical capitalism.

Probably all of these are right, at least in the short term. What has been described as the biggest financial crisis in history clearly has to leave a significant residue. The issue for chief executives is how much has really changed and what to do about it. So how do CEOs change their leadership styles not only to cope with a significant shock to capitalism but to win in the very different circumstances of its aftermath?

"The reset is an evolving issue and no one quite knows where it will end up and what will become the ultimate new normal," says Brian France, chief executive of NASCAR, the US company that governs stock car racing. However, there is some good news: our research found that the crisis has developed many CEOs as leaders and forged closer teams within their organizations. As the crisis waned, the best CEOs refocused their companies from survival mode to an obsession with business performance and efficiency. Now they are moving beyond performance to business leadership.

This is a new world order. We need to run the business as if that's the case

As Andrea Jung, chief executive of Avon Products and a director of Apple and General Electric, says: "The going-in assumption is that this is a new world order. We need to run the business as if that's the case." So what exactly has changed and how should CEOs adapt?

Divergent global markets

Conventionally, capitalist economies move through boom and bust cycles but, at least in the short term, this has been replaced by what Sir Martin Sorrell described as "LUV". Using a phrase originally invented by Thomson Reuters correspondent Stella Dawson, he said there will be an L-shaped recovery in western Europe, denoting a very slow, protracted improvement that takes a while to take hold. In the US, he went on, the recovery will be U shaped – a quicker but relatively feeble upturn. Only in Brazil, Russia, India, China, and the next 11 fastest-growing developing nations will the recovery be rapid and V shaped.

Ferdinando Beccalli-Falco, CEO of GE International, agrees. "We see a reset world of more regulation and greater interface with government," he says. "We see scarce growth rates in the developed markets of the US, western Europe, and Japan and aggressive rates in the emerging markets. There'll also be intermediate markets like Australia and Canada."

Putting meat on these bones, Steve Forbes, chief executive of the eponymous publishing group, forecasts annual growth of 8 percent for China and 6 percent for India, which he says could achieve 10 percent with greater government action for business. In turn, Harriet Green, chief executive of distribution group Premier Farnell, attributes the sluggish forecasts for North America to government actions to "make business pay" for President Obama's redistribution of wealth plan. "Capital is now and will continue to be a challenge in the next two to three years," she says. The problem for western businesses therefore is securing growth in their core markets. Lord Heseltine, chairman of Haymarket Media Group, the UK's largest privately owned publishing group, puts it succinctly. "There's a constraint called economic limitation," he says. "Of that, there is no doubt."

Capital is now and will continue to be a challenge

Mike Laphen, chief executive of American outsourcing giant Computer Sciences Corporation, believes US growth will be particularly hard to come by in the reset world. "It's going to be an unusually slow recovery," he says, "because this recession, particularly for the US, is going to be quite different from recessions of the past. Typically, the US has bounced out of recessions pretty fast and got back to prosperity, but the anomaly we have this time is what has happened to consumer spending.

"For the past ten years, the US consumer has been spending at very high levels and saving at very low levels and that has now completely switched positions. We have a 6 percent savings rate that I don't think has ever happened before. What's different this time is two forces have intertwined and are impacting the consumer. One is the pension crisis; the other is the collapse of the US property market. They have scared consumers and it's going to take much longer for US consumers to bounce back from that. So we're going through a transition period during which capacity adjusts to the new norm of spending."

Strong prospects in Eastern markets

Few western commentators doubt the continuing growth and future promise of the East. Lord Levene, chairman of Lloyd's insurance market, sits on the board of China Construction Bank, China's second biggest bank, and is adamant. "There is not a reset economy in Asia," he says. "They haven't had the problem. The speed at which China is developing is extraordinary."

KV Kamath, chairman of India's ICICI Bank, elucidates further. "We had a very shallow V-shaped recovery in India," he says. "We had recovered in six months. We took our hit in two months of inventory repricing. Growth dropped from 8.5–9 percent to 7 percent." He adds: "Today in India we see strong infrastructure investment, a mood change in Indian entrepreneurs. Everyone's interconnected, but we're only connected through global debt and capital markets and the exchange rate, and not by much as we don't borrow all that much internationally."

In China, Yu Minhong, chairman of New Oriental Education and Technology Group, says the upside is even greater. "For the private sector in China only 10 percent of the potential has been tapped into," he says. "For thousands of years, businessmen were prevented from doing business." Now, he adds, they're making up for lost time with a vengeance, capitalizing on the size and quality of the workforce, China's lower cost base and huge hunger for industrial consumption.

Eastern governments also broadly continue to nurture the development of robust economies and to support state champions and overseas expansion.

Constraints in the West

It's not necessary to retell in detail the events of 2008, the collapses of Bear Stearns and Lehman Brothers in the US, and the government bailouts of Citigroup, Royal Bank of Scotland, and Lloyds Banking Group, to name just three western examples. The damage done is well known.

Eric Schmidt, CEO of Google, says: "The blame is largely in the United States, not in Europe, not in Britain. It was fundamentally because a low-interest policy created too much money. It was an easy-money policy and eventually an easy-money policy catches up with you."

Eventually an easy-money policy catches up with you

Steve Ballmer believes that this has left the West facing huge challenges. "For the past 25 years," he says, "the world has certainly enjoyed incredible, incredible global growth. Average incomes around the world grew at unprecedented rates, millions of people moved out of poverty into the middle class for the very first time. That expansion was built on three things: innovation, globalization, and increasing debt.

"But over the last period of time, the balance has really shifted. Instead of innovation and productivity driving growth, it's really been unsustainable levels, particularly of private debt, that have been a key driver of economic growth. The hard truth is this, in my opinion: The private sector of our economy has borrowed too much money, businesses and consumers alike, fueled by a lot of different things, some notion that housing prices would go up for ever, that you could borrow money cheaply. The bubble has burst. We can no longer rely on consumption by refinancing our homes or inexpensive money to fuel economic growth, and that's certainly had a huge impact."

The immediate repercussions are a scarcity of capital and a drying up of mergers and acquisitions and initial public offerings. While the latter trends are easing as companies take advantage of depressed prices to snap up prized assets, capital is set to remain scarce in the West for many companies, which will also have to contend with much greater regulatory intervention.

In the UK, this has taken the form of increased taxation on the highest-earning individuals and a windfall tax on bankers' bonuses. However, corporate governance rules are being revised in most western markets and many observers believe the regulatory reaction has gone too far.

"There's a risk in the aftermath," says Michael Spencer. "You get a blame culture. Somebody somewhere must be blamed. Culprits must be found and culprits must be punished. The politicians seem to have decided that the easiest and most obvious choices are the bankers, rather forgetting the culpability of the politicians, the regulators, the central bankers and rating agencies. They all, in varying degrees, have their fingerprints on this crisis. No one is exempt. So we have a witch hunt almost and we run a risk of a material overreaction."

> The politicians, the regulators, the central bankers and rating agencies all have their fingerprints on this crisis

Ian Powell, chairman and senior partner at Pricewaterhouse-Coopers, the world's largest accountancy group, is also concerned about overregulation of Britain's financial services industry. "Everybody's getting tarred with the same brush because one or two may not have behaved in the way you would want them to," he says. "People talk about breaking up some of our financial services institutions. I don't think that's a sensible or viable thing to do unless it's done on an international basis. Ultimately, the only way out of this recession is to grow out of it, so any regulation that puts this country at a disadvantage in terms of encouraging investment and restricts growth opportunities is what I'm most afraid of. Some of the legislation coming in now has been designed pretty quickly and the implications of it need to be pretty carefully thought through."

Lord Levene is also extremely concerned. "I understand all about the anger about the bonuses. I get it. I know what the mood is out there," he says. "But nevertheless, the end result of that is hammering businesses in this country."

All three fear an exodus of companies seeking less restrictive domiciles and Ferdinando Beccalli-Falco agrees that this is a real risk. "We see a reset world of more regulation and greater interface with government," he says. "Companies are reconsidering their domicile in the light of state interference, growth markets, and tax and regulation."

Nor is this a problem just for the UK, though America's stringent penalties on companies seeking to redomicile deter most. General Electric, for example, has relocated its research and development operations to India. Other US companies may also selectively move certain divisions and activities.

LESSONS FOR THE WEST AND THE EAST

It is clear that regulatory change is inevitable and probably unstoppable in the West. But the reset involves a new perspective on moral hazard too, particularly for financial services companies.

Says Sir Terry Leahy: "The special feature of this one was the cause of the recession – the financial crisis – and there it is not clear that we have learnt the lesson. At the heart of it is moral hazard and we have to recognize that it is wrong that the banks make a profit and the taxpayers take a loss."

Adds Eric Schmidt: "The number of people who were hurt by the activities of the financial industry is so large, it is very hard to have a lot of sympathy with that industry, given the very high-flying nature of its behavior. If your assessment is that there is a greater and greater concentration of large financial companies that are too big to fail, well, they need to be more regulated. You cannot have a situation where you only win and do not lose in capitalism. At Google, if I lost $10 billion in one day, I would be likely to lose my jacket."

You cannot have a situation where you only win and do not lose in capitalism

The perspective of some eastern observers, moreover, is that western leaders can learn from eastern practice. "I think that first there is moderation," says Deepak Parekh, chairman of Indian housing finance company HDFC. "Even after 32 years with HDFC, I only own 0.1 or 0.2 percent of HDFC. Where in the USA, top salaries at a firm might be 100 times those at the bottom, in India, that would only be a maximum of ten times." Then, he suggests, there are lessons in how western leaders should approach their employees. "Our competitors are riddled with militant unions but we have none," he says. "It's about how you deal with your people – total transparency."

It's about how you deal with your people – total transparency

This is also true of how CEOs conduct themselves in the reset, for the financial crisis has shone a fierce spotlight on how business people behave. Asda, the UK supermarket group owned by US giant Wal-Mart, sensed the zeitgeist in 2009 and commissioned extensive market research on what its customers wanted from the company in terms of openness and transparency. The upshot is that it is putting webcams into its factories, distribution centers, and headquarters in an effort to improve consumers' trust in the business, an aspect that scored very low in the research. Asda chief executive Andy Bond recognizes that this has implications for not only how he communicates with customers but how he goes about his job. "Having a 'fly on the wall' of the life of a CEO wasn't that appealing to customers," he says. "But what was appealing was: 'Does this guy live the values of the company? Is it really true that the chief executive travels economy when he flies to the US?' Because that's really quite remarkable if it's true."

Indeed, Bond says he always travels to the US in economy on outbound flights and often on the return leg too, though he does fly business class if it's overnight and he has a meeting the next day. "It's now an Asda-wide rule," he says. "I've stayed firm on that. You can't have a low-price business unless you have a low-cost business and this saves us £2 million a year."

Of course, this growing demand for transparency rubs both ways. Western business leaders counter that Indian and Chinese companies have often been highly opaque and impossible for outsiders to fathom. In the reset financial world, they will come under pressure to have transparent structures as well as financial reporting systems.

Says Lord Levene: "They're moving from institutions which are wholly owned by the state to ones where there are outside shareholders. When they were setting up China Construction Bank's current structure they went around the world and looked at who has the best corporate governance and settled on Germany, with its supervisory and operating boards. Having sat on the board of the Deutsche Borse, I'm not sure I would have held that up to be the best model, but that's what they've done so we have a supervisory board and an operational board. They have taken from European best practice, but the end result will also be shaped by local markets and conditions."

Jeff Immelt sees compromises between business and government in both East and West. "The global economy and capitalism will be reset in several important ways," he says. "The interaction between government and business will change for ever. In a reset economy, the government will be a regulator and also an industry policy champion, a financier and key partner."

There is certainly increased pressure in both West and East for companies to focus not merely on shareholder returns. In the West, the drive for sustainability (discussed in more detail in Chapter 3) has been building momentum for some time. However, many Chinese CEOs are also concerned about the right role for private-sector companies in society. This is partly because of the historical state mistrust of entrepreneurs, but it is also growing to encompass concerns about pay, corruption, and the environment.

"We have to balance social obligations and entrepreneurship," says Liu Chuanzhi, chairman of Legend Holdings. "People and customers are key but public welfare comes first," adds Cheng Siwei, former vice-chairman of the Standing Committee of the National People's Congress. "So of course pay a good salary and bonus, but also you must practice people-focused management. People must be at the core."

Xiang Bing, Dean of Cheung Kong Graduate School of Business, states: "The percentage of the economy's assets owned by millionaires is higher here than in Japan. Our model today can only create wealthy people, not great institutions. If our entrepreneurs are to get recognized, they should care not just about money but also the use of that money."

GREATER BOARD OVERSIGHT NEEDED

Much has been made of the failure of boards of directors at banks and other companies in the West to employ tight risk-management controls before the credit crisis and recession. In the reset, there will be a near-compulsion for boards to provide much more active governance and counsel. Boards of directors need real governance to monitor their companies' biggest risks, assess the wisest options, and push their corporations to fight hard once again to explore the best opportunities, maintain and extend their brands and reputations, and engage with customers and staff.

Says KV Kamath: "The role of boards and supervisory structures has changed for ever. Boards need to be better informed and if action needs to be taken, they need to be involved – but without becoming involved in the day-to-day operations. The narrow issue is, is strategy going to be dictated by boards? This is where dialogue will be more important – where board meetings need to be more than an hour and a half."

For example, ICICI's credit committee reviews 60 percent of the bank's loans by value, meets one to two times a month, and a group of nonexecutive directors make up the majority of the number. The group's customer service committee meets once a month. "The board's role becomes one of counselor and you need to be informed to be a good counselor," he says.

Lord Levene too, for his part, wishes that China Construction Bank's board meetings were longer than an hour – especially when he sees the five-inch-thick folder of files in perfect English that he is supposed to digest beforehand. "I wouldn't hold up US corporate governance as necessarily being a higher model, but corporate governance in China is certainly changing," he says.

SO HOW ARE THE BEST COMPANIES RESPONDING?

Any military leader will tell you that the worst battles have to be survived before an attack can start again in earnest. Business is no different. At the height of the crisis in the West, the sensible option was to hold as much cash as possible. Mike Laphen at CSC, which employs 82,000 people in 80 countries, recalls: "You have to have a different mindset in a crisis." Like other businesses in the downturn, he says, the executive team quickly assessed the situation, reduced costs in line with falling sales, and took a more aggressive position on client credit risk.

You have to have a different mindset in a crisis

CSC traditionally borrowed about $600–700 million through 30- to 90-day short-term commercial banking facilities, but at the heart of the financial crisis its banks started switching these facilities to overnight lending. In order to ensure that its capital structure was robust and stable, CSC drew down a $1.5 billion line of credit, or backstop, that it had negotiated several years before. "We elected to call in that backstop of $1.5 billion so we had complete assurance that, notwithstanding what happened in the banking community, we were well protected with working capital and the cash to do business," Laphen says. "And today, even though the markets have improved dramatically, we carry much more cash on the balance sheet than we have done historically. We have about $2.25 billion of cash on hand whereas we traditionally carry about $600 million. We will continue that until we're convinced that the market is healed and we'll also watch the interest rates closely. So you have to deal with things from a lot of different aspects, but we've weathered the storm pretty well."

Brian France agrees that there was a phase where companies simply had to survive. "Given that everything was so unstable, there was a tendency to pull back just to be sure that you did not put your company in an even tougher spot," he says. "Most CEOs were trying to zero in on the right expense control and the right prices to keep customers."

Now, however, there's a realization that to be truly sustainable and long term, companies need to emerge from a protective mindset and build a new generation of truly great global businesses that can adapt to the emerging world. This is not an easy task, not least because the strength and attractiveness of many traditional corporate role models waned in the crash. "We used to admire GE hugely, but today even great firms like GE and Microsoft face big challenges," says KV Kamath. "I'm struggling to think of any firm I truly admire today. All the global banks we admired are now in difficulties."

It is not yet clear who the new corporate icons will be, but it is likely that they will need to be more nuanced, respecting elements of leading western and eastern businesses alike.

GOING FOR GROWTH AGAIN

Top CEOs are adopting an entrepreneurial mindset, espousing global ambitions, and exploring the use of global resources. At Tesco, for example, Sir Terry Leahy plans for the company to generate an additional £1 billion of profit through new initiatives ranging from a mobile phone business to a new banking venture.

Procter & Gamble, the consumer products giant, has also moved from an initial defensive, protective mindset to focus on growth. By the time of Bob McDonald's promotion to chief executive in June 2009, P&G had put in place a short-term initiative to reinvigorate sales by boosting spending on marketing, cutting prices on 10 percent of its product lines, and dropping its 2010 diluted earnings per share growth below its long-term double-digit target in order to rebuild market share. The company returned to growth in the third quarter of 2009 and is now engaged in an aggressive expansion drive.

"In five years, we're going from reaching 4 billion consumers using our products to 5 billion consumers," says McDonald. "We're going to go from the average consumer in the world spending $12 a year on P&G products to $14 a year. And we have all the building blocks that lead to those results."

Andrea Jung says Avon Products is another example. In 2009, the cosmetics group responded to the recession by launching the biggest recruitment drive in its history to hire new door-to-door agents in 44 markets. In the first quarter of 2009 alone, it increased the number of its self-employed agents by 200,000 in the US. "My philosophy was 'let's go on the offense not the defense,'" says Jung. "It's easy in these kinds of times to hunker down, cut everything, and wait for sunnier days. But if you study businesses in the worst economic periods, that's when heroes can be made. More market share can be lost or gained in tough economic times than in other periods."

More market share can be lost or gained in tough economic times

At Cisco Systems, John Chambers says the company provides real evidence of this truth. "In every economic downturn that's occurred in our company's history, we have emerged from it dramatically stronger than when we went into it," he says. "Almost without exception, we've come out with a dramatic increase in market capitalization, profitability, market share, and movement into new markets. So each time one of these downturns has occurred, even though it has been brutal for us and for others, we have executed pretty well." He believes that now will be no exception. "You've never seen such a combination of global spending combined with central bank action," he says. "But you can view it as the biggest challenge that many of us have seen in our lifetime or you can see it as the greatest opportunity."

Jeff Immelt agrees that there is a massive opportunity. "The current crisis offers the challenge of our lifetime," he says. "I've told our leaders at GE that if they are frightened by this concept, they shouldn't be here. But if they're energized and desire to play a part in transforming the company for the future, then this is going to be a thrilling time to be a part of GE."

Western businesses need to continue to innovate and to focus on a long-term mindset if they are to compete with entrepreneurial companies from the East that have not had to downsize. Says Steve Ballmer: "America really has to return to growth that's built on innovation and productivity, rather than leverage and private debt. That must happen."

The good news is that there are plenty of visionary companies with great assets to help them do that. Some have the advantage that they are positioned in areas of technological or market growth. "We do benefit from the world going digital," says Enrique Salem. "If everything is digital, then more and more informational technology is needed. The digital storage market is doubling every two years. People are taking more pictures and more videos and creating more information and so the trend of more data is good for Symantec. We benefit by needing to protect people from increased threats."

Jeff Bezos, chief executive of Amazon.com, adds that a lot of the growth drivers that existed before the financial crisis are still there for companies bold enough to focus on the long term. "Some of the things that we have been able to fix and do could never be done with a short-term mentality," he explains. "I see some companies who are very focused on the next three months. In the long term, I am super-optimistic about our economy and our nation and actually the whole world. And the reason is that everywhere I travel in the world I meet people who are so inventive, so engaged in building a better future. And our world is going to get so much more productive over time because of that inventiveness. For me, it's very motivating."

Indeed, some companies chose never to slow down. Says Eric Schmidt: "From a Google perspective, we never stopped hiring but we told our team again and again that we are increasing our hiring rate and our investment rate in anticipation of a recovery."

The challenge is to match the entrepreneurial and talent-oriented mindset in the East. Says KV Kamath: "When I came in as CEO, it was hugely exciting. We saw an opportunity, in the face of loud skepticism, to create a retail bank. But we had to create a retail market, a brand and product, processes and operational suites. The core team was an entrepreneurial set of people but it wasn't easy. The mission wasn't all that clear at the time. We had to be so entrepreneurial. There weren't clearly set goals but an entrepreneur sees opportunity. Definition comes later." Even as we talk of growth, it's good to remember that ICICI's growth hasn't been wholly linear. In 1996 it culled 15 percent of its 1,000 employees and another 25 percent two years later. "We needed a younger, more entrepreneurial team," explains Kamath. "It was also a meritocracy with a clear, formal evaluation process because the big risk was talent. Then we focused on brand, products, technology, and capital."

An entrepreneur sees opportunity. Definition comes later

Deepak Parekh at HDFC, where mortgage loans have enjoyed 25 percent annual compound growth for five years, adds that the company sees its executives as professional entrepreneurs, not just professional managers.

At Reliance Industries, moreover, chairman and managing director Mukesh Ambani, the wealthiest man in India, admits that the group's global ambitions were set extremely high. "We always wanted to be a Top 500 firm when people had written India off," he says. "But the most important thing was to do transformational stuff. It was always a mission – never status quo stuff. We were always building businesses with the new India in mind."

In China, Yu Minhong adds: "Innovation is more important than the annual performance of a branch company. If you cannot be the number 1 in your sector, you should do something you're good at!"

> If you cannot be no. 1 in your sector, do something you're good at

FOCUS ON ENTREPRENEURIAL, ORGANIC GROWTH

Merger and acquisitions markets have already begun to revive, with companies taking the opportunity to buy assets at lower prices. Exxon Mobil's $31 billion acquisition of US gas producer XTO Energy is a good example. Cisco Systems has also consistently used stock market down cycles to make bolt-on acquisitions. In the short term, capital will continue to be more expensive and harder to source, so acquisitions need to be truly strategic. If such hurdles can be overcome, big, opportunistic plays should not be ruled out, especially as governments may be less inclined to block deals on competition grounds in some markets and situations.

Generally, however, limited capital means that companies need to explore the full growth agenda and place greater focus on more innovation and entrepreneurship for organic growth and smart partnering. Wim Elfrink, chief globalization officer for Cisco Systems, based in Mumbai, says: "We make conscious decisions about how to capture market transitions – through building, buying or partnering – and for what reason."

India's richest woman Kiran Mazumdar-Shaw, chairman and managing director of Biocon, India's largest bio-pharmaceuticals group, says: "We have partnered with a research lab in Cuba. Cubans are extremely innovative and we found a very rich biotech culture and with their embargoes they have found it hard to commercialize their innovations. My message would be innovation happens everywhere, so you have to look for innovation everywhere."

In China, Xiang Bing adds: "For Chinese firms to date, success is built on the failures of their peer companies. We do not innovate like MySpace and Honda. US firms create new business spaces. We need to look not at the moon from the earth but at the earth from the moon."

Adi Godrej, the billionaire chairman of Indian consumer products conglomerate Godrej Group, has built growth innovation into the heart of the group. He says: "Young talent is more important than anything. We use talent in their late 20s or early 30s to make a corporate radar. They look out for all the threats to the company and report to the executive every quarter. We have a thinktank of non-CEOs working on the future. We have a red and a blue team working on our strategy. They have total freedom and resources, but they are not allowed to talk to each other. They present back to each other and to the executive."

Indeed, technological change will continue to provide opportunities for growth. At Cisco Systems, John Chambers is using the next phase of internet technology to facilitate a new, collaborative way of working. Cisco has designated 26 objectives to increase its $39 billion turnover by 25 percent for five years, ranging from bringing Web 3.0 to China to installing routers in space, conquering cloud computing, and coming up with a strategy for Mexico, Brazil, and Russia. "In sports and entertainment," says Chambers, "give us a couple of years and we will have our wiring in most of the sports stadia around Europe. We will change the way you watch that entertainment."

How can a company attack 26 such gigantic goals simultaneously? Chambers' answer is a slide entitled "The Future of Countries, Companies, and Citizens," showing Cisco's top 250 people on 26 company councils and boards, one for each objective.

This is collaborative planning Cisco style, and Chambers gets involved, sitting on such bodies when he feels they need a particular push. "We're doing what we think has not been done before in business," he says, "with a replicable process that allows you to scale and grow and to add flexibility. By doing this we can have 26 priorities, whereas in the past we might have had one or two. If this works, this will be probably the most fundamental change in business over the last couple of decades."

Growth markets can also be used as inexpensive test-beds for experiments. Kanwalinder Singh, India and South Asia president of US microchips supplier Qualcomm, says: "India's a phenomenal laboratory. For example, if you install a mobile telecoms base station, then it reaches capacity almost immediately. We drove the cost of a handset down from about $100 to less than $20." He observes that in the West, customers now want to connect devices, not just people, wirelessly. "We are using the technology developed in India to fulfill that need," he says. "It may be that discoveries here would not have happened elsewhere." As Kiran Mazumdar-Shaw adds: "The cost of failure is very affordable in India."

HONE VERY POWERFUL, TIGHT TEAMS

Developing the best talent, as we continually reinforce in this book, is the key to ensuring that your business can adapt and succeed in new climates. As CEOs look for growth in more difficult western markets, utilizing the different skill sets within your organization becomes even more important.

"You change how you get growth as economies go through their cycles," says Brian France. "At the bottom of the cycle, the cost cutters in your organization are very important, but it is the value-creating people who will grow your business. These people were in the limelight for the 15 years or so before 2008 and they will be so again in the reset. There are lots of opportunities for growth in the green economy, for example. You just need to get the people who can take advantage and drive growth focusing on doing that again."

Clearly, both cost control and entrepreneurial skills are needed. But crucially, the experiences of executive talent in the downturn can be utilized to unite management teams and harness determination and togetherness for future growth. "Do not be blind to emotional loyalty," urges D Shivkumar, chief executive of Nokia India. "Identify the young people who had the stomach for the rough 2009 ride. We look for 60 percent agreement but 100 percent commitment."

Marc Bolland, the Dutchman who transformed British supermarket group Morrisons and is now chief executive of Marks & Spencer, agrees that talent is key to the kind of challenge that winning in the reset represents. "There are three elements of management," he says. "It's about the belly, the heart, and the head. They should be in balance. When I make an analysis of people, I look at analytical skills, which come

Management is about the belly, the heart, and the head – in balance

from the head, the ability to make judgment calls, and what I call 'shaping', which goes very much through the belly. People who have a very strong belly feel have a very strong understanding of what you can do and what's needed. Retailing is very much about reaction to markets and understanding what customers want. This all goes through the belly but at the same time the heart is where you have passion for the business. For me, it's impossible to do a turnaround with 130,000 people and not to get them passionate about something."

DON'T LET STRUCTURE GET IN THE WAY

Shivkumar also believes that corporate structures have to evolve in response to the economic environment. "Structures divide people; people unite structures," he says. "So we need to find leaders who unite people."

KV Kamath agrees: "We've always seen structure as living and play about with it as much as we can. But it always hardens eventually. In 2008, we had a huge opportunity to pull everything out. We literally dismantled the whole structure and put it in again and not too many people were complaining."

Companies are discovering that there's a new code to crack: capturing, disseminating, and renewing their knowledge, especially when a change in leadership is coming. It's not easy and for Kiran Mazumdar-Shaw it can be "like trying to drink from a fire hydrant".

Harriet Green believes that this means change in the ways CEOs operate within their organizations. "I don't think you can think, with all this technology and change going on, that a CEO can sit any more at the top of a construct," she says. "People have to be thinking in much more circular, more connected, more viral ways of getting things done."

"The big challenge CEOs have is that they know everything," adds Kamath. "Most organizations tend to ring-fence knowledge because knowledge is power. Our philosophy is that knowledge is to be shared. It is a pool that will never deplete; it will always increase."

> Knowledge is a pool that will never deplete; it will always increase

At drugs giant GlaxoSmithKline, CEO Andrew Witty is committed to avoiding what he sees as past mistakes made by his industry and his company. Why, he asks, does an industry that prides itself on innovation still operate around a business model that hasn't changed for 50 years? He has also pledged not to reprise the drug-pricing controversy that initially blighted GSK's anti-Aids treatments in Africa, and says it's essential to have sensitivity to the specific characteristics of local markets. "To some degree it's personal," he says. "I've lived in Africa, I've lived in Asia. I've spent a lot of my career outside Britain and a big chunk of it in the emerging world, and I think there's tremendous scope for companies like GSK to play a very constructive role. I'm very pleased that we've been able to lay out some of the challenges to the old way of doing business, which I must say are the right challenges, and we'll continue to do so."

Fluid and flexible corporate structures are going to be necessary for corporations to thrive in the reset economy. Says Mukesh Ambani: "Today our focus is structuring all our knowledge and we do not see any of the big firms we respect doing this. If we can get 100 percent knowledge integrated, we can transform our business."

Speed is a new competitive weapon

Speed of decision making, execution, and delivery is everything in global markets. In engineering, for example, Harriet Green says that the critical element is time to market, or how quickly design engineers can translate ideas into designs and prototypes. "Our research shows that, while project lifetimes on average used to be 18 months from conception to completion, the average is now much more like 18 weeks, so there's enormous time-to-market pressure," she states.

The best CEOs are responding by institutionalizing rapid-response mechanisms within their organizations. This begins with strategy. States D Shivkumar: "Today, you need to revisit strategy every three or six months rather than every three years. We review our strategy every three months – you need to be very nimble."

Organizational speed needs to spread into every department and every initiative, however. KV Kamath says that at ICICI: "We have a 90-day rule: from concept to beta to market in 90 days. All projects follow this rule and most get done."

Similarly, Unilever chief executive Paul Polman has installed a new system in which the company's plans have to be executable within 100 days or the group will not carry them out. The main change is that the group now focuses its innovation efforts on a smaller number of bigger brands, such as Lipton pyramid tea bags and its Magnum Temptations ice cream, in Latin America and Europe. The group's hair-minimizing deodorants and clear shampoos are being rolled out to 32 countries, whereas in the past it limited pushes of such new products to 12 or 13, and the roll-outs are quicker as well as bigger. Polman also insists on a "30-day plan" for each product innovation or attempt at troubleshooting. If the plan isn't working after a month, it has a good chance of being ditched.

Operating at speed also doesn't have to mean limiting corporate ambitions. At Glaxo, for example, Witty believes that a global group employing 99,000 staff should be more than capable of pursuing several goals at the same time. "I'm quite a generator of new initiatives," he says. "I'm a big believer that a company of the size of GSK can employ multiple agendas in parallel, so I'm not intimidated by the notion that we can redesign our US operation, put in place a new R&D strategy, do a small acquisition, and get consumer growth. We can do all that at the same time, so I am quite demanding of people's bandwidth. I expect the organization and senior people in it to be able to cope."

Localize properly – West to East and East to West

Emerging economies, particularly China and India, are vital markets for most global companies, so thriving and flourishing there constitutes a very real challenge for western businesses. However, there are considerable cultural and structural differences that require changes of mindset.

"We see a lot of businesses in our industry trying to run Asia just like North America," says Harriet Green. "In fact, it's a totally different environment and requires leadership teams that are much more agile and experienced in multi-cultural dimensions. You need different talent and different capabilities because the old construct of hierarchy has changed. The West is no longer at the top of the hierarchy of world order. All these developments pose very real challenges."

There are also challenges for eastern companies wanting to move West. "Not many Chinese firms have the makings of a multinational. We will have to gradually learn how to localize," says Qi Shu, former senior vice-president at Hewlett-Packard China. "And Chinese firms will not be welcomed like multinational organizations coming into China were," warns Edgar Hotard, chairman of Monitor Group (China).

Companies have to be culturally sensitive. States Liu Jiangnan, CEO of Alcatel-Lucent China, "Americans are better, but Europeans have the traditional colonial mindset of 'I'm here to help you'. Today, the environment has changed. Multinational corporations need to have a very peaceful, calm mind. They need to change their mindset. In the past we welcomed multinational companies as guests, but now we have a different mentality. We think multinational companies are here to take a piece of our cake." Adds Shu: "Multinational organizations have to lose their superiority complex and we have to lose our inferiority complex."

ADOPT AN OBSESSIVE FOCUS ON TALENT DEVELOPMENT

All this is very hard. So the talent shortage and hence the competition for talent are going to be hotter than ever. The best companies are putting talent at the heart of the company – just as they would the customer. Deepak Parekh describes this philosophy as "hiring ordinary people but making them do extraordinary things".

It is also about understanding demographic as well as cultural differences and recognizing that young talent in particular is different from its predecessors. Elio Leoni-Sceti, former chief executive of EMI Music, states: "Being in the music business, which is so rooted in the young generation and so present in everyday life, I see quite a lot of the trends among youth and we are very engaged in understanding them because we have made that a mantra about what we do. One of the key things that the generation of this decade has demonstrated is an unbelievable flexibility and adaptability, which is fairly unprecedented in previous times. It's a flexibility and adaptability to evolving models, to technology, to a change in the political and social scenario. That curiosity, participation, and readiness for change is amazing and there are fascinating opportunities for us to engage with it."

Kate Robertson is UK group chairman of advertising agency Euro RSCG Worldwide and co-founder of One Young World, the London conference for 18–25 year olds that has been dubbed "Young Davos". She cautions that this generation of talent may have been more shocked by the financial crisis than their older colleagues: "We have an age group of young people and we have seen this in delegates from China, India, and Africa, who have a grasp and it may be a frightened grasp on systemic risk." Countering that cautious impulse, she comments, is the enlightened attitude this generation has to technology, media, and globalization. "Everything they address in the future, the good and the bad, is actually about a single world. Digital platforms make the sense of that possible for them and that is a completely different world. And digital platforms also offer them a chance to be heard in a way that's never been possible before. This generation live in a different world and they have different tools, but they are genuinely different and incredibly well informed."

While such talent has the potential to rejuvenate stuffy workplaces, the challenge for companies is that it has fundamentally different demands from older generations. Says Harriet Green: "They expect a level of transparency and openness and being able to communicate with their 3,500 closest friends on LinkedIn or Facebook, in a way that I don't think people saw as their right in the past. This generation that we have created has a totally different view of work. Someone who has worked for us for a year saying that they want to take a year's sabbatical and work for our business in Pakistan for no apparent reason other than that they wish to may not appeal to us as leaders, but it certainly does to them."

This generation has a totally different view of work

Rather than automatically spurn such requests, she sees a greater engagement with the wishes of young workers as part of rebuilding trust in corporations. "Engaging with the trust agenda is one of the most important elements of the reset from the recession," she says. "This desire for transparency, honesty, and giving something back to the communities we work in is no longer just some trendy, cool thing that neat CEOs do. It's a requirement from our people."

Jacob Hsu, chief executive of Chinese research and development outsourcing company Symbio, adds: "We have incredible employee loyalty because we appreciate that ideas, resources, and assets can come from outside. For example, we have just completed a three-way merger and all the founders from previous mergers are still at the firm." He was inspired, he says, by researching companies in Finland, where he found a very mature research and development and innovation infrastructure.

"The question is how we manage our talent," adds Mukesh Ambani. "My dad said to me: 'I took 20 years to learn this. You'll learn it in five and you'll be twice as smart'. Reliance can be world class if our 65,000 people can beat any other 65,000 people in a one-on-one. From textile spinners to top managers, they have to compete on knowledge, courage, competence – all of it. They have to be better on every single metric, granularly, not just the average."

Of course, this kind of ruthless continual self-improvement needs to start at the top and be cascaded down through the organization by example. "You become obsolete every year," says KV Kamath. "So can you take up to 10 days to retrain yourself? Especially in the early days, I would stand up to my colleagues and say I'm going to get trained for 10 days. Now human resources have made it a rule that all colleagues get eight days' training every year."

EMBRACE THE OPPORTUNITIES OF THE RESET

Some CEOs remain skeptical that the events of 2007–09 mean that things are going to be radically different from now on. There is, for example, a camp who believe that what transpired was little more than one of capitalism's regular crises. "Reset is a pretty little word," says Sir John Parker, "but there are always upturns and downturns. What we've been through is just a particularly harsh example of the latter."

Then there's the view that whether or not there is a reset is not a day-to-day concern for CEOs. Ron Sandler, chairman of UK mortgage bank Northern Rock and closed life insurer Phoenix Group Holdings, argues: "Public policymakers and regulators in particular need to think very hard about this question. They need to decide whether or not we need different models of regulation and apply those models in different ways, and I can well understand why that debate is highly relevant for that segment of the economic population. But when it comes to running a business like Northern Rock or Pearl, the day-to-day running of those businesses is not actually governed by those sorts of considerations. Clearly there are issues to do with reward and with trying to inculcate the right attitudes in people so that the right balances are struck, for example between shareholder and policyholder interests. But those don't stem directly from a consideration of whether or not the world has undergone some step change or not or whether the Far East and Europe are going to be on very divergent paths. The world of running businesses is much more micro and much less macro than that."

Equally, for some CEOs the dominant facet of the economic reset remains the divergence of the world economy into Eastern and Western economies and their very different growth rates.

"We're on a two-lane highway," says Lakshmi Mittal, chairman and chief executive of ArcelorMittal, the world's largest steelmaker. "Clearly, developing economies are in the fast lane and Europe and the US are in the slow lane. Between the US and Europe, I think Europe is lagging behind. Because there's no growth in demand in these economies, we'll have to continue to invest in research and development, continue to work on improving our productivity and efficiency, and reduce our costs so that we remain competitive in Europe and the United States. We do not plan to move our operations from Europe, but clearly Arcelor Mittal's ratio of businesses will move more towards developing economies. We will build new plants there and we will grow those businesses faster than those in Europe and North America."

Ultimately, which view CEOs take doesn't change the fact that they need to discover ways of winning in whatever climates they find themselves. It is clear, however, that a majority of CEOs do see the reset as a real and important phenomenon. The reset world provides bold CEOs with a once-in-a-lifetime window to reinvigorate their business, grasp organic and acquisitive growth globally, and offer opportunities for a new breed of ambitious, global talent. Those who do not will, particularly in the West, be rewarded by no growth and low levels of profitability.

3

THE FIVE REALITIES OF THE NEXT DECADE

In the next decade the business world will change on an unprecedented scale. Most CEOs think the secret to success in those ten years will be understanding how to:

❑ Compete globally in the first decade of hard globalization.
❑ Position your company to deal with the environmental challenge and play a wider role in society as a sustainable business.
❑ Exploit the promise of Web 3.0.
❑ Lead your business through particularly extreme cycles of capitalism.
❑ Be a winner in the first world war for talent.

In this chapter, we take you through all five realities and provide advice from leading CEOs on how to navigate them successfully.

PROFITING FROM HARD GLOBALIZATION

"To succeed in the global bazaar requires a global mindset."
Narayana Murthy, chairman and chief mentor, Infosys

Chief executives see coping with globalization as the most important reality for the next decade. Globalization has been talked about for years, but we're seeing a dramatic shift as India and China reintegrate into the world economy and are expected to surpass developed nations. The recent global financial crisis has done little to dissipate this trend.

Philip Green, chief executive of United Utilities, sees China as "the second industrial revolution", while Ed Zore, chief executive of Northwestern Mutual in the US, says: "Globalization is a trend for the next 200 years." Sir Martin Sorrell adds: "We've not witnessed growth on this scale for 200 years and not at this speed. China and India are going back to where they were in 1819." Then, the two nations generated 49 percent of worldwide GDP, due to silk, spice, and porcelain trading. By 1973 this had shrunk to 8 percent, but they're forecast to hit 49 percent again by 2025.[10]

India is expected to be the fastest-growing economy in 2010 with 8 percent growth, according to the World Bank's 2009 Global Development Finance Report. Deutsche Bank expects China to overtake the US in economic output within a decade. It believes emerging market economies will account for 70 percent of global GDP growth in the next decade. "We're watching something unstoppable that will cause a painful transition," says Sir Martin Sorrell. "The West was on the right side for 200 years and will be on the wrong side for 200 years." It's difficult to see better opportunities for sustained growth than Asia, where huge numbers of people are set to be lifted out of poverty and the educated labor force is multiplying. China and India are leading the way, so global businesses have to be there.

However, there are substantial risks to operating in emerging markets, not least forgetting the West. In real terms, economic power will remain in the West in the medium term, as the US and the EU are expected to have real GDPs bigger than China or India in 2025. Given their huge populations, Chinese and Indian consumers will still be much poorer individually than their western counterparts.[11]

Higher growth means greater risks

Growth at the rates being achieved in China and India is unstable, unpredictable, and prone to crises. China and India are facing structural issues. They're seeing wage inflation and a war for talent for information technology and call center staff. They may be hostages to soaring commodity prices and heavily dependent on oil and coal.

They've sacrificed large swathes of land and taken their toll on the environment in the quest for growth, especially in China.

There are massive infrastructure problems, with transport grinding to a halt in Chinese and Indian cities, and barriers to entry for western companies in some sectors. Both economies are also in the early stages of liberalizing. "The problem is that, as Gandhi said, only 20 percent of what gets sent out by Parliament is spent at its destination," says Vijay Mallya, chairman of United Breweries and Kingfisher Airlines. "What's missing is not resources but accountability."

What's missing is not resources but accountability

A cardinal error is treating the two countries similarly. Narayana Murthy says: "China has a system of governance whereby leaders in Beijing can wave a magic wand and get action. In India the electoral strength is in the rural communities, where there are 650 million people."

The secret of hard globalization

A conception of globalization as either a westward or an eastward flow is flawed. Wipro chief executive Azim Premji says the Indian IT company is building customer relationships in Canada and the Middle East and tapping talent in eastern Europe, Mexico, and the US. "Globalization for Wipro is not just about getting customers in the US and western Europe and talent in India. It's about many other things and places."

Bajaj Auto chairman Rahul Bajaj adds: "We have no choice but to globalize. It may be not only in our interest now but also a question of survival in the future." He wants to raise the proportion of production that's exported from 20 percent to 40–50 percent over five to ten years.

True global competition has started. So how should CEOs compete in hard globalization?

Adopt a global mindset

"Go-out" globalization will be a strategy for failure. Hard globalization starts in the mind. The essential first step is for the CEO and the business to suspend their domicile and stop thinking of themselves as having a "home" base. Every problem is then solved by reference to global best practice and through the application of globally sourced resources. Companies need to adapt and improve best global practices, accept worldwide competition, and produce products and services that compete with the best.

Says Narayana Murthy: "Globalization is about sourcing capital where it's cheapest, sourcing talent where it's best available, producing where it's most efficient, and selling where the markets are. It's about operating without being constrained by national boundaries." Lord Browne adds: *Cooperation and open innovation are the future* "Easy globalization is planting a flag because you have an easy advantage, such as technology. Hard globalization is when everyone's competing. The right view is the truly international one." Liu Jiren, CEO of software company Neusoft, comments: "Now, no one is independent. All the resources are dispersed. Cooperation and open innovation are the future. How to open, to communicate, to improve self are the challenge to East and West."

Create a global strategy and business model
Your strategy for competing globally has to be in your corporate bloodstream. It has to affect the structure of the business and the manner in which it functions. Unless it does, you will fail to think globally while acting locally.

Sir Terry Leahy advises: "Adopt very local business models, be very focused, and don't enter too many countries." Tesco, he says, is flexible in its investments in each country, uses multiple formats for new territories, and concentrates on transforming capability, not relying on scale. "In time, build brands" is his motto.

Joint ventures and partnerships can help. Bringing in local partners with detailed knowledge of their markets can give you the expertise you need at grass-roots level. It's not a question of what you need to own but of what structure you need to procure the most leverage and influence in the markets you're targeting.

Thras Moraitis, head of group strategy and corporate affairs at mining group Xstrata, advises: "Construct joint ventures and ecosystems to help you achieve what you want to achieve. Control will not be at such a premium in the future, so do it now." Tan Pheng Hock, CEO of Singapore Technologies Engineering, argues that we've entered the age of "co-opetition", the ability to cooperate across company borders with sometime competitors in order for both to win.

Fix strong global values
Chief executives need to institute strong universal values that are modeled and celebrated in every culture in which their companies operate, while still leveraging local conditions. Says Azim Premji: "We're focused on never losing sight that applying innovation to help make our customers successful is what makes us successful, never losing our sense of humility and fairness, and being unyielding on integrity. Globalization doesn't change but only accentuates the importance of these basics."

Embrace devolved power
Letting go, resisting the temptation to micro-manage, is one of the hardest management skills to learn when running a global business. But it is absolutely vital to devolve power to ground operations to stimulate enterprise and creativity and ensure you get an authentic local feel and character to what you're doing in each locality.

"Trust the team and let go," urges Mike Turner, chairman of Babcock International and former CEO of BAE Systems. Narayana Murthy adds: "It's very important to decentralize. Articulate your vision, lay out the norms for reporting and the delegating of authority, and formulate a clear escalation mechanism. You need a protocol understood and practiced by various cultures."

Set global minimal standards
Devolution of power needs to be accompanied by complete transparency so that head office can see what local operations are doing. And you need strong central decision-making capabilities to sort out any problems that emerge from actions that have gone wrong. "You should make the decision at the point where the most information is," says Thras Moraitis. "We devolve power from the group

in exchange for transparency. At group level we raise money, manage shareholders, conduct transformational acquisitions, and assist in incremental acquisitions at the request of business leaders. The business units are left alone to run businesses, but give total transparency on results and operational data."

Create a global company clock and live globally
Globalized companies need to learn to cope with working 24 hours a day, 7 days a week. The fact there is always a light on in some part of your global operation brings opportunities for productivity and heightened customer service. It also means time and location can no longer be used as buffers.

Leading a global organization also requires a lot of travel. Many CEOs we interviewed spend 40–50 percent of their time on the road. At GE, chief executive Jeff Immelt operates a "swing" system, swinging into a country for a week to speak to customers, top management, and politicians. This gives him a level view of a nation and allows him to understand market challenges, test his vision, and see how management is responding. After that, he can do things by telephone.

As Tan Pheng Hock says, "You cannot be hands on but you have to breathe the air." Thras Moraitis says you have to be effective straight after your flight lands; something much easier if you've learnt Lord Davies's lesson about sleeping on an aeroplane. Being there, and alert, is not enough. You must ensure that people from all cultures understand you. Communicate simply and directly, laying out clear roles and responsibilities. Leave local nuances to local leaders.

DECODING SUSTAINABILITY

"Climate change will be the single biggest business issue of the next decade. You've got to be on the right side of that."
> James Murdoch, chairman and chief executive, News Corporation
> Europe and Asia and chairman, BSkyB

Sustainability is one of the corporate buzzwords of our time, but it is not well understood. The United Nations' 1987 Brundtland Commission's definition is "development that meets the needs of the present without compromising the needs of future generations". Many CEOs now see sustainability as mitigating climate change, but it's also about social responsibility and companies' role in communities.

Brad Mills says: "There's an increasing backlash between this thing called capitalism and this thing called community. We don't understand the environmental effects and long-range problems communities face; they don't understand business pressures of cost and competition. The challenge is to try and change the world by creating a different model which is much more life-affirming to people."

So how can CEOs meet the sustainability challenge?

Accept that greener business is here to stay

Skeptics said that corporate commitment to sustainability would wane in the recession, but it's still high on the agenda. "Some businesses facing real financial problems have to cut costs to stay alive and may cut some of their environmental efforts," says BAA and Invensys chairman Sir Nigel Rudd. "But businesses that believe they're going to be there in the future will look at the new legislation and at ways they can reduce costs by actively embracing new technology. Good businesses are still prepared to invest in that future."

Corporate environmentalism will encompass all industry sectors over time. The UK government has pledged to reduce the country's carbon emissions by 80 percent by 2050 and Carbon Trust chief executive Tom Delay says the task cannot be underestimated. "The next five to ten years are going to be enormous in the efforts to reduce carbon," he says. "There are incredibly difficult decisions if we're to get anywhere near."

The effort will be long term as governments build low-carbon economies. John Roberts, chairman of Royal Bank of Canada: Europe, says that by 2050 the UK will have virtually carbon-free transport and low-carbon power generation from renewables, nuclear energy, and carbon capture and storage. "The level of CO_2 from energy generation – currently 500g per megawatt of electricity produced – will be about 70g," he says. "And we will have stabilized the level of CO_2 in the atmosphere at around 550 parts per million, compared to 430 now and 280 before the Industrial Revolution."

Cautious voices do exist. John Richards, former chief executive of property group Hammerson, gets "worried by the eco-warrior mindset that says that if anyone does not have a zealot-style enthusiasm for it or dares question the science of the environmental lobby, they have to be shouted down." Skepticism also still exists in the US. James Berrien, Forbes Magazine Group president, says: "Most CEOs in the US see it as important from an image and branding point of view but I'm not sure people see it as core to their business."

"Environmental sustainability is now core to business," counters Samir Brikho, CEO of engineering group AMEC. "You like it or you don't, but you can't ignore it. Sustainability is the way of the world. Otherwise move to another planet."

Although there is cynicism in the West about the response of emerging markets, environmental concerns are rising up the agenda there too. The Chinese government has made environmental action core to its five-year plan and is increasingly making this a very high priority. Unipart Group chief executive John Neill is optimistic. "For the first time I can think of, we can have alignment between all the players," he says, "Governments, corporates, and individuals; the world has a common enemy to fight against."

Connect with broadly defined sustainability

Enlightened companies are moving on to define sustainability much more broadly. Says Lord Davies: "Tomorrow's story is that what you're doing to help the planet be a better place will be part of your brand promise." As well as being "green", this means connecting on social issues, including poverty, health, and homelessness.

Two key drivers of this trend are consumers and employees. Says James Murdoch: "Sustainability for our business is first and foremost about being customer driven. It's about understanding customers' needs and caring about what they care about and not being caught out." As well as becoming the second FTSE100 company to go carbon neutral, BSkyB offers audio description for blind and visually impaired people and a remote control that makes life easier for those with manual dexterity problems. It has also pioneered new ways for parents to control the programs their children watch.

Tesco is also being led into social sustainability action by customers. Says Sir Terry Leahy: "The battle to win customers will increasingly be fought not just on value, choice, and convenience but on being good neighbors, being active in communities, seizing the environmental challenges and behaving responsibly, fairly, and honestly." At BT Group, surveys indicate that customers who rate the company highly for its corporate and social responsibility work are 70 percent more likely to return than those who don't.[12]

Attracting and engaging staff is another powerful motivation for action on broadly defined sustainability. "Talking about profit is a complete waste of time if you want to motivate people," declares Barclays chief executive John Varley. "Am I am able to motivate 120,000 people here by telling them I want them to make more profit? You can forget it. You might as well go and talk to the birds. You have to have an emotional motivation. Our people are motivated by something very deep: the human instinct to help."

Roger Carr, chairman of Centrica and former chairman of Cadbury, says sustainability credentials enable a company to hire the right staff. "It's in the culture of the business," he says. "All of this is in the company's DNA. You don't have to force-feed it to Cadbury. A lot of the people who work for Cadbury joined the business because they like the values." Aviva chairman Lord Sharman adds: "Sustainability is very important in terms of the employer brand. A few years ago, the first question of new graduates was about when they were going to get a car. Now they want to know what your policies are toward sustainability and the environment."

Take advantage of opportunities to reduce costs
Sir Nigel Rudd says there's enlightened self-interest in BAA rebuilding major parts of Heathrow Airport to environmental standards. "We have incorporated a huge amount of effort in reducing the carbon footprint of these buildings and trying to use the environment to our benefit by measures such as using waste water and reducing the amount of heating required from fossil fuels," he says. "All those kinds of things are eventually going to reduce costs."

Justify the position of the business in society
"If you become divorced from your communities, it's potentially quite dangerous and threatening because corporations have no sense of loyalty any more and communities have become increasingly hostile to business," says Brad Mills. One extremely senior UK chairman and former chief executive frets whether this will threaten western capitalism itself. "I worry about the sustainability of the economic model I grew up with," he says. "There's a real threat to capitalism. Only about a billion people in the world participate in free markets. Capitalism has to prove it's the best way to run an economy. The jury is still out."

Similarly, the chief executive of one major British high-street retailer admits his business is "very vulnerable" to the child labor issue. "There are 4,000 garment factories in Bangladesh; you cannot check them all," he says. "And the impact on the population of Africa is such that if you do things wrongly there, that can kill people."

Leaders know that sustainability is the right thing to do. "We do this because our role in society is something multifaceted and very important," says James Murdoch. "I just think businesses can be better."

Make a difference
Former GE Healthcare CEO Sir Bill Castell says: "Companies can be more effective in solving some of the world's problems than politicians. The best CEOs have a vision for their company's impact on the world for 20 or 30 years ahead." Businesses are also much

better than governments at innovation and think beyond geographical boundaries, ministerial systems, and elections. Global
businesses are not the problem; they're actually the solution.

Anglo American CEO Cynthia Carroll says when she arrived at
her job the group had a huge problem with workers dying in its
platinum mines – 29 deaths in the first half of 2007. A senior executive said fatalities would happen whatever the company did. That
night, he reported another fatality, so Carroll shut the mine and
brought 28,000 people out of the ground. "It was clear we were out
of control," she says. The mine was closed for staff retraining,
safety audited and an infrastructure study conducted. Now its
death rate has more than halved while lost-time injuries are down
33 percent. "This fundamentally changed probably the whole mining industry," Carroll comments.

Embed CSR in your business

Business needs to move beyond a focus on inputs and resources to
thinking through its environmental and social footprint. Says
Nandan Nilekani, co-chairman of Infosys Technologies: "Truly
global companies will need to develop a compelling vision that
enables sustainable, profitable development of their business
while benefiting society at large."

Paul Polman says it's possible to create a better world while
boosting shareholder value. He recalls a mother in Cairo explaining
how she collects water from a well to wash clothes and prepares a
fire to cook meals: "I asked what happened when her husband got
home and she said mostly she gets beaten because the laundry
isn't clean enough and the food doesn't taste good enough. If we
can make slightly better washing powder and give her a Knorr
product, for example, with a slightly better taste, it will really
improve the quality of her life."

Explore CSR metrics and engage with stakeholders

Leading companies are developing metrics to measure sustainability
initiatives. Tesco has added "community" to the "growth wheel" that
drives its store managers' work. At Cadbury, Todd Stitzer says: "It's
specifically included in each senior leader's objectives that their

businesses must invest in education and health in their communities." Long-term value will only be built by sustainable businesses in the next decade. Says Sir Martin Sorrell: "If you want to build a business for the long term, you'll take into account the interests of all your stakeholders, so you're not going to foul up the environment, you're not going to annoy governments, nongovernmental organizations, or employees." Sir Bill Castell wants much more cooperation between industry, government, and NGOs to increase accountability and win trust from society. Investors should also benefit. Goldman Sachs sees a correlation between sustainability and better stock market performance, while there are now more than 300 European socially responsible investment funds.

SURFING THE THIRD WAVE OF THE WEB

"The next five years will see a faster rate of change in consumer behavior than ever before. What took 50 years will take 5."
　　　　　　　　　　Mark Clare, chief executive, Barratt Developments

The internet, once widely dismissed in corporate boardrooms as a passing fad, is in its second phase and entering its third. Its ramifications will touch all businesses, and yet 61 percent of CEOs admit they don't know enough about emerging technologies.[13] Clearly, there's a generation gap. CEOs who suffered in the bursting of the dot-com bubble in 2001 or overinvested in preparing for the Y2K computer bug also have deep reservations about technology investments, and most chief executives don't come from technology backgrounds.

Caterina Fake, co-founder of photo-sharing website Flickr, is blunt. "At Davos, again and again companies would say: 'We've crossed the chasm. We've gone digital. We get it'," she says. "But going online is not going to suffice. The new religion is you cannot sleep and rest on that. When corporate leaders say to me: 'We've done that', I say: 'Wait until you see what's coming around the bend.' It's tiring. You can't rest."

The three waves of the internet

Wave one was about businesses establishing a web presence, safe-guarding intellectual property, and opening for e-commerce. Most "old economy" businesses made the transition. Wave two has optimized the web as a way of connecting people, making it essential to everybody, not simply technology geeks. Chad Hurley, co-founder and chief executive of YouTube, says: "The movement itself is just getting started. It is leveraging the power of people, leveraging the power of a community, giving everyone the chance to participate."

Web 2.0 creates business opportunities and massive disruption

Brent Hoberman, co-founder of Lastminute.com, explains: "The web will disrupt more and more industries and major corporates will be faced with a choice to cannibalize themselves or wait for a startup to do it to them. Very few have the bold, courageous leadership to do this." Indeed, he knows of one board that only adopts

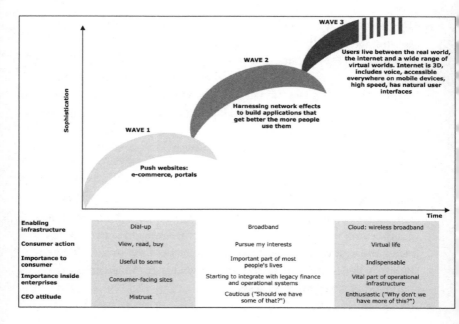

	WAVE 1	WAVE 2	WAVE 3
Enabling infrastructure	Dial-up	Broadband	Cloud: wireless broadband
Consumer action	View, read, buy	Pursue my interests	Virtual life
Importance to consumer	Useful to some	Important part of most people's lives	Indispensable
Importance inside enterprises	Consumer-facing sites	Starting to integrate with legacy finance and operational systems	Vital part of operational infrastructure
CEO attitude	Mistrust	Cautious ("Should we have some of that?")	Enthusiastic ("Why don't we have more of this?")

technology when enough of its members' grandchildren start using it!

It can make traditional businesses much more efficient
Sir Terry Leahy highlights the breadth of internet applications at Tesco.com, which has grown online turnover from nothing to £2 billion. "The role of the internet as a medium for creating new retail businesses is growing in significance," he says. "Its role in enabling efficient operations is gathering pace. And its role as a place for developing relationships with business is growing rapidly." Liu Jiren adds: "When we design hospital IT solutions now, we're seeking to get all parties to collaborate: doctors, families, hospitals, our systems. Web 2.0 will be vital to that." Sir Bill Castell adds: "The internet and information are going to fundamentally transform lots of industries in the next decade, especially healthcare. The ability to engage patients in their own health will allow true personalized treatment."

It enables closer customer relationships
Trail-blazing businesses are going far beyond using the web as a shop window for e-commerce and as a brand-building tool. Nike, for example, allows consumers to create their own shoes on a company website. Nike USA chief executive Mark Parker says, "Web 2.0 is enabling a fundamental shift in power that really is giving the power to the consumer to engage, connect, and create and to do so on a scale never seen before. That's going to have so much ripple effect in ways we don't know."

Electrical components distributor Premier Farnell is also asking customers what they need in a sophisticated online forum. Chief executive Harriet Green says Web 2.0 is enabling the company to evolve into a much more interactive, value-added distribution business.

It helps businesses evolve and refresh employee relationships
Web 2.0 will allow companies to minimize inappropriate command-and-control structures and enable more sophisticated, flat structures. John Chambers believes collaboration technology

and other Web 2.0-related innovations will increase productivity by between 1 and 5 percent by 2012. "We see the next wave of productivity reaccelerating around the world," he says. Philip Rosedale, founder of Linden Lab, owner of virtual world Second Life, believes CEOs have to manage differently with Web 2.0. "If they maintain a rigid, top-down, command-and-control structure in the future, they will probably fail," he says. "Improved technology leads to radically greater transparency, which leads to looser management and lower cost."

Bill Amelio at Lenovo set up an online "cultural compass" blog to allow greater dialogue between all levels of the company and was very impressed to see the number of "undiscussables" raised. Says Michael Dell: "We commit the same resources to listening to our teams as we do to our customers. We've gotten great feedback from our teams about how to improve Dell as a workplace, and also for our customers." Google president of global sales operations and business development Nikesh Arora says the development of consumer web tools has forever changed the face of business technology. "Employees now expect the same ease of use at work and flexibility of access as they have with applications in their personal lives," he adds. "This means sharing information and collaborating on projects in the same way as they share their photos, chat on social networks, and invite people to comment on their blogs. Information sharing is as important, if not more important, within organizations as it is to individuals."

Web 2.0 challenges

Web 2.0 presents businesses with vast opportunities, but CEOs find it difficult to disrupt the market and can be thwarted by tensions with core businesses. It can also be difficult to get sufficient cross-functional collaboration between functions such as IT, marketing, and the line businesses to implement the technical and institutional changes required. It's hard for companies to modify their traditional structures to create a business that effectively harnesses the energy and initiative of workers from the bottom up. Then there are challenges of intellectual property rights management and revenue sharing.

None of these is insuperable and the rewards are immense, so it's well worth CEOs embedding the web in their businesses. Azim Premji at Wipro states: "We use the web for training, employee self-service, asset management, collaborative teamwork, risk management, and as an internal marketplace for jobs. Every function, every business, every group uses it. It's completely integrated into operations as a driver of efficiency, immediacy, and collaboration."

Wave Three: What Next?

Another transforming change is coming. In Web 3.0, users will live between the real world and a wide range of virtual worlds. The internet will be three-dimensional, will include voice command, and will be accessible from everywhere on mobile devices. It will operate at high speed and have natural user interfaces. The key entry point will be wireless broadband and the web will, at last, be compelling and indispensable to most consumers.

Web 3.0 will be vital to the fabric of life

Tomorrow's adults will take the internet and mobile telecoms for granted. For them, the world has always been connected. In the developing world millions of people are coming online, often leapfrogging technologies and moving straight to mobile broadband. Worldwide users will become increasingly used to accessing the internet at any time and in any place.

Cloud computing is also becoming increasingly prevalent. Here, both the software and the information accessed through the software live on centrally located servers rather than on a single user's computer, which means users can access information they need from any web-enabled device. In practice, this means that if your laptop breaks when you're on a business trip you don't also lose all your work, because it's stored in a data center and you can access it from any device.

It will engage businesses and consumers in collaboration

Narayana Murthy sees Web 3.0 enabling much more interaction between customers, vendors, and competitors in making life better for customers, as well as allowing better collaboration on business problems. "There needs to be a shift in mindset," he says. The challenge is communicating to chief executives just how much more transformation Web 3.0 can bring. John Chambers says, "I think it will be dramatically bigger than the first wave both in terms of network volumes as well as productivity and business model changes. It's going to change business models in a way that will make the first phase of the internet look small. That's what this next decade is about."

It will be vastly more compelling and enjoyable
The web is already a forum for some of life's most important inter-actions; the high degree of personalization that Wave Three will encompass will also make it a core channel for content consumption. Jean-Marc Frangos, senior vice-president of technology and innovation at BT Group, predicts: "Web 3.0 will be a rich personality repository; it's a window on your true interests. We've only seen the beginning of personalization for online consumers and we'll see it in enterprise applications too." Neusoft is excited about the prospects raised by virtual worlds, though Liu Jiren adds a note of caution. "These worlds present challenges to legal systems," he says. "People may be hurt. People like to live in both worlds, real and virtual. I don't know if that's good or bad. This may be a new crisis for our society."

Words of caution
———————

Technology flattens the world but doesn't solve its core problems. Companies should still focus on what they have to do to win and figure out how to do that using the best available methods, including but not limited to the web. "Fundamental business principles have not changed. You need to understand the consumer," says Martina King, former managing director of country operations for Europe, Yahoo!.

"You have to ask what your core proposition is," adds Russ Shaw, director of innovation at Spanish telecoms group Telefonica. "What will the customer pay for? Then, you need to create a seamless experience." Web 3.0 will also increase the price of operational mistakes. Reputational damage in the Web 3.0 environment will be swift for companies that are caught out, because of the speed at which information can spread around the world.

Security is a big issue. Val Gooding, former chief executive at health insurer BUPA, says: "Putting out personal information can lead to people hounding you. I see a lot of violence and intrusion of privacy if more information is opened up." There are also huge risks regarding the protection of consumer data.

Lastly, remember that technology adoption always takes longer than you think. "When I worked at Intel in the 1980s, there were posters on the wall reading 'Have you emailed today?'" remembers Subrah Iyar, founder of WebEx. "I also recall a friend at Bell Laboratories telling me that it took 15 years for people to adopt the push-button telephone over the radial dial."

RIDING THE CYCLES OF CAPITALISM

"A manager's job is to manage in the good times and the bad times. Great managers use difficult times to position for competitive advantage."
Archie Norman, chairman, ITV

The recession that followed the effective closure of western capital markets as a result of the US subprime mortgage crisis that infected the wider debt markets in 2007 is reckoned to be the biggest recession in the history of modern capitalism. A key challenge is managing capital through such cycles, with the higher cost of finance and the weakening of consumer demand in current western markets in sharp contrast to the preceding five years, which were typified by cheap debt and solid growth.

That is also only half of the capital story. Even prior to the downturn, CEOs were wrestling with a rapid transformation in their sources of funding. The "capital" in capitalism has become more complex and globally diverse than ever before. Significant inflows of capital can now be gathered not only from institutional and private investors, but also from private equity firms, sovereign wealth funds from Asia and the Middle East, and hedge funds.

So how do CEOs adapt their leadership style to ensure they can succeed, whatever stage the cycles of capitalism are at?

Survival comes first, so capital and cash are king

Survival is the first priority in a downturn. This means ensuring the balance sheet is strong, the business is adequately capitalized, and the company is generating the cash it needs to meet debt covenants.

"Cash is king, so keep the balance sheet strong," advises Ian Coull, CEO of property group Segro. "You will have the fire power to take advantage when things settle down."

Barclays CEO John Varley believes in keeping the balance sheet as efficient as possible, even in a downturn. "You have to form a point of view about how much capital you need to run your business," he says. "You have to be prudent in that and you have to be analytical. You have to determine that number and that's what you've got to have."

Critical to operating within capital constraints is efficient cash generation, as Rahul Bajaj explains. "In a growing business, sometimes operating efficiency and working capital take a back seat and businesses bloat up. This can hurt in a downturn. However, if the business is always run lean with a continuous focus on increasing efficiency, then no special effort is required in a downturn."

In tough times the temptation, exaggerated by feverish markets, is to cut deep and early, a move often presented as "decisive and brave". However, take great care not to be short-sighted. Philip Green thinks that "leadership is about the tough prioritization calls. Yes, you have to cut costs but what you consciously do *not* cut is just as important," he says. "We will continue to invest in our priorities – especially talent, training, and climate change."

Alan Rosling at Tata Sons says: "Leaders need to balance the immediate issues, which will lead to greater caution, cost reduction, and a more careful risk profile, with the need to maintain the long term. Investment in brands, training and development of people, technology and innovation, and the opening of new markets all need to continue even while the immediate performance of the business is maintained."

Focus more intensely on organizational performance and talent

Archie Norman believes it's critical to clear the decks straight away. "You must try to avoid continuous surprise," he says. "It's much better to try to 'panic early': declare your losses, get any luggage over board, and get your people facing the bad news."

Andy Hornby, the former HBOS CEO who is now chief executive of Alliance Boots, says that ensuring operations are really slick is critical during turbulent times. CEOs should "surround themselves with people who don't mind having to take tough decisions," he states. "From the finance director to divisional chief executives, people should be comfortable with saying 'no'. You need to get people around you who have the strength to say no when things are not right."

Equally, some of your high fliers will need more attention in a downturn. Warns Ian Coull: "There needs to be more hands-on activity, as many of the high fliers will not have experienced it before and they could panic." Archie Norman agrees: "You have to get people motivated and facing the recession. They must not feel bad that there's a global recession – it's not their fault!"

Have radar and act fast

Speed is of the essence in fast-changing markets: a long delay can mean missing a crucial opportunity that could make or break the company. Raising finance at the right time is a key example. "Capital markets are like the tide," says Andy Hornby. "You have got to catch the tide. Once it has gone out, you are left high and dry." Managing capital in a constrained market requires CEOs to take advantage of limited opportunities.

Pulling off such deals requires a very responsive business. "It is really important when doing something like this that your lines of communication are short and effective," says John Varley. "The kind of shorthand that you get from knowing each other and trusting each other is very valuable in the intense period of activity around a big transaction like this."

Down cycles are opportunities too

Former Prudential chief executive Mark Tucker is insistent: "Often a downturn brings opportunity – that's why boldness becomes vital." He adds: "There needs to be a preparedness to take these opportunities. The difference at this juncture between good and mediocre is that the mediocre will tend to be overcautious or reckless, rather than bold and decisive." Many CEOs believe you should look to grow market share and competitive advantage with the same intensity as before the downturn.

This assertion is powerfully illustrated in the financial services industry. Bob Diamond, chief executive of corporate investment banking and wealth management at Barclays, which bought the US assets of collapsed investment bank Lehman Brothers, says: "Most foreign banks have not succeeded when they've entered the US market. It's counter-trend to be investing in the US, but we see an opportunity to move into the top three or top five."

Liu Jiren advocates a careful review of how you can take advantage of the change in circumstances across your organization, saying companies should consider their ways of operating and search for new business models that may help them focus on exploring long-term industry possibilities. "During any economic recession, it is much easier to complete a buyout or merger at a lower price than usual," he says. "Any economic downturn could be a strategic time for enterprises to invest for the future."

Even in recessions, there will be great opportunities for organic growth, in particular in emerging markets. In Alan Rosling's view: "The emerging world will become relatively more influential as a result of a slowing in the developed world. Good western companies will continue to grow their businesses in emerging markets, while emerging-market companies will gain relative position."

CEOs' advice for a downturn

As in any major shock to business, downturns put the CEO in the spotlight. Experienced CEOs offer the following advice.

Be visible and have a roadmap
It is very easy to be knocked by a tough economic climate. Carolyn McCall, CEO of Guardian Media Group, says: "The most important thing is the posture and language of my top team. It's very easy for directors to seem beleaguered in a downturn and that is very dangerous. Leaders need to bring energy and belief to their teams."

The bottom line is that all your people need reassurance during tough times. CEOs stress the importance of communicating clearly and frequently with employees, so they are reassured and can reassure customers. One CEO sent an email to his whole business explaining the need for a rights issue and by lunchtime he had had 2,000 responses. Another confided: "People will follow you through almost any troubles if they know the business is facing reality and has a roadmap ultimately to get to a good place in the future."

Believe in yourself
It's in times of downturn that you can make the right decision for the medium or long term and still watch your stock price plummet by 60 percent. This is where it is a lonely personal burden to keep an eye on the long term. Being a CEO at these times is not a popularity contest and analysts and commentators have little idea of what's going to happen to the economy. "The reality is you have to go more with your gut," one FTSE100 CEO told us, "because the markets and analysts don't give you credit for doing the right things for business in the long term at this stage of the cycle."

Stick by your convictions about the business
In tough times, CEOs come under harsh financial performance pressures and it can be tempting to do business that does not fit with your long-term strategy. You must resist. "During tough market conditions we need to make sure we stick to our principles of not writing business for a short-term gain, maintain our longer-

term view and financial discipline, and don't succumb to the temptation to please the market with robust sales growth at the expense of profitability," says Mark Tucker. Ultimately, you must not be distracted by the market and must continue to turn out great business.

Discipline also requires you to safeguard the assets you'll need to capitalize on during the economic recovery. "Of course you have to get the costs down, but if you cut too hard and too fast and too near the bone, you cannot come out of the crunch fast enough," says Carolyn McCall. "When palpable opportunities reappear, you won't have the resources to take advantage."

WAGING THE FIRST WORLD WAR FOR TALENT

"Human capital is more important than financial capital."
                    Sir Bill Castell, chairman, The Wellcome Trust

"My ideal people have Ivy League brains and blue-collar brawn."
                    Andy Haste, chief executive, RSA

In our survey of FTSE100 CEOs, 68 percent ranked talent and human capital as top priority. However, global workforces are becoming much more unstable and complex to manage. Graduates entering the workforce today will have 13 jobs by age 38.[14] Companies need a new approach.

Talent tops the CEO agenda

"One of the biggest issues is attracting talent," says Sir Martin Sorrell. "If you have the right people running the business units, it works magically. It's like turning up the volume." Why, he ponders, do analysts fret about capital investment when two-thirds of WPP's turnover goes straight into the pockets of his company's greatest assets? BT chairman Sir Michael Rake agrees. "The biggest challenge for global companies is to unleash the power of our people," he says. "It's not easy, as cultural issues get in the way and it needs common values. But the more diverse the employees, the more innovative, richer, and more likely you are to find a global solution that will succeed."

Kevin Whiteman, chief executive at utility Kelda Group, thinks along the same lines. "We've all seen dysfunctional teams at the top," he says. "They destroy organizations. The biggest keystone is the unity and clarity and purpose and togetherness of the top team." Recruiting and managing the right talent is critical, even in a solidly performing business, says Richard Pym. "If you look at a senior team of 50 people, you normally only have to change two or three to make a difference." Fresh blood can supercharge performance in a turnaround situation. Archie Norman adds: "Changing means changing people. You are what you recruit. Your success depends on it."

Walking the talk

"CEOs don't make time to put talent on the agenda," says one HR director. "We ask the right questions, we really want to drive it. And they believe it and buy it, but don't give it time. It comes back to us, and it stays an HR initiative. They get it but are not executing."

Some CEOs do make sure they address this issue. Steve Holliday, chief executive at National Grid, aims to allot 20 percent of his time to talent development and has his personal administrator calculate his performance against the target every two months. "If you get really good people, it's amazing the difference they can make," he says.

Michael Dell agrees. "I was asked why we hadn't articulated 'people' as one of our five priorities," he says. "The answer is simple. They're the ultimate priority. I spend a good portion of my time on talent."

Eric Daniels tracks his hit rate. "You cannot hire someone to engage all the staff and make sure you have the talent that you need throughout the organization," he says. "That's something the CEO must do. Hiring is a pretty random walk, but a person who is a bad fit has a very profound negative effect on the company. I spend a lot of time researching and trying to figure out how people are going to add value. I'm very conscious of the cost of a miss."

A step change in HR performance

Many CEOs are scathing about the HR profession. "Few HR depart-ments are able to deliver HR's potential," complains Philip Green. "The low appetite within businesses for HR is depressing, as is the scarcity of excellent HR professionals. HR is a critical function: it should be an enabler for the general managers in the heart of the business." Brent Hoberman adds: "Most corporate HR teams are not great, as they are inflexible and can't respond to the packages required for the new world of work."

Command-and-control businesses required only a mechanistic service from HR: an efficient compensation and benefits system and slick hiring and firing process. This has created a strong process orientation in many HR directors. Says Archie Norman: "The trouble is that there's an HR profession which is a menace. They bring with them a process. They flaunt at you regulation all the time. That's their trump card. When you find they've won every other argument, they say 'Ha, ha, but you've got to have a consultation', and when you have a consultation they manage to make a great meal of it which is designed to make everybody miserable."

Former Granada CEO Sir Gerry Robinson adds: "The key to suc-cess is getting the right people. There's a tendency in HR to try to do more than that. HR has a tendency to get involved in things that don't contribute as they should at the sharp end."

CEOs require a much more substantial contribution from HR, which should in turn be regarded as a strategic partner. At Cadbury, Todd Stitzer says there has been an HR person on the board for the last 30 years and that talent development, succession, and the identification of external talent are given two prime hours at every monthly executive committee. At such companies HR is regarded as a truly strategic function and people value the department's judgment in discussions of strategy and organizational design. Carolyn McCall believes HR has to be an enabler at the strategic level. "I work with my human resources director in a discursive way," she says. "Once every six weeks we meet and understand issues and team coaching and support. She sees the business in a fresh way and suggests ways to do it. I ensure she has good operational HR people to deliver."

HR professionals need to be drawn from a commercial background or rotated through roles, so that they truly understand the reality of the business. Says Eric Daniels: "Most banks have lousy HR departments, so none of the candidates for my head of HR were from a bank. I looked for an extraordinary executive with a pattern of success."

HR must also be truly global. Globally dispersed leadership teams need an HR framework to support them. Lord Davies says, "As businesses go global, talent management by necessity becomes more bureaucratic. The leader cannot just walk down the corridor to see his people. Therefore HR becomes a strategic partner to the CEO."

Search is outdated

Can chief executives simply go to external search consultants to bolster their internal HR function and deliver their talent agenda? The answer should be yes, but many CEOs don't rate the search industry, perceiving it as too transaction based and unready to be a strategic partner. One says, "Most consultants have a narrow geographical or sector focus and are transactional, driving you to do the highest number of searches as quickly as possible. I don't think any could give me a list of the top 1 percent of global talent."

"I've never met a headhunter with in-depth knowledge of my sector," says Val Gooding. Krister Svensson, founder of executive mentoring firm CMi, adds: "Headhunters rarely challenge perceived wisdom. They often seem to take orders like a *maître d'hôtel*."

Richard Baker says that chief executives need a talent partner from the search industry. "They need radar on the industry and on perceptions of their company," he states. "The search partner should be like a deputy HR director. They should be in the CEO's diary every month."

Apply the talent mindset

Talent-magnet companies will make it a critical objective to attract the top 1 percent of the best people globally and structure their businesses to ensure they provide attractive and stimulating routes for that talent. "You need a single, integrated approach to talent to succeed in a global, integrated world," says Sir Bill Castell. "You need to be global and give the opportunity to grow leaders outside the home market."

Liu Jiren adds: "There will be no difference between eastern and western leaders in the twenty-first century, because the world is now a small village. Western and eastern leaders have the same language and ability so will compete together. Although cultures will not merge, abilities will."

In acting globally, talent-magnet companies self-consciously aim to be talent scouts. Great businesses continuously scout for talent that can form a semi-warm bench of potential recruits for when a succession looms. Talent scouting will result in workforces that are characterized by difference. Never forget that talent is about individuals, whether you're trying to attract, retain, or develop people. Scouting for talent proactively will turn up irresistibly attractive, exceptional individuals who do not fit any particular predefined hole. So break the mold.

"Businesses are all about balance between control and innovation," says John Richards. "If you want to lead rather than follow, you have to make space for and tolerate the odd maverick. These characters don't always file their expenses on time; they can be easily coaxed into compliance, but they are inevitably going to reoffend. I am prepared to tolerate that because we want this person's contribution to the success of our business." Former Royal Mail chairman Allan Leighton adds: "You have to have a balance of 10 percent mavericks and 90 percent nonmavericks. You're not balancing that enough if a manager doesn't have the capability to have three or four people who don't fit the usual mold."

Talent tactics
_____

Talent-magnet companies will employ distinctive tactics to attract, develop, and retain the top 1 percent of global talent. Todd Stitzer says, "I want to surround myself with the smartest people I can: people with the same value set in how they treat others and a desire for accomplishment." Adds Richard Baker: "I always look for personal qualities and who's got an edge rather than technical competencies, and when I do that I inevitably get it right."

Most CEOs do not know even their top 100 people in detail, but to have a true focus on individuals the CEO and HR must know the aspirations, motivations, morale, and capabilities of the business's talent. True individualization leads to flexible action. When an employee hits a personal crisis, for example a death in the family, the company's reaction will forever color his or her relationship with the organization and colleagues. HR and line managers must be close enough to employees to spot these issues and must be empowered and bold enough to push through genuine short-term actions to help. This level of commitment to talent takes a huge amount of time. In response, some companies split HR systems maintenance from the talent function.

It's important to recognize that you will not have a 100 percent success rate in hiring. Fire fast if you make a mistake. Archie Norman comments: "The ones that don't work out, you've got to get out of the business again and you do it fast, because otherwise you accumulate people who are halfway successful or no good at all, and because you've got investment in them, it takes you two years to figure out you made a mistake. My best performance was recruiting somebody and parting company with them the same day they arrived. It was the right thing to do. It was obvious it wasn't going to work for him and it wasn't going to work for us."

A central role for the CEO
_____

The CEO needs to drive the talent agenda. Greg Dyke, former director-general of the BBC, points out: "If you want to change the culture of an organization, human resources can only do it if it has the chief executive with it." The CEO must also make the talent agenda a priority for everyone in the business. Talent attraction, retention, and development must be made key responsibilities for all line managers, who must be incentivized on this. Companies should be just as ruthless about underperformance on talent as they are on growth and margin targets. CEOs of many companies will find that their HR function will need repositioning and upgrading.

Winning on talent is hard. Shire Pharmaceuticals CEO Matt Emmens says: "It's like you're on the train and running the engine and changing the wheels. It's controlled chaos. You're changing all the systems while they're in place."

Sir Terry Leahy and Jeff Immelt are CEOs fully engaged in the talent agenda. Sir Terry chairs Tesco's "people matters" group, and says that employees are managed as rigorously as commercial or financial assets. The committee examines Tesco's work levels four and five – about 400 people. At GE, Immelt is actively involved with all 180 VPs and 450 senior executives. Sir Bill Castell says that at GE Healthcare he was actively involved in the assessment, development, and succession of more than 460 people and spent 60 days a year on talent issues. Great CEOs are continually asking how they should set up the business to get the best from talent and develop it effectively – and they never stop asking.

The best CEOs have an external radar that informs their strategies. They are also able to simplify and prioritize, giving their teams and business clarity. Keeping front of mind these five realities and how they influence the profit dynamic for your business will help you give the guidance your organization needs.

PART II

LEADING AT THE TOP TODAY

"There is not one answer to leadership: one is trying to find the keys to the answer for one point in time."

John Pluthero, Cable & Wireless

So there you have it: CEOs are worrying about a huge range of problems that affect their businesses, but five critical trends stand out in their minds. We think that many companies will struggle to cope with the trends we examined in Part I and so we spend Part III looking at how some of the best CEOs are reshaping their organizations to profit from these testing times.

Before we examine how businesses are likely to change, in Part II we think it's important to examine the way CEOs are actually leading their businesses today. What have the best leaders learnt about how to lead?

❑ How do top chief executives really run their businesses?

❑ Where have they come from?

❑ What motivates and drives them?

The first insight from our analysis is that most current CEOs are really professional managers. It seems clear that the start of the new century has been characterized by the replacement of the 1990s' publicity-hungry, "celebrity" CEOs with professional managers. The latter are typically more risk averse and, wary of eye-catching ventures and personal publicity, may prefer to make incremental adjustments to their company's core businesses rather than seeking to promote dramatic change.

The second insight is more heartening. In contrast to professional managers, top CEOs are far-sighted leaders who are open to radical change but not set on it, and who paint a sophisticated and compelling picture of the future for their employees, customers, and shareholders. Not for them a bland three-year planning cycle: these CEOs are always impatient and looking to push the boundaries of their organizations.

The third crucial insight is that top-quartile CEOs fall into five distinct categories. In fact, we were surprised by quite how different the operating styles of our top CEOs were. In this part of the book we define these leadership types and illustrate how they work through detailed profiles of leading examples. We have found that these types hold true wherever in the world leaders are from.

Note that we did not set out to "pigeonhole" CEOs' leadership styles. We have here identified the characteristics these top leaders have displayed up to this point in their careers, and in the leadership situations they have faced. It is not impossible that their leadership styles could evolve in the future, or that they have strengths that have yet to be brought out by their experience.

Equally, any classification brings clarity but risks simplification. It is clear that the individuals we profile are superb, broadly based leaders and will also exhibit characteristics that are associated with other leadership types. The truth is that great leaders outperform most of us on most elements of leadership, but also have particularly pronounced strengths that characterize their style. We have tried to focus on our profilees' most instructive clusters of strengths (and weaknesses) in the following chapters.

In outline, the five leadership types we've identified are as follows.

Commercial executors focus on how the business is trading: "What are our like-for-like store sales this week?"
Commercial executors have a driving focus on achieving the best results in their industry, combined with a relentless attention to detail in order to ensure that operational and strategic ambitions become a reality. Tesco chief executive Sir Terry Leahy and Avon Products' CEO Andrea Jung are our prime examples.

Financial value drivers focus relentlessly on the financial worth of their business: "What's the business worth today?"

Financial value drivers recognize that business metrics are essential, but what really keeps them awake is the group's valuation and where the next value-accretive deal might come from. They understand the metrics of their industry and are often highly skilled in identifying value-enhancing corporate transactions or realizing value from portfolio disposals. Xstrata chief executive Mick Davis and Kraft Foods chairman and CEO Irene Rosenfeld illustrate this type.

Corporate entrepreneurs live their business: "What's happened to my baby today?"

Corporate entrepreneurs have something to prove. They disrupt industries because they believe in a better way of doing things. They excel in spotting breakthrough opportunities and making them a reality. We feature Sir Martin Sorrell, who founded WPP, now one of the world's largest advertising and marketing businesses, and Michael Spencer, chief executive of inter-dealer broking giant ICAP.

Corporate ambassadors worry about the global impact of their business: "How can I transform the geopolitical landscape of my industry?"

Corporate ambassadors have a global vision that has a broader societal impact; they operate at a geopolitical level and often deliver transactions that transform industries. Lord Browne, the former CEO of BP who is now forging a new career in private equity, propelled BP from a mid-ranking European company into the third largest oil company in the western world. Sir John Parker, chairman of Anglo American and National Grid, is another key example of the model.

Global missionaries wake up every day and renew their personal mission: "How do I make my company and the world a fundamentally better place for all my stakeholders?"

Global missionaries want to make a significant personal difference and at the same time make their companies great. They are typically customer champions and lead by inspiring people and energizing them to tap into their potential. Two of the best examples are Cisco Systems chief executive John Chambers and Zhang Ruimin, CEO of Chinese conglomerate Haier.

In the following chapters we set out the measures of success that most resonate with these leaders, the situations in which each type generally excels, the industries in which they are most commonly found, their particular strengths, and the risks with which they are most often associated.

We hope that this part of the book will help you gain a better understanding of how *you* lead, the likely gaps and shortfalls in your leadership approach, what skills to look for in potential team members, and whether the industry and situation you are in are the most appropriate for you.

4

COMMERCIAL EXECUTORS

Commercial executors are so named not for their skills in chopping heads or cutting costs, but for their ability to get things done. They combine a driving focus on achieving the best results in their industry with a relentless attention to detail in order to ensure that operational and strategic ambitions become a reality. There are two types of commercial executor: driving personal leaders and team marshals.

Driving personal leader commercial executors are focused on industry metrics. In the retail sector, commercial executors like Tesco chief executive Sir Terry Leahy have instant recall of the latest week's like-for-like sales. In insurance, commercial executors like Mark Tucker, former CEO of life and pensions group Prudential, compete fiercely on quarterly new business figures and on the industry's embedded value metrics that measure the value of in-force policies.

Industrial commercial executors, such as Phil Cox, CEO of International Power, and Steve Holliday at National Grid, are driven by a quest to raise productivity and eliminate waste. Holliday has a relentless focus on continuous improvement, which he manages through business metrics. "A lot of people think that if you do 5 percent better than last year, that's very good," he says. "But if you just improve by 5 percent, you leave a huge amount of opportunity on the table. You have got to really inspire people with vision. It can't just be the old rhetoric about all having to go up the hill together."

Team marshal corporate executors, meanwhile, accent the development of their team as their engine for success. Examples include Virgin Active chairman and former Alliance Boots chief executive Richard Baker, Capita CEO Paul Pindar and Paul Walsh, chief executive of Diageo. Often self-effacing individuals wary of media exposure or celebrity status, they exhibit a genuine interest in the people around them and the roles all team members can play in meeting business targets.

Says Paul Walsh: "You've got all these people managing in the right direction in the same boat. You've got to make the destination compelling. Whether it's an ambition to be the best company on the planet or something else, you have to orchestrate your forces and modify the profile of skills you have got in accordance with the objective. To my mind, the CEO should be called the chief engagement officer. There are so many people you have to pay attention to."

This all sounds very cosy – but can team marshals deliver with this "soft" focus on people? Fear not: they're true to their commercial executor type and their people management is distinctly hard edged.

"When I joined Asda, the then chief executive Archie Norman told me that the hardest thing to change is people," recalls Baker, "so I was to interview everyone in my new department and fire four of the 30 by the fourth Friday of my tenure and then hire replacements fast. I've kept this focus on quality. By the end of my first six months at Boots, I had fired two direct reports. It gave me space to hire new people and signaled change. By the end of my tenure I'd changed everyone in the top team."

PROFILE OF A DRIVING PERSONAL LEADER:
SIR TERRY LEAHY, CHIEF EXECUTIVE OF TESCO

As chief executive of Tesco since 1997, Sir Terry Leahy has turned that company from a good business into a great one, making it Britain's biggest retailer and then taking its operating model to Asia, Eastern Europe, and the US.

When he became chief executive, the name of the game was still fierce rivalry with Sainsbury's for the position of Britain's top retailer. However, great driving personal leaders excel not only at pushing their companies to deliver but at spotting new battlegrounds to win in. When the City began to doubt whether Tesco could continue its UK growth story amidst a planning clampdown on new out-of-town superstores, Sir Terry took the battle to the high street, stunning the City with the acquisition of convenience stores group T&S Stores for £337 million. In one swoop, the acquisition boosted Tesco's still fledgling high-street operations by 862 convenience stores.[15] Later, he surprised analysts again by buying a £100 million majority stake in Dobbies Garden Centres, a new area of business for Tesco.[16]

Acquisitions are just one tool in Sir Terry's kitbag. He has proved that he can grow Tesco organically in the UK, building its share of the nation's wallets to today's position where it accounts for £1 out of every £7 spent in the country.[17] He has also demonstrated that he can expand overseas, quietly amassing retail operations in more than ten countries in Eastern Europe and the Far East before embarking on Tesco's long-awaited push into the US. "We have more space outside the UK than within," he told the *Daily Telegraph*. "It's an extraordinary statistic. We're highly profitable outside the UK and growing rapidly, and yet the number of expatriates in our overseas operations is less than one in 1,000, so we have been able to achieve all these things with a relatively light investment in management."[18]

It's instructive that Tesco began its international expansion in 1995, two years before Sir Terry's appointment. Corporate executors don't always need to be the people who start trends or come up with innovation; their flair is for turning strategy into successful reality. Sir Terry did not lead on this initiative, though he was on the board that backed it. However, his eye for detail, organizational excellence, energy, and relentless focus on results have made the expansion a huge success. "It was a big decision for Tesco," he says. "Retailing is the most local of industries and it was far from certain there could be an international industry. But we felt that if we were to stay in the front rank of our industry we would have to be international, to seek out the best competitors, and to learn from them. We knew that it would always take time to put down sufficiently deep roots in a market to provide a platform for long-term success."[19]

The international story is only one element of Tesco's transformation under Sir Terry's leadership. Other components include the power it has accumulated in "nonfood" areas like consumer electronics and music retailing, the growth of its Tesco Extra hypermarkets, the astonishing success of its Clubcard in driving customer loyalty, and its successful diversification into financial services products such as home and car insurance.

All these strategic moves have been accomplished with little fanfare and without simply following fashion. Key is Tesco's focus on carefully chosen business metrics and peer comparisons against which to measure its performance, as well as a constant opportunism for chances to extend the brand.

This opportunism is underpinned by a commitment to the values that Tesco has associated itself with: simplicity, economy, and excellent service; all the values that underpin the CEO himself. Rather than this being a case of an egocentric CEO putting his stamp on the company he leads, it seems that Sir Terry's 29-year career at Tesco has engrained the business in him. Indeed, it's hard to see where Tesco stops and Sir Terry starts. There's no doubt that his relatively low ego by CEO standards, strong family background, and dry wit, including his long-suffering support for Everton Football Club, keep him grounded in reality.

Sir Terry on being a driving personal leader

"In business, the important thing is the relationship between the firm and its customers. I've always had a very strong sense of what's important. It's what the business is for. It's its customers. All you can do is leave the business better than you found it. What else is there? That's enough. The radar comes from working with customers. What do they need in their lives? You're talking about where they are heading, what they want, what's changing. The talent radar is easier because retailers are managers of people. That's what you do. So through the process of managing people you're managing talent.

"What you don't do also matters. That is why we tend to be internally focused. That's what matters, not the cocktail circuit. It's not driven through the lash; it's driven through the culture. A lot is driven through giving people confidence to make decisions for themselves, for the customer. It's not to be driven by fashion. Our presentations to shareholders don't change over the years; we concentrate on the same things."

Formative roots and career

Terry Leahy grew up in a prefabricated maisonette on the Lee Park council estate in a working-class part of Liverpool, UK. The third of four brothers born to a greyhound trainer who worked as caretaker on the council-owned farm where they lived, he went to a Catholic grammar school before gaining a business science degree from Manchester University. "My brothers all left school at 16, but my parents worked very hard so that I could stay on and do my A levels," he says on his former university's website.

After university, he worked for the Co-op for a year and a half as a graduate trainee before quitting to move to London with Alison, now his wife. There he joined Tesco, initially as a casual worker stacking shelves, aged 23. He soon joined the marketing department and before he turned 30 had become Tesco's marketing director. Eight years later, in 1992, he was appointed to the board of directors, and by the time he was 40 he had worked his way up to become chief executive.

Sir Terry's family background has given him a down-to-earth approach with a solid connection to day-to-day life and "ordinary" people. He eschews a chauffeur-driven car, does not sit on other companies' boards, and prefers pacing his shop floors to networking at glitzy receptions.

"Being centered must come from your upbringing," he says. "I had loving parents and a very secure background. My Catholic education brought me up to serve, not to judge people, and to know that no one is better than you but you're not better than anyone else."

Core beliefs and values

Sir Terry's ordinariness is not a front or a stunt. He is obsessed with the company he runs and is committed to making sure that it stays in touch with its customers and with trading trends. His biggest motivation does appear to be helping people lead a better life, but he is no dewy-eyed bleeding heart; he knows that Tesco's resonance with value-focused shoppers is what gives the stores group its *raison d'être*.

This commitment is genuine. "Sir Terry is the sort of man who feels more at home discussing football in a Liverpool pub than among London's glitzy set and this is the root to his rapport with Tesco's customers and staff," said a BBC report.[20] "Coming from Liverpool hasn't given him airs and graces," added *Management Today*, "and it has equipped him to ignore them in others."[21]

Sir Terry is tough and during the early part of his career he was known for an aggressive management style. Although the aggression has long softened, he remains impassioned, believing in the importance of employees and customers, ensuring that Tesco is a company where people can succeed regardless of their background, and driving the business with consistency and relentless customer focus. And you still have the sense talking to Sir Terry that he is eyeing you just as he would a sample product from a new supplier – coolly and piercingly.

Sir Terry on managing business

"Intensity is to some extent harnessing the skills in the business because, as a retailer, Tesco has a lot of people. These people tend to be from ordinary backgrounds, so they feel that they have to work hard to get on and so there has always been extraordinary energy. So we harness these assets: Focus that energy and it can be tremendous. And with energy comes discipline. People work hard and don't obstruct action unnecessarily. At a senior level, you have to drive consensus; you need a lot of discipline at the top because then you need to project that out, in our case to 400,000 people. In two competing businesses, the one that projects the vision out furthest wins.

"[In making a strategy] you tend to start with where the growth will come from, perhaps not if it's a new business, but usually you take up a business with strengths and weaknesses. Before answering that, you look at the assets of the business. And what those two really lead to is the purpose, because it's necessary to answer what the business is for because you need to align everybody.

"Purpose is really for employees: this is what we get up every day to do. Then there is a secondary use of the purpose for explanation to people outside. Strategy then comes underneath the purpose and the values – it expresses how you make the growth. And you have to make it as stretching as possible. The objectives we have laid out are really about the vision (what are we here for?), the values (how do we behave?), and the strategy (what do we do for growth?).

"So that's the sequence. The next great thing was the balanced scorecard, because you need to connect these things to the complicated wiring of the business. Retail is about people, property, and products, so you need to structure your time to face these.

"In Tesco, people are managed as assets like property. Most of the top people have grown up in the business. There's tremendous loyalty and they have always been stretched so they don't feel held back. They've always had new opportunities when ready.

"There's quite a good culture. People feel stretched but valued. Generally, you feel your boss is on side, not your biggest problem. This is not Wonderland but generally people feel challenged, not judged. There's quite a lot of empowerment. People don't realize that Tesco tends to run on trust and confidence. We do a lot of work on motivation.

"The biggest challenge is maintaining the values of the business as you go to new countries and face new expectations. If the business stays close to customers and retains its values, it can go anywhere."

Work–life balance

Sir Terry lives a comfortable but unglamorous life with his wife, a medical doctor, and their three children. He cites his wife as a major support.

"You do have to have a work–life balance and an even keel, but it is not easy," he says. "There's often less pressure at the top than in the middle, because you have more control and an inner self-confidence so that you can leave things alone much more easily. For people in the middle, it is not their judgment. They're trying to work to the judgment of others.

"I think I have a work–life balance. The more difficult challenges are physical travel and external stakeholders who want the CEO in person. Managing £1 million is much like managing £1 billion and managing 100 stores is much like managing 1,000, within reason."

Life after Tesco

It is difficult to conceive of Sir Terry running a company other than Tesco. He said in an interview back in 2003 that he'd lost count of the calls he's taken from headhunters in his near three decades with the company. None was entertained. "Some people are stayers and some are movers," he told the *Financial Times*. "I'm obviously a stayer. I think it is partly in your personality. I make a joke about it: one wife, one football team, one firm. I remember saying to myself: 'What would make you move?' In the end, I concluded I would stay at Tesco up to the point that the business stopped me from contributing in the way I wanted to contribute. It never did."[22] Nor is it easy to imagine him "going plural" with a portfolio of non-executive directorships or spending all his time on a golf course. Barring a corporate disaster, Sir Terry looks likely to be inseparable from Tesco for some time.

He told us, "Professionally, Tesco means everything. No other job could compare because all my relationships and experience have been here in Tesco and it is important work – it matters to people. How long I do the job has never been an issue because it's genuinely not for me to decide. That's for the board, though I have some say. So don't worry about what you can't control.

"The best thing you can do is concentrate on the business. It's not necessarily decades for me but it is for the firm. You always think long term. The days and months take care of themselves."

From the Tesco perspective, this presents several challenges. One is ensuring that the company does not begin to believe its own publicity and loses track of reality. While there are millions of happy shoppers who love its cheap prices and convenience, the company has attracted criticism for its planning policies and its impact on communities. It also remains to be seen whether Fresh & Easy can replicate Tesco's success in other markets and avoid becoming one of the many British retail ventures to fail in the US.

Another clear challenge is succession. One secret of Sir Terry's success has been the strong and dedicated core team he has assembled in Richard Brasher, Phil Clarke, Andy Higginson, Tim Mason, and David Potts, who have almost all been with the business for at least ten years. However, their quality and Sir Terry's longevity must beg the question of whether there will be more high-profile departures like that of John Browett to become CEO of electrical goods retailer DSG International. Can Tesco manage Sir Terry's succession and the growth of his lieutenants successfully?

PROFILE OF A TEAM MARSHAL:
ANDREA JUNG, CHIEF EXECUTIVE, AVON PRODUCTS

Andrea Jung is on the boards of Apple and General Electric – by common consent the two most-respected companies in the world. In 2009, she was ranked by the *Financial Times* as the second most important woman in world business and was placed fifth on *Fortune* magazine's list of best-paid women. Having celebrated her tenth anniversary as chief executive of US cosmetics group Avon Products in 2009, she is also the longest-serving female CEO in the Fortune 500.

It is her success at Avon, of course, that has propelled her into all these other positions. Arriving at the company in 1999, she has turned around a once-ailing firm by tripling profits and revitalizing its dowdy image and "Ding-Dong! Avon Calling" catchphrase. Nevertheless, there have been some very tough moments when she needed the robust people management skills that characterize team marshals in their pursuit of business success.

One came in 2005 when she decided to rid Avon of its "grandmother" image, shedding one third of its managers through "delayering" and revitalizing the brand by more than trebling spending to nearly $400 million a year. Jung has since recruited actress Reese Witherspoon as Avon's global ambassador, brought in Yasmin Le Bon, Tess Daly, Louise Redknapp, and Lisa Snowdon to front campaigns, and plowed another $200 million into sales training and internet ventures.

In 2009, Avon responded to the recession by launching the biggest recruitment drive in its history, hiring new door-to-door agents in 44 markets. It increased its agent headcount by 200,000 in the US alone in the first quarter of 2009 and now has more than six million self-employed direct sales representatives worldwide.

Avon began in the US in 1886, arrived in the UK 50 years ago, and became the first major beauty brand to sell online in 1997. It now claims to reach more than a billion customers in over 100 countries, distributing 600 million brochures a year in 25 languages. Worldwide, it sells four lipsticks and two mascaras every second, employs 40,000 staff, and develops 1,000 new products a year. In the UK, one in three women is an Avon customer and 10,000 orders are processed every day.

Like other team marshal corporate executors, Andrea Jung ascribes the company's success to its people and has a passion for nurturing and developing talent.

Jung on being a team marshal

"First and foremost is to have passion: to love what you do. For me, passion has been the foundation of my most critical career decisions. Sometimes leaders have to make tough decisions. But, even as we make these decisions, compassion and the protection of the human spirit and dignity must always be the first concern. A business is nothing more and nothing less than its people. And caring about your people is a hallmark of great leadership. And it's okay to cry – even in business settings – and to express your feelings for the people you care about.

"This was brought home to me in a very personal way in late 2005, when we made the very difficult decision to cut the number of layers of management in half. Our goal was to eliminate bureaucracy and streamline decision making. It was the absolute right thing to do, but it meant that over the course of four months, we actually eliminated 30 percent of the senior management ranks. Many of these people were my close friends. I had pneumonia at the time, but I got on a plane and traveled around the world and spoke personally to our 1,000 top leaders. I looked them in the eye and explained why we had to eliminate one third of all positions. I assured them that no matter what, we were going to be fair, honest, and open throughout the process.

"Following these meetings, people sent me emails of encouragement, telling me that my message was really difficult to hear but they were glad that I had taken the time to come and explain it to them in person. They told me I was doing the right thing for the company. Their feedback and support were incredibly energizing, and the quality of compassion enabled all of us to get through a difficult time and emerge even stronger."[23]

Formative roots and career

A Canadian born in Toronto, Andrea Jung was a high achiever at school, skipping first grade and beginning college at 16, then graduating *magna cum laude* in literature from Princeton in 1979. Her father was an architect from Hong Kong, her mother a pianist and chemical engineer from Shanghai.

Jung began her career with ambitions of doing "something philanthropic" then tried to become a journalist, but switched her sights to retail and consumer businesses after she was turned down for an internship at the recently closed *Boston Globe* newspaper. She progressed to senior vice-president positions at luxury department store chains Neiman Marcus and I Magnin and Company, and then joined Avon in 1994 as president for product marketing in the US.

Jung admits to impatience in her youth. "Early in my career I was in a job that wasn't very interesting," she admitted. "And I said to my parents: 'I don't love this. I think I might quit.' And they said: 'Are you kidding? You can't quit. You've got to start at the bottom and move your way up.'"

There were the business challenges of her gender, too. She admits that she felt discriminated against in the early days of her career. And when she arrived at Avon, the company had never been led by a woman and the top management was full of men.

Her initial job interview, however, convinced her that Avon was a progressive company. "The chairman was a man who truly believed in women in the workforce," she recalls, "and he had a plaque behind the desk that had on it four footprints: a barefoot ape, a barefoot man, a wing-tipped shoe, and a high heel, beneath the title 'The Evolution of Leadership'. I said to him: 'That's a very interesting plaque. Do you really believe it?' And he said: 'Some day, a woman will run this company.' When I got the CEO job, he sent me the plaque.

"It's very different today. The opportunities for women are great now and I feel it's a privilege to be a female leader in a company that walks the talk. We are *the* company for women."

That claim extends to Avon's charitable activities also and Jung is proud of the company's success in raising more than $700 million for breast cancer and anti-domestic violence charities. On a personal note, her mother was diagnosed with cancer at a hospital that had received donations from Breast Cancer Care, which Avon supports; she is now cancer free.

Jung on her core beliefs and values

"It's not easy when you've been a CEO for ten years. That's 40 company quarters. What keeps it meaningful and purposeful is that it's about doing good, not just doing well – making some kind of difference.

"On a bad day I go out and meet our Avon representatives and they really do inspire me, because they'll tell you stories about how from nothing this company has given them an opportunity to change their lives. I meet people from villages all over the world who say they have been able to send their son or daughter to the UK or US for education. No matter what kind of day I'm having, that's a hugely satisfying and gratifying thing.

"We're offering women an opportunity when times are tough and unemployment is high. Women are turning to us for additional income for their families. In the emerging world, women are coming into a socioeconomic status where they're wanting to earn. We're one of the largest micro-lenders in the world because every time a representative joins us, we give her a small loan by supplying her with her initial products up front. With credit drying up in the world, we have more money lent to women than any other business."

Personal drive to succeed

Despite her success and commitment to her team, Jung admits she is motivated by a fear of failure and frets that whatever made her successful in the past few years may not be enough in the years ahead. What sustains her is advice from CEO coach Ram Charan three years ago.

She explains: "He said: 'You have to go home every Friday night and ask yourself this question: If you were fired and a new CEO started on Monday, what would that person do to your strategies, your team, and your thinking? Would they keep everything? Or would they look at it in a way that you can't because you're too tied to it? If you can think like that, you'll have the objectivity and the courage to do things or perhaps stop things that you yourself put into place and therefore reinvent the company and your next legacy.'

"I'm a huge believer in reinventing myself all the time. You have to as a leader stay fresh and develop new skills. I sit back and think: 'Let's be totally self-critical. What am I doing wrong or what could I be doing better?' You're in the corner office. It's not that easy for people to come in and tell you what you're doing wrong. It's just not human nature, so you have to do it yourself. GE in particular has been like a business school for me. Every time I come back from there, I feel I've learnt so much."

PITFALLS OF THE COMMERCIAL EXECUTOR MODEL

While commercial executors can operate in any industry, they are not usually effective in professional services; they're best in businesses that need to be taken from average to great, where pragmatism and an honest confrontation of reality are hugely valuable. Corporate executors excel at setting and meeting targets and combatting obstacles to ensure that operations and future strategic ambitions become a reality. They are ruthlessly competitive and have a precise eye for comparing and measuring themselves against their peers, so are typically most focused on business metrics as their measure of success. They're not usually primarily motivated by a wider societal mission.

Therein lie the dangers of the model. One is that the relentless battle to lower costs and increase sales may take too much out of key executives and cause burnout. Another is that without careful management, a commercial executor's company can become overly challenging, with executives vying to outshine each other or seeking to massage their metrics. Then commercial executors risk being unable to attract the best talent, which may be more attracted to value- or entrepreneurial-driven opportunities elsewhere.

Corporate executors have an obsessive focus on customer needs and delivering to meet them, but relying too heavily on customers telling you what they need is always dangerous; no one asked for an iPod, remember. Corporate executors therefore run the risk of being outflanked by a disruptive corporate entrepreneur who changes the rules of the game by spotting a niche in the market and a way of serving customers better. Suddenly it doesn't matter how efficiently commercial executors are running their models; in order to compete, they need to learn to play a whole new game.

5

FINANCIAL VALUE DRIVERS

inancial value drivers, the category of chief executives that is arguably most loved by the City, focus relentlessly on shareholder value. They are highly skilled at identifying value-enhancing corporate transactions or realizing value from portfolio disposals.

Financial value driver chief executives speak the same language as bankers, analysts, and investors. They're obsessed with generating returns for the shareholders who put up capital to start or grow the business. Value generation is their mission and a single-minded focus on shareholder returns is how they aim to deliver it.

Value drivers want to create the leanest and most streamlined business in their industry; they're aiming to be fat free and rigorously transparent. To reach this objective, they believe in extensive delegation and decentralization, matched with crystal-clear accountability and sheer hard work. In return, they offer exceptional financial rewards to their executives, who in turn have to be comfortable with the unremitting scrutiny and unrelenting assessment that come with working for a value-driving chief executive.

The financial value driver model is best suited to situations where the strategy depends more on smart identification of opportunities to release value, flawless execution, and smart finance and financial control than on inspirational visions, transformational technologies, intellectual property, or highly complex government relations.

While value drivers are rigorous in their focus on shareholder value, the best are not sociopathic accountants unable to inspire people. On the contrary, the value driver model, depending on highly decentralized operations, is heavily reliant on exceptional, supremely motivated executives who are willing to be held to account for meeting, or failing to meet, stretching targets.

Mike Turner, chairman of Babcock International, is one example. "You have to get the team right, make sure you have people telling you what they really think, make sure your objectives are clear, and then delegate," he says. "You need to keep communicating and remember you're a role model and people will watch what you do very carefully. It's about delegating to people and then holding their feet to the fire. Don't feel guilty about making people do things that are difficult. Don't do it for them. You need to have a very clear strategy. When people say they don't understand the strategy, it's often because they don't like it."

Stephen Hester, chief executive of Royal Bank of Scotland, shares the focus on value. "I think conceptual statements of purpose and values can be overdone," he says. "Companies have to create value or do not exist. Someone will dismantle you."

Delegation is also central to effective value drivers; their skill is partly in identifying which decisions and initiatives will make a difference in the required timeframe. Paul Thompson, partner at Pamplona Capital Management and former chief executive of closed life insurance funds consolidator Resolution Life, is another financial value driver. "There are about five or six really good decisions you make every year," he says. "It's about selecting those five and releasing some of the 250 other decisions and getting them done quickly. So you delegate them and people feel they are empowered. I get horrified when I hear about CEOs sending out 150 emails a day. That's far too much detail. You have to delegate things to the people you hire."

Mike Turner agrees. "Home markets have to be managed semi-autonomously by a local, so I have to trust my six home markets CEOs to run their market," he says. "Often I can't even know about all projects being undertaken for clients. I'm constantly aware that I'm an alien when I'm on Capitol Hill. Trust is key."

In contrast, Stephen Hester emphasizes the need for the CEO sometimes to get into the detail. "Intelligence, drive, and communication skills are important," he says. "It's also important for a CEO to move strategically from the big-picture stuff to the nitty-gritty detail. That's not because you have to do the nitty-gritty. That's what you leverage other people for. But to manage people effectively you do have to dive deep into the organization."

Financial value driver chief executives are found most often in diversified industrial businesses, but also in financial services. Both are sectors where complex businesses frequently require portfolio rationalization or "buy-and-build" strategies where mergers and acquisitions are seen as the engine for growth. Financial value drivers measure their success in the same way as the City: through earnings per share and the share price.

PROFILE OF A FINANCIAL VALUE DRIVER: MICK DAVIS, CHIEF EXECUTIVE, XSTRATA

Mining group Xstrata did not exist before 2001 but, under the leadership of Mick Davis, it has barnstormed its way to become not only one of the biggest minerals groups in the world but also one of Britain's largest public companies. Its phenomenal growth is partly due to being in the right place at the right time. The huge demand for minerals and base materials from China in particular is fueling a commodity metals boom that has seen all miners experience exponential rises in stock market valuations. However, a great deal of the credit has to go to Davis, who put Xstrata in that place at that time.

Before Xstrata was formed in October 2001, its operations were subsumed in the Swiss-based metals group Glencore, which saw an opportunity for a minerals group to join a select band of mining companies attracting London investment. Glencore looked for a chief executive who could drive its idea of transplanting some of its ferroalloy and zinc businesses to a London listing and using this vehicle to consolidate the highly fragmented mining sector. It found Davis at the very top of the industry. He had worked in a similar minerals transplant as chief financial officer of Billiton, a London company formed out of the assets of South Africa's Gencor. He was a key architect of the merger that Billiton then fashioned with Australia's Broken Hill Properties to form BHP Billiton.

Xstrata started with a value of about $500 million ascribed to assets injected into it. Davis then raised nearly £1 billion through a flotation on the London Stock Exchange, simultaneously acquiring Glencore's Australian and South African coal assets for $2.5 billion. The company immediately entered the FTSE100 and proceeded to use its new paper on a series of acquisitions in Australia and Canada.

Today, Xstrata is the world's largest producer of export thermal coal and ferrochrome, one of the top five producers of coking or metallurgical coal, the fourth largest global producer of copper and nickel, and one of the world's largest miners and producers of zinc. It's also the fifth largest diversified metals and mining company, with operations and projects in 18 countries and top-five market positions in each of its major commodities. With the exception of the short-lived phenomenon of the first dot-com boom, it's hard to think of any other British company achieving so much in so short a time.

Davis on driving a business for value

"I wanted a new company that was nimble and sure-footed and would add value for shareholders and that's what we've built. There was space for us. To be a high-quality CEO, you should be able to lead a company irrespective of which industry it is in or the position it is in. People have leadership capacity or they do not. Whether they are finance people or engineers is not relevant. The reality is that things happen to companies because the person running the company has the flexibility to be able to manage the risks he is dealing with. You have to wake up every day saying, 'Yesterday was not good enough. Today we have to do better.' Growth is important to me, but it's not growth for growth's sake. You have to protect your values and make sure that you understand the core risks of your business. If you don't do that, your whole business can implode. Making sure that a company can cope with its risks is the CEO's job."

Formative roots and career progression

Davis was born into a Jewish family in Port Elizabeth on the Eastern Cape of South Africa and enjoyed what he calls a "normal middle-class" upbringing with his two brothers. His family was not wealthy, but Davis was always keen on going into business. After training as a chartered accountant with KPMG, he worked for South African electricity utility Eskom before joining Gencor, where he served as executive chairman of Ingwe Coal Corporation and later as chief financial officer of Billiton.

The roots of his restless ambition were already apparent. Davis left KPMG because he was not made a partner, even though such an appointment would have meant he was the firm's youngest ever partner at that time. He prospered at Eskom, becoming finance director at the age of 29 under the tutelage of the company's boss John Maree, whom he ranks as his biggest business influence. However, Davis left the firm for similar reasons of unfulfilled ambition three years later after failing to get the chief executive's job – a perhaps unreasonable expectation given that he was still only 32. "My career has been one of leaving companies because they would not recognize the potential I recognized in myself," he says. "I always had the view that I was capable of running the company." At Gencor, Davis joined a young and ambitious team fashioned by then chief executive Brian Gilbertson and nonexecutive director Derek Keys.

Davis was hired as a "young Turk alongside people like the now BHP Billiton chief executive Marius Kloppers", says his right-hand man Thras Moraitis. "All the hires were smart, eager, strong-willed, and willing to stand their ground. I think the seeds of Mick's mental model were sown there. Gilbertson molded the young Turks by delegating authority to them."

Davis became chief financial officer, working closely with Gilbertson, but then came Billiton's merger with BHP. He was offered the role of chief development officer in the enlarged group and once again felt he was being undervalued. "It was the right deal," he told *The Times*, "but the result was a completely different company to the one I joined. I didn't think my personal assets would grow."

"I'm speculating," says Moraitis, "but I think that to some degree Mick wanted to show that he was the intellectual force behind Brian Gilbertson when he was managing director. I think there's a sense, perhaps, that he felt he was always the unrecognized number two."

Management style

Davis has very deliberately set about building a value driver model at Xstrata, taking advantage of the company's newness to fashion a group in his image. He describes his management style as "short on process, short on bureaucracy, and long on values" and says that Xstrata has a "unique" business model that relies on complete decentralization.

Davis is a heretical miner. In his view, the mining industry operates on the basis of the myth that you need a large center as a risk-control and scale mechanism, and that head office has to be able to second-guess what people in the field operations are doing. He also doesn't believe that scale in shared information technology and purchasing is essential for a diversified mining company. His insight has been to give full profit-and-loss responsibility to the leaders of each of Xstrata's business units, who get complete operational autonomy but are held tightly accountable for results and compliance with group safety and technical standards. Business units can collaborate to share back-office functions and garner the synergies that most mining companies would seek to exploit through a large corporate function, but they are not obliged to.

Likewise, while the center executes transformational deals, the business units are under no obligation to use corporate assets in acquiring smaller companies, within their own capital expenditure limits, though they may apply to do so. Thus Xstrata's slim central operations, overseen by Davis, only retain control of the money, targets, health and safety, and technical standards. "I give people the space and support to do their jobs well," he told *The Times*. "I tell them when they haven't."[24]

At Xstrata mistakes are tolerated, as long as they are not repeated and have been made in the context of sensible business risks. The center promises the operations "transformational mergers and acquisitions" that will give them opportunities to make economies of scale within the business units. In return, headquarters demands that the business units deliver operational excellence, meet their financial targets, and never cover up mistakes. Businesses will always be held to account for their actions and inactions.

In effect, Davis has built Xstrata on a form of social contract. Power is devolved from the group in exchange for transparency. "We won't fail" is the strapline to both sides of the deal, but, as he emphasizes, "you have to deliver." At the center of the value system, Davis has a reputation as a robust manager who doesn't suffer fools gladly and has very high intellectual expectations. Definitely not a touchy-feely chief executive, he's also not happy at high-profile dinners, preferring to work and to mix with his management team. "He's very comfortable with silence," says one Xstrata executive. "I've been on executive jets with him and he's not said a word for three hours. He can be awkward in groups at times. He really cuts through it and gets to the crux, to the Achilles' heel of an argument. He frustrates bankers because he'll take their presentation, flick through it, find the slide that really matters – even if it's slide 48 – get the point, and get up and leave."

Acquisitions are where Davis has really made his mark. He has proved a skillful negotiator, strong enough to leave deals on the table if the price is not right. When he does do a deal, he also disciplines himself to be fast and delivery oriented in his decision making, giving himself 30 days to decide who's out of the new combined management team. "He's single-minded when in pursuit of an opportunity – he won't look at even a good deal while doing another," says Moraitis.

But Davis is not a ruthless, cold-hearted accountant. His value driver model is constructed on a compelling vision of building the most valuable mining group in the world and empowering delegation, creating the freedom and opportunities for ambitious entrepreneurs to build something valuable for the company and themselves.

Moraitis believes that Davis is one of the best delegators he's seen. "He gives a task, he's patient and will watch you flounder with the task and will not intervene, but will wait for you to come for help," he says. "Of course, he'll intervene when necessary. He's not a great, charismatic leader – he's a very shy man – but he is an intellectual giant who lets people get on with stuff. He thinks expansively and excites people, taking them places they would not normally go. Mick paints pictures people would not paint for themselves and gets them to believe they are achievable. He's inspirational."

As a consequence, Davis has been able to hire executives of the highest caliber to drive the phenomenal growth that Xstrata has seen in recent years. "We get the best entrepreneurs in the industry who are self-motivated and stand up to be counted," notes Moraitis. "Our people are not here just to run plants; they are here to find value. Mick has a saying: 'If you tread water for long enough you'll eventually sink.' Momentum is ingrained into us. Everyone is comfortable with accountability and having a bright spotlight on them."

Davis on his management style

"The market has a view that I am a tough individual who does not suffer fools gladly, but there is a softer side to me. If people get themselves into difficulty, my instinct is to help them, not cut them off. We're very loyal to our people. We encourage them to take risks and when they make mistakes we will support them, provided they do not make the same mistake again. We support people so they are challenged, not threatened.

"I go into the business and test the talent. It destabilizes the situation. We give complete freedom and total responsibility to individuals. They get big financial rewards if they deliver and we hold them accountable if they do not. If I can see a weak link in a business unit, I would say 'I am not sure about Joe Bloggs', but I would never say to them 'Fire Joe Bloggs'. The rule in this company is that you don't give instructions to somebody else's subordinate, but there is no problem with asking somebody else's subordinate for information.

"I have close relationships with people in the organization and try not to be hierarchical. I believe in a style of openness. My natural disposition is to discuss everything with everyone.

"I don't feel lonely. The only time I feel I am alone is when a decision has to be taken about whether to pursue a company-transforming acquisition. My job then is to ensure that I absorb the risks. Absorbing the risks is what I am paid for. I am alone in absorbing those risks. I am not alone on a daily basis, but at the end of the day, it is my decision.

"There's no formula. Anyone who tells you there's a formula is lying. The reason why people get into trouble is they like the myth that they generate that they are omniscient; that they did things because they knew things were going to happen."

Life after Xstrata

Davis is matter-of-fact about Xstrata existing only as long as its shareholders want it to, and he is likely to take a similar view about his own long-term commitment to the company. In some ways his model is similar to that of a private equity firm, and he will be similarly unemotional about selling or leaving the company if he feels that the opportunity is good enough.

He draws personal strength from his Jewish faith and is rounded enough not to be taken in by his own success. "I'm very committed to my career," he told *The Times*, "but it's not those kinds of things that make people intuitively happy. It's things like a decent set of friendships and other interests. I think we all do work–life balance unsuccessfully. It is a big challenge. I do have a life outside work, but I don't think I can claim to have achieved a balance. There are times when I get overburdened."

Like most value driver chief executives, one day he may decide there is more value to be driven elsewhere, whether at another business or in his own personal or religious interests. He continues to nurse an interest in charitable donations and in teaching, and he mistrusts celebrity. "Celebrity CEOs are a danger because in this market people like to see failure," he says. "They do not like to see success. If you have celebrity status, people will seek your downfall and ultimately you will fail, not because you did anything wrong but because you ran out of luck. There are so many things that you don't know you don't know that no matter how good you are, you are going to be faced with uncertainties. There's a danger of linking a company too closely with its CEO. The reality is that it is not the case that a company's success is limited to and attributed to one man. That has never been the case. I don't know where I will be in five or ten years' time, but I am determined it will not be here. When you stay too long in a job, you become less and less effective."

"If someone bought us tomorrow Mick would not shed a tear," says Moraitis. "He's not about building a legacy mining company.

He is first and foremost about value for the shareholder." This may also present a challenge for Xstrata under Davis's management, however. His cold management style and frankness about his willingness to exit may lead to difficulties in motivating employees to continue the success story.

PROFILE OF A FINANCIAL VALUE DRIVER: IRENE ROSENFELD, CHAIRMAN AND CHIEF EXECUTIVE, KRAFT FOODS

Irene Rosenfeld was catapulted into the international spotlight in 2009 when, as chief executive of America's Kraft Foods, she stunned the stock market with an audacious hostile takeover bid for chocolate maker Cadbury. Yet her climb to the top as a financial value driver has been studied and meticulous and had already been noted, with *Forbes* magazine ranking her sixth on its list of the world's most powerful women.

Like Mick Davis, however, her route to the top has not been smooth. She had to leave Kraft and succeed elsewhere in order to get the CEO job she desired. After that, this Long Island-bred executive, who admits that patience is her "most challenged virtue", wasted little time before reshaping the tired brands portfolio that she said had "lost its heart and soul" amid cost-cutting drives that had affected quality.

When she came back to Kraft as chief executive in 2006, she set out on what she called a "rewiring" of the US food group. Inside two months, she removed half the top executive team. Then, still in her first year, she bought the biscuit business of Danone of France for $7.2 billion and sold off Kraft's cereal business for $1.7 billion.

A 25-year veteran of the food and drink industry, Rosenfeld's recipe for change was to prioritize innovation and decentralize decision making. Describing herself as an "insider with an outsider's perspective", she went outside the company for new executive talent, bringing in five of the ten-strong executive committee from competitors.

Under her leadership, Kraft has reversed some cost-cutting measures that had lost customers, such as a reduction in the cheese content of its famous Macaroni & Cheese packaged dinners. She also launched new lines, such as a soft cake version of the best-selling Oreo cookies and "live active" versions of Kraft cheese, resulting in double-digit growth in those categories. The overall new direction was to take advantage of consumers' desire to economize by opting for low-cost, home-cooked meals, while also embracing the health and wellness agenda. The result has been a boost in overall sales, with revenues up by 17 percent to $42 billion in 2008.

Kraft, which employs 98,000 people worldwide, now has its products in about 150 countries and in 99 percent of American households. The group has nine brands with revenues of more than $1 billion, including Oreo, Philadelphia, and Maxwell House coffee, while more than 50 additional brands have revenues greater than $100 million. More than 80 percent of its revenues come from products that hold the number one position in their categories, while more than 50 percent of revenues are driven by categories where the group's market share is twice that of its nearest competitor. The company was rewarded for its focus on financial performance in 2008 when it joined the Dow Jones index.

Three years after Rosenfeld returned to Kraft, her unrelenting focus on financial value had put the company into the sort of shape where it could bid $17 billion for Cadbury to strengthen its confectionery business. "I have been repeatedly asked: 'Why now?' she told the *Financial Times* about the bid approach. "The answer is simple: Why wait?"

Rosenfeld as a financial value driver

Like Mick Davis, Rosenfeld has used a combination of merger and acquisition activity and a focus on operational productivity to drive financial value, while employing a decentralized business model that incentivizes managers to deliver.

The deal making is central to her approach. "Divestitures [are] an important part of our strategy," she says. "I laid out a strategy and I tried to get the organization to think about growing their brands, I wanted to give them the time to do that and see which could be grown and which could not and as I told many of our investors, some of our businesses were on a shorter leash in that regard than others.

"We looked at a couple of different criteria, we looked at just their relative market share, their growth potential, and their overall profitability, and we used that as a screen as we looked across the portfolio and that really helped us to identify where we wanted to invest and not. So we have a clear set of acquisition and divestiture priorities."[25]

Rosenfeld's operational focus utilizes her qualities as a brand guru who, after a quarter of a century in advertising and marketing, is well qualified to cast a critical eye over brand performance and prospects, nurturing and developing stars and weeding out also-rans. Her long-term aim is for Kraft to grow its sales consistently by more than 4 percent, while seeking a 9–11 percent annual improvement in profits. This might suggest cost cutting, but actually Rosenfeld is wary of overdosing on such measures, telling an audience at Cornell in 2006 that the tremendous focus on cost cutting, restructuring and headcount reductions prior to her appointment as chief executive had left Kraft "tired, raw and somewhat disillusioned".[26] "It's hard to get up every morning when cost cutting is your end, rather than a means," she added.

She prefers to use innovation as a key financial value driver. "We are engaged in a transformation of Kraft to get the company back to its rightful position as a top-tier food and beverage company," she says, "and a big part of that is what we call reframing our categories, which is just to look at our categories through the consumer's eyes. For a long time, we were apologizing for the categories in which we participated and we looked in a number of our other peer companies and we said, 'Well if only we made this or if only we made that, we could be growing at much better, much faster rate.'

"I've really encouraged the folks to think about reinventing those categories rather than apologizing for them and to that end we've been using a framework that we call the growth diamond, which is just predicated on the growing trends that we see around the world in food and beverages. It's about health and wellness, it's about snacking, it's about quick meals. Everyone is pressed for time and everybody is looking for ways to eat and fuel on the fly, so it's about quick meals and it's about premium quality in developed markets and affordable quality in developing markets. Those are really the four trends that we are focused on as a company and each of our categories is engaged in thinking about their own category through that lens."

Like Davis again, Rosenfeld has also focused on decentralizing corporate decision making to ensure the most relevant choices are made. "The first thing I'm trying to do," she says, "is to let the marketers in Indonesia market to Indonesians and to make sure that the managers of that market are mostly local nationals, because a lot of our staffing historically in our international organization was through expatriates and I think we can benefit greatly by having more locals managing their local markets.

"As we are decentralizing the company, the mechanism to try to capture the synergies that come from one geography to another is to set up category councils that are comprised of the leaders of the categories in each of the key markets, so that they can share some of their best practices and that they can begin to learn from one another. We have not had good success having a separate global group who acts as a facilitator; typically those individuals do not have any profit and loss responsibility and so they're not able to be very impactful. So we can benefit greatly by having the business managers participate in the process.

"The second [key] is to make sure that we have incentives in place that actually incentivize people to cooperate with one another. Our international strategic plan had more synergy across all regions than we have seen in the history of our international business, despite the fact that we had taken away the global group who used to be responsible for coordinating it."

Rosenfeld on driving a business for value

"What we can bring the party as a branded manufacturer is the equity of our brands, the consumer relationship with our brands, and in many cases technology that we are prepared to invest in or proprietary technology that we've developed through our own R&D capabilities that can allow us to be successful.

"And so a key part of our transformation is the reinvestment in brand equity and product quality and in proprietary technology that leads to new products. That's how we're going to win.

"For example, if I think about some of our new product introductions, we have a snacking cheese that we introduced with probiotic cultures. That's a proprietary technology that allows us to make a great-tasting snacking cheese that delivers on consumers' desire for greater digestive health.

"That's the kind of thinking that allows us to capture higher margins, gives us a proprietary point of difference, and it's something that's not easily copied by some of our competitors, both private label or branded. So the key to it is really the ability and the willingness to make the necessary investments in the equity of our brands and quality of our products and then in the thinking behind our innovations.

"I spend a lot of time with investors, because they basically run our company together with the board. They have a very strong stake in our programming and our success, and they have a good sense of what they'd like to see and what they wouldn't like to see. For the most part, I think those who have chosen to invest in the company are quite supportive of our strategy. They're pleased by the progress that we've made. They understand that this is a fairly large ocean tanker that we're moving and it's not going to move overnight."

The Cadbury takeover: Financial value driving in action?

Despite Rosenfeld's value-driving achievements in her first four years in charge of Kraft, her leadership of the Dow Jones company will ultimately be judged on the success or failure of the Cadbury acquisition, achieved after a vigorous bid battle culminated in an agreed takeover worth $18.9 billion in January 2010.

Like most such tussles, the hostile takeover showed up management and leadership weaknesses as well as strengths, and it is instructive to assess these against the financial value driver model. First, Rosenfeld's initial approach to Cadbury chairman Roger Carr, delivered via a message on his mobile phone requesting a meeting, demonstrated her highly cultivated value-spotting skills. When the two met, she made an unexpected cash and stock bid. Having gone through a demerger of its soft drinks business in mid-2008, Cadbury was pushing management to meet aggressive financial targets. However, the results of the action had yet to show and shareholder activist Nelson Peltz (also a Kraft shareholder) was putting pressure on the company to demonstrate progress. Crucially, the demerger had made Cadbury highly vulnerable, leaving it focused on a single sector and dangerously exposed to predators. Rosenfeld struck at exactly the right moment.

She was successful in landing her target, albeit at a higher price than first offered. However, her execution fell short of the "flawless" characteristic of the financial value driver model in two key ways. First, Rosenfeld, an American who had never before made such a large acquisition outside her home territory, demonstrated naivety in dealing with Britain's financial media. This is much more aggressive than its US counterpart, with many more national newspapers and a much more questioning attitude among journalists. Secondly, Rosenfeld allowed Kraft to get into political trouble over the company's pledge during the takeover battle that it could keep open a plant near Bristol that Cadbury had been planning to close. However, three weeks after the takeover was clinched, Kraft retracted, saying the closure plans were so far advanced it would be "unrealistic" to reverse them. One worker told the BBC that Kraft's earlier statement had been "a bit fat lie". Kraft promised there would be no job cuts for Cadbury factories for at least two years in a bid to defuse the mistrust, however Rosenfeld attracted more ire for failing to attend a House of Commons committee to be questioned herself.

The result of these flaws in execution is that there remains a debate about whether Kraft will deliver value from the Cadbury deal. After agreement had been reached, Carr said Rosenfeld could probably have bought Cadbury for less if Kraft had read shareholder sentiment more effectively and if she had not been affected by political events. Warren Buffett, Kraft's biggest shareholder, also said he thought Rosenfeld had overpaid. Time will tell, but the charge of overpaying is one no financial value driver wants on their record.

Formative roots and career progression
_____

Rosenfeld was born Irene Blecker in 1953 to Jewish parents Seymour and Joan in the small town of Westbury, 25 miles outside New York. Growing up in Long Island, Rosenfeld was ambitious from an early age, admitting that as a child she dreamed of becoming US president. Her accountant father was born and brought up in The Bronx by parents of eastern European origin and Rosenfeld was top of her class at West Tresper Clarke high school in Westbury, as well as playing basketball and three other sports. She worked on the student newspaper, sat on the student government, sang in the choir, and was a member of the school's theater group. In the Brownies she became treasurer – a post that she jokes was her first public role – and she spent summers at Tyler Hill children's camp in Pennsylvania.

After graduating from high school, she studied psychology at Cornell University, admitting that she chose the Ivy League college partly because of its reputation in sports, but broke her leg in her first season in competitive basketball there. She then completed a Master's degree in business administration and a doctorate in marketing and statistics, before starting work in advertising at the Dancer Fitzgerald Sample agency in New York. Her career in food began in 1981 at General Foods, which was later combined with Kraft after both companies were bought by Philip Morris. She gained the name Rosenfeld through marriage to her first husband Philip Rosenfeld, whom she met as a student; she kept the name after he died and she wed investment banker Richard Illgen.

She progressed up the Kraft organization, leading the restructuring and turnaround of key businesses in the US, Canada, and Mexico. She also led Kraft's integration of the purchase of food group Nabisco in 2000 and worked on plans by Philip Morris to spin off Kraft as an independent company. She left the group in 2003 to head the Fritolay unit of rival PepsiCo after Roger Deromedi was named Kraft chief executive. There, she led the division to increased growth in healthier products and developed a pipeline of health and wellness offerings. However, Deromedi left in 1995 and Rosenfeld was called back to Kraft as chief executive, adding the chair of the company in 2007.

Rosenfeld's management style

As well as being direct, forthright, and strongly focused on financial performance, Rosenfeld prides herself on being approachable and accessible. She had the security lock on the door to the main executive suite at Kraft headquarters removed soon after her return. "Probably the most important lesson that has guided my leadership is the golden rule," she says, "and it's about just doing unto others what you would want done to you. It has helped to guide a lot of my managerial actions.

"It's guided my ability to tell my boss bad news. If you apply the screen 'If I were on the other side of that situation, how would I want it to be handled', I think it gives you a very clear set of operating principles and I have found that that has served me well.

"So I will never ask someone to do something for me that I wouldn't do myself. I would like to be able to anticipate things that my bosses have asked for in a way that I would want as well. I think that has really served me well and I think has made me more accessible as a result as a leader."

Rosenfeld has also retained her love of sports, still enjoying rollerblading and citing tennis star Martina Navratilova as a "tremendous inspiration".[27]

Life after Kraft

Rosenfeld says she is "passionate" about her job, admitting: "It's great to go to cocktail parties where everyone has an opinion about what you do. I really enjoy figuring out why people behave the way they do, using those insights to develop new products or building stronger relationships with our consumers."[28] Though she has spent most of her career with Kraft Foods and its forerunners, however, Rosenfeld exhibits a mentality far from that of a one-company woman. When she leaves the company, her focus on financial value may tempt her into private equity or another role at a mature business where financial value driver skills are needed to propel moribund performance into life.

PITFALLS OF THE FINANCIAL VALUE DRIVER MODEL

One element of value drivers' agreement with their executives is that they will provide exceptional personal returns. In so doing, they encourage a close alignment of wealth creation for shareholders and the personal enrichment of the management team, particularly the chief executive. When value driver chief executives are successful, therefore, they tend to reap rich rewards in the shape of bonuses and long-term incentive schemes, which also act as valuable carrots to tempt talented executives.

However, the rich rewards that value drivers offer their teams can lead to some key risks. Because this category of chief executives are driven by financial returns, they and the value driver executives they recruit can be difficult to retain once they've been successful and become independently wealthy. Executives who have striven hard for years, motivated by the promise of financial rewards, may become less committed when they are enjoying the fruits of their success. And as they do so, the job of keeping the talented executives underneath them who have helped in their achievements becomes harder too. Although the best value-driving businesses develop strong value systems, there can be a lack of glue bonding people together beyond wealth generation, and this can leave gaping holes at the top of hitherto successful organizations.

Another major risk of the model is that driving value, with its three-year mission plans, can be swiftly overtaken by industry shifts or economic downturns just as the payback for earlier cost cutting, restructuring, or exceptional acquisition-related costs is supposed to be reaping big rewards for shareholders.

There is also a risk that when value driver chief executives make a large acquisition or significant restructuring, the high profile that their returns for investors and personal wealth creation have given them can be their undoing. "People get built up more than they deserve," says Stephen Hester, "and then they get ripped to pieces more than they deserve."

6

CORPORATE
ENTREPRENEURS

Corporate entrepreneurs have something to prove. They disrupt industries because they believe in a better way of doing things, they excel in spotting breakthrough opportunities and making them a reality, and their vision for their companies is their life vision.

There are comparatively few corporate entrepreneurs in the UK but more in India and China, where executives have had to be entrepreneurial to take advantage of opportunities as these markets have opened up. Take Liu Jiren of Neusoft. "When I founded the company, there was no market, a shortage of capital, and a shortage of talent," he says. "The challenge was the lack of conditions usually required to found a company. We didn't know how to run a business, so our approach was to challenge and to learn through making mistakes and by trying."

Corporate entrepreneurs are also more common in the US, mainly because of the lead in innovation that has long been established by California's Silicon Valley. Obvious examples are Michael Dell and Oracle co-founder Larry Ellison and, more recently, Yahoo!, Google, and Second Life.

Dell fits the model well, saying that he was sustained through the hard early years of founding his computer company by the fact that "we could clearly see our customers' needs". He adds, "Answering those needs better than our competitors was a terrific motivation. Even during the hardest of times we were clear about the opportunity before us and the advantages of the direct model, which was like rocket fuel for our business." A classic entrepreneur, he believes: "When you use input from your customers as your compass, the right answer is almost always clear."

Corporate entrepreneurs are brilliant visionaries and have the energy, drive, and charisma to bring their business ideas to reality. They start companies not always because making money is their number one priority, but because they believe in something and want to change the way a particular business or industry works. However, that same disruptive mindset can also make them deeply mistrustful of the stock market, the City, and the corporate environment.

Some of Britain's best-known entrepreneurs, therefore, have chosen largely to eschew the quoted environment. Sir Richard Branson and Sir Alan Sugar did so because they had mixed experiences at the hands of analysts and fund managers in the periods during which parts of the Virgin Group and the whole of Amstrad were publicly quoted. Sir James Dyson, on the other hand, has chosen never to bring the company behind his revolutionary bagless vacuum cleaner to the stock market, but summed up a classic entrepreneurial attitude when he told us: "You have to focus on the product and make sure it is appealing. It's about technological breakthroughs and having an edge. I have stepped back from being a professional chief executive; my ultimate role is in being the ongoing creative and innovative force."

Opponents of the public company route cite the increasing burden of regulatory compliance, the dangers of restrictive corporate cultures emerging, and the worry that the City will not understand their entrepreneurial mindsets or be long term enough to back their ideas without immediate returns. Thanks to the growth of the venture capital and private equity industries, moreover, they can find capital from sources other than the traditional equity markets, so they do not always need to overcome their aversion to the capital markets.

Arguably, the best-known corporate entrepreneur is Steve Jobs. As chief executive of Apple, he has shaken up no fewer than four separate industries; the computer, animation, music download, and mobile telecom markets. He has also done so in a publicly quoted environment, though the fortunes of Apple have fluctuated wildly during his two stints at the company.

Elsewhere, an example of a corporate entrepreneur outside a publicly quoted environment is James Bilefield. "I see myself at the growth end," he says. "I like things when they are growing from 0 to 100. I am less interested in 100 onwards. The main thing is belief. You have got to really believe and fight your way. You have to have an end place in mind, but to other people you are ridiculous. It may be a mad idea, but if you have absolute belief in that idea and a team with ability behind you, you can make it happen."

Technological industries are natural breeding grounds of corporate entrepreneurs, as is biotechnology. Chris Evans, founder of Merlin Biosciences, a specialist venture capital and advisory company dedicated to the biotechnology sector, is a good example. He has set up 20 different biotech companies that are now valued at more than £1 billion, including four businesses that have floated on the London Stock Exchange. He says he sees himself as a "commercially driven scientist" whose companies generate ideas and solutions for everyday problems. Elsewhere, the media, consumer, and professional services sectors tend to attract corporate entrepreneurs.

PROFILE OF A CORPORATE ENTREPRENEUR:
SIR MARTIN SORRELL, CHIEF EXECUTIVE, WPP GROUP

Back in 1986, WPP Group, one of the world's largest advertising and marketing businesses, was yet to be born and the corporate vehicle that would grow into that behemoth was still a shopping-trolley manufacturer called Wire Plastic Products. Martin Sorrell, who until then had been building a career at Saatchi & Saatchi, bought the company, appointed himself chief executive, and began to use it as a vehicle to acquire "below-the-line" advertising-related companies. In 1987, he stunned the advertising and marketing world with the $566 million hostile takeover of J. Walter Thompson (at that time 13 times WPP's size). In 1989, Sorrell followed this with another dramatic hostile deal, this time paying $864 million for Ogilvy and Mather, twice as big as WPP. Over the next two decades, WPP became the driving force for consolidation in the global advertising and marketing industry. In 2000 alone, it completed 35 acquisitions.[29]

Today, WPP has amassed one of the largest media-buying groups in the world, Group M. And with its giant creative agency networks, JWT and Ogilvy and Mather, the group is one of the four major players in the global advertising and marketing market. WPP's stock price has soared and – although the company has been through difficult times, including a period in 1989 and 1990 during which it was on the verge of collapse after having overleveraged itself – Sorrell's determination and business acumen have led to significant growth. WPP now has billings of over £31 billion and revenues of over £6 billion.[30] It has more than 100 brands in more than 100 countries, employing over 100,000 people worldwide and providing national, multinational, and global clients with advertising, media investment management, information and consultancy, public relations, public affairs, branding and identity, healthcare, and specialist communications services.

WPP is now valued on the London Stock Exchange at over £7.5 billion and it is more than a decade since Sir Martin led the company into the FTSE100[31] – not a bad growth story for a company that had a market capitalization of only £1.5 million back in 1986.[32] Sir Martin is widely respected throughout the advertising and marketing industry, with his words being scrutinized and quoted by many within the sector; his famed remark that the recession at the beginning of the 2000s was "bath shaped" was one of the most-repeated quotes. Indeed, many industry observers credit him with the fact that the UK still has an independent, vibrant communications industry.

Sir Martin as a corporate entrepreneur

Sir Martin built the world's largest advertising and marketing group through daring acquisitions, but he is not simply an aggressive financial wheeler-dealer. What makes him a leading example of a British corporate entrepreneur is that he not only built up WPP Group from nothing, he also successfully diversified its offering in terms of product mix and geographies, growing the group to cover four separate product segments and becoming truly global. As well as doing all that, he developed world-class business acumen to guide WPP's acquisitions. His personal review of the company's fortunes and the wider global economic and business outlook in its annual report has become compulsory reading for anyone wanting to understand the way the global economy is moving. He has a detailed knowledge of modern economic history and an encyclopedic recall of facts and figures, allied to an ability to interpret them seamlessly.

Underpinning all these attributes are the classic characteristics of a corporate entrepreneur. Sir Martin is motivated by proving that he has a better way of running an advertising business and wanting to build something that's better than the offerings of rivals. He's proud of what he has created and the legacy he will leave when he finally retires. As an entrepreneur, his motivation is customer centric; he is always looking for better ways to serve customers and he has a pragmatic vision to profit from the opportunities that he finds are available. This pragmatism extends to his favorite metric, cash. "Cash tells you what is happening to expenditure, what's happening to acquisitions: the whole thing," he says. "It's not an earth-shattering response, but it's very important. I started in 1975 and actually the same pieces of information we had in 1975 are still as relevant today as they were then."

His is a restless, hands-on management style. He will insist on being personally involved with the first three or four layers of management, taking part in recruitment, and wanting to know details of what's going on in all the businesses. WPP's model places a premium on his personal expertise, market knowledge, deal-making brilliance, and the importance of his physical presence at big pitches to clients. Sir Martin is the critical source of energy in the business.

Sir Martin on being a corporate entrepreneur

"If you start something in a room with two people and you have now got 100,000 people, you're much more emotionally involved with it. We started this business with two people in one room. Moving it from there to whatever demanded a set of characteristics, qualities, attributes, strengths, and then to move it again in another five years demanded another set.

"It's different for me because I started this business. It's the closest a man can come to having a baby. It tends to be very different because it's like the famous Liverpool quote: Football is not a matter of life or death, it's more important than that. WPP is not a matter of life or death; it's more important.

"When we win business, I'm delighted; when we lose, I'm physically and mentally upset. That's the founder's difficulty. We started 25 years ago and built it brick by brick.

"Entrepreneurialism means taking risks, so our industry is not entrepreneurial. People in it mean independence when they talk about entrepreneurialism. They mean taking risks with the company's money, not betting their houses. So there are not many true entrepreneurs. There are people who are good at starting things and people who are good at running things, but rarely do you find the same characteristics in the same person.

"It's hard to find someone who's entrepreneurial and managerial. I have been called a trumped-up beancounter many times. We started like a beginner, but we wanted to be a big banana. You had to do it by acquisition. Clearly, the most powerful thing to a shareholder is not to grow by acquisition – it's the top line. What's the variable? What drives success? Well, having the best people round your business, getting the strategy right, getting the people right, and then dealing with all the communities."

Formative years

Sir Martin once described himself as a "spoilt only child", qualifying the statement by revealing that he did have a brother who died at birth.[33] He was born into a business background, with his father working as chief executive of an industrial holding company that had a retail electrical division. "From a very early age, when I was 13 or 14, I remember meeting the chairman of my father's company and him asking me what I wanted to do," he recalled.[34] "Somewhat precociously I said, 'You know I want to go into business' and he said, 'Well, if you want to go into business you should go to Harvard Business School'."

The young Sorrell did go to Harvard, after first taking an economics degree at Cambridge. He was a member of what Sorrell recalls the admissions dean called the "most naive class" at the Ivy League business school. Sir Martin always loved business. Even while he was at Cambridge he wrote an article called "Management today". He remembers going with his father when aged about 12 to look at existing stores or potential new sites. "I think it has always been in the blood," he says.

After Harvard he worked for US consultancy Glendinning Associates, Mark McCormack's International Management Group, and James Gulliver Associates. Then he became the first finance director of Saatchi & Saatchi, an advertising business that was two years old when he joined. "In all these jobs, I profited from the focus, intensity, and determination that I'd gained during my time at Harvard," Sir Martin recalls. "Harvard's hothouse atmosphere stayed with me. Fear of failure drove me. The trouble was that we were made to feel that we could run the world."

Sir Martin on his roots

"I've had two mentors – a lawyer friend in New York and my father – but mentor is not the right word. It's someone you can talk to, someone whose view you can rely on to be independent, someone who has no agenda. I used to talk to my dad four or five times a day. I used to talk to him about what was happening in the business.

"He was an extremely close friend, I think probably the closest friend I've ever had. He was somebody that I could talk to in a very open way and get a view. He was a very clever man, probably never fulfilled his potential. I think certainly he could have done much more than he did."

Sir Martin on his management style

"It's all apple pie and motherhood. No one has any magic formula. It's pretty commonsensical. I think you can over-intellectualize these things. Keeping it simple is pretty important. Everyone obfuscates and makes it too sophisticated. Having a clear purpose, vision, and strategy, having the right team, and having them aligned is what's important.

"People accuse me of being a micro-manager. I take it as a compliment. I think the detail is incredibly important.

"I am like a referee in that I bring all the parts of the company to work together. I am the only person, or one of very few people, who sees the whole picture. My Pavlovian reaction is to have everybody in the corporation working together. The Pavlovian reaction of anybody running one of the brands, whether it's 100 companies or 12, is to see it from their point of view.

"My natural inclination is to think of the WPP brand. That is where I am different, in that I was born with this thing and therefore I've seen most and I know 80 to 90 percent of what is there in fairly intimate detail. Therefore I know more about what goes on than most and what the capabilities are. We've got some very good creative people and some very creative insights, so making those available in the corners of the empire is very important. So my role is one of a referee and sort of consolidator or cooperator.

"I don't change. You are what you are. If I'm right I'm right and if I'm not I'm not. I'm not a great believer in the mentor-style approach; I think it's too stylized. I think individuals are very important. Individuals drive businesses. This is not voguish. It's counter to modern theory about leadership and teams, but I still think that individuals are key and probably unreasonably so."

Work–life balance

Sir Martin has never made any pretense of the fact that he lives for his business and has no separation of his business and personal lives. As with all pure corporate entrepreneurs, WPP is his life. "The three circles that matter are family, career, and society," he says. "There are very few people that manage to balance it. I certainly haven't been able to. You could probably balance two, but balancing all three is phenomenally difficult.

"Traveling a lot has caused disruption from a personal point of view and has probably made my personal life more difficult. I haven't actually moved home a lot. I've only had two houses, because I've always made my base in the UK. So, that, at least, has not been a problem."

He does feel that being a chief executive is a very lonely business. And his business life may have been successful at the expense of his personal and family life. In the papers for their divorce, Lady Sandra Sorrell stated that his infidelity, globetrotting, and the long hours he spent building up WPP were the reasons behind the marriage's collapse. She said they led to Sir Martin's workaholic lifestyle, in which she felt "marginalized", "dehumanized", and "discarded".[35]

In fact, it is possible that whenever Sir Martin leaves WPP, it will be the nearest corporate experience to a divorce. He admits that his own succession is one of the biggest threats to WPP's sustainability and one of the biggest issues for the board. "I'm obsessive about things not because I think I can do them better," he told CNN, "but because I am interested. And that's the problem. I'll never be able to let go. Someone will have to tap me on the shoulder."

Just as he is one of Britain's clearest examples of the positive attributes of a corporate entrepreneur, therefore, Sir Martin also illustrates the potential risks of the model. First, corporate entrepreneurs may experience problems in finding people to scale up their businesses without losing the vital entrepreneurial spirit. And while corporate entrepreneurs rely on their vision and brilliance to attract great people, this can also be their downside, resulting in people-related problems that may include allowing themselves and others to get burned out by the demands of their roles. Critics of Sir Martin in particular say that he is so authoritarian and fast moving that staff sometimes cannot keep up. He remains proud of his legacy, however, and is adamant that he would do it all again.

"Some people can start a company and can't run it and some people can run a company but they can't start it," he told CNN. "I'd like to think that I can do both, so the epitaph should read: 'He was partly responsible' or 'was responsible for initiating the growth and development of the finest advertising marketing and services company in our industry'. It's very pretentious, but that's probably what it's about."

Sir Martin on life after WPP

"There is no such thing as stress, it's just that you're not having fun. Lots of opportunities to deal with problems you might describe as stress, but I think that can be fun. The stress occurs when you feel you can't do it. When people say they're stressed it's because what is coming at them or what they're having to deal with is either too difficult or they feel it's impossible to deal with or they're not doing their job properly. That doesn't mean that I haven't had times when I've thought this is very difficult and how am I going to deal with it.

"I ultimately chose my direction, so I am very fortunate that I decided at the grand old age of 40 to start to do something. We have to be political, in a sense, but I've chosen a direction and I didn't have to kow-tow. I happened to fall into the advertising business and I've been able to carry on doing what I regard as fun. Our industry is you are as good as your last ad, so the barriers to entry are not that great. You know every day whether you are succeeding or not; there's no hiding. You do a good ad, you win a pitch, you lose a piece of business, you win a piece of business, and you know instantaneously. It's like the entertainment business and sports, you get results very, very quickly.

"My succession is probably one the biggest issues for the board to deal with. I would find it very difficult not to have something central to my work life. I am a doer, not a chairman. If I didn't do this, I would try to do something not dissimilar. I would start again."

Profile of a corporate entrepreneur, Michael Spencer, chief executive, ICAP

Michael Spencer, founder and chief executive of inter-dealer broker ICAP and treasurer of the UK's Conservative Party, is frequently described as one of Britain's City grandees, but this is no testament to his background. Although Spencer spent much of his childhood in Africa and was privately schooled, his success came in one of the most testosterone-fueled sectors of London's financial district, where he had to fight his way up the ladder. Ever since he can remember, he says he has wanted to make money and that has involved him consolidating the global market for inter-dealer money broking.

Spencer co-founded the company that was then called Intercapital in 1986 and has built it into the world's largest voice and electronic inter-dealer broker. The company now employs 4,600 staff and has operations in 50 countries, making a fortune of more than £1 billion for Spencer, who owns 17 percent of the company. ICAP is active in the wholesale markets in interest rates, credit, commodities, foreign exchange, and equity derivatives. It has an average daily transaction volume of more than $2.3 trillion, more than 40 percent of which is traded electronically.

Spencer as a corporate entrepreneur

The financial sector is not well known for producing corporate entrepreneurs, though there are noted exceptions such as the heavily risk-taking Lloyd's of London insurance market. Spencer's credentials as a leading corporate entrepreneur, however, stem from the fact that, despite operating in one of the most competitive sectors of the City, he has wrought transformational change, building ICAP from scratch into the world's largest company of its type.

He set up Intercapital initially to concentrate on the new interest rate swaps market. As a specialist financial derivatives broking firm, Intercapital grew from the original four people to over three hundred worldwide, with offices in London, New York, Sydney, Singapore, and a joint venture in Tokyo. In 1998 Intercapital merged with EXCO, a listed money broker, and formed Intercapital plc. Nearly a year later, Spencer executed another merger, combining Intercapital with money broker Garban to form Garban-Intercapital, bringing together Garban's traditional strength in government and corporate bonds, interest rate products, and money market instruments with Intercapital's strengths in interest rate swaps and options, commodity swaps, illiquid securities, and foreign exchange options. The name of the group was changed to ICAP in 2001.

Although Spencer didn't found ICAP on his own, the company has long been shaped in his image. He is a feisty trader and inveterate gambler who once lost £10,000 in a night at backgammon and is said to have started a market in the number of lace-up shoes under a table at a City lunch. He has been involved in a few scrapes in his time, being sacked twice early in his career for trading errors, including racking up huge losses in the gold market. More recently, he was investigated and cleared over suggestions of insider dealing over a £5.5 million purchase of shares in Marks & Spencer after meeting his friend Stuart Rose. At the time he was being lined up by retail mogul Sir Philip Green to help with a mooted takeover. Inter-dealer broking is a fiercely competitive sector and Spencer has also had well-publicised battles over alleged poaching of staff from rivals.

Despite the macho environment – Spencer and his co-founder banned women from working for ICAP in the early days – the company has an altruistic side. In 2009 it held its 17th annual charity day, donating the entire £11.5 million gross revenues of the day's trading to good causes. "Unquestionably it is the most exciting and fun day for the firm every year," says Spencer. Indeed, celebrities ranging from Prince William to Cherie Blair and Denzel Washington have been known to drop in, while ICAP's staff in 50 offices worldwide whoop it up in fancy dress. "There was an entire desk of Michael Spencers, all with spectacles and fake bald patches one year," Spencer laughs. "I was Sergeant Pepper."

Spencer on being a corporate entrepreneur

"I wanted to go into business from about 15. I was one of those fortunate people who didn't worry about what they were going to do after they went to university. I knew I didn't want to be a civil servant, take any professional exams, join Procter & Gamble, or go into accountancy. I didn't bother with any of that. I knew I wanted to work in the City so I just went where I wanted to go.

"The single thing I am most proud of in my life is setting up ICAP in 1986 with three colleagues and £50,000. Twenty years later in 2006, seeing ICAP go into the FTSE100 was a moment where I pinched myself a little bit. One should never be hubristic, but I am very proud of that.

"I don't regret anything in my business career, but I would give myself lots of advice if I could go back and start all over again. Work hard. There's no substitute for hard work. And read a lot, particularly if you want to work in the financial sector."

Formative years

Spencer, the son of a civil servant, spent his childhood in Malaysia, Sudan, and Ethiopia. He says he decided at the age of 15 that he wanted to work in the City and make money. While a physics student at Oxford, he made £300 dealing in shares.

His first job was at stockbroker Simon & Coates, but he was fired after making a losing bet with his own money on the gold market. His second employer was US bank Drexel Burnham in London, but he was fired from there too after a $110,000 trading error. He then worked for money broker Charles Fulton before forming Intercapital.

"Growing up in Africa had a huge impact on me really," he says. "The exposure to the poverty of Africa, the simplicity of Africa, and the scale of Africa really made an impression. I go back there a lot now and am building a house in Kenya, which is very exciting for me. So in a subtle and subliminal way, I think Africa has been a very tempering component in my life and in my soul.

"I haven't really had a mentor in my business career. I was certainly influenced by my tutors at school. I was very lucky in that I had some very good tutors who helped me through my A levels and motivated me very, very much. My father was a great influence on my life. Although he was a civil servant, he was a very motivational guy and he really gave me a lot of passion. Actually, I wanted to set up in business from quite a young age. In terms of other great figures in history, there are lots of people who have influenced me, whether it be JP Morgan, Andrew Carnegie, or more modern entrepreneurs such as the founders of Google and Microsoft or Li Ka-shing, chairman of Hutchison Whampoa in

Hong Kong. But there's nobody who I could say was a big personal mentor to me. I have never read a business book in my career, I am embarrassed to say. Over the years I've been given quite a few, but they're collecting dust on my bookshelves. I think actually that business is something you feel in your bones and in your blood and are driven passionately by."

Life after ICAP

Spencer admits that he initially wanted to divide his life into working first in business and thereafter in politics, but he has settled for his unpaid role as Conservative Party treasurer and no longer hankers after a political career.

"I was fascinated by finance and by politics and fortunately I have been just about able to combine both of those in my career," he says. "I always wanted to do business for half of my life and to go into politics after that. I set up ICAP in 1986 when I was 30 and I originally intended to do that for about ten years, make some money and then perhaps go into politics, but I found the whole project of setting up a business that within ten years had become reasonably successful as very absorbing, so I gave up my aspirations for a political career and focused on business. Politics is not for me now."

He is more than likely to leave ICAP eventually for some other business venture, possibly in private equity; he has already made investments in stockbroker Numis Securities and spreadbetting firm IG Index. Like Sir Martin Sorrell, it is difficult to conceive of ICAP without Michael Spencer, but that's exactly what will happen one day. Like all corporate entrepreneurs, Spencer needs to prepare his company for life without its founder.

PITFALLS OF THE CORPORATE ENTREPRENEUR MODEL

Corporate entrepreneurs tend to rely on their vision and the brilliance of the opportunity, rather than their personal leadership, to attract talented people. The failings of corporate entrepreneurs are therefore typically related to their ability to find, organize, and keep the managers, technicians, and staff they need to make their great ideas work.

The risks of the model are that people burn themselves out, there is inadequate succession planning for when the founder of the business retires or moves on to do something else, and there is difficulty attracting the right people to grow and scale companies. Corporate entrepreneurs can be weak at managing businesses that are not growing exponentially but are in a steady state; they may have chaotic systems or be distrusting of attempts by managers to instill process and order to their organizations. And they may cause investor disquiet by betting the whole company on a disruptive technology or marketing that may be ahead of its time.

One example of this is the move by Charles Dunstone, one of the few corporate entrepreneurs leading FTSE100 companies, to offer "free" broadband services to customers of his Carphone Warehouse mobile phone retailer. In less than six months, the company signed up 525,000 broadband customers. But its shares dived as it revealed that its TalkTalk broadband offer had become a service nightmare, attracting too many customers to a service that was not ready for that number. "It was an idea that went out of control," Dunstone said. "I thought, 'We've got all these people coming into the shops, what else can we sell them?'"[36]

Actually Dunstone, whose fortunes have now revived, doesn't accept that he meets the description of the corporate entrepreneur model. "I'm no entrepreneur," he has said. "I haven't started loads of great businesses. I'm a one-trick pony. I was lucky enough to realize that the real market for mobiles was not giant corporations like BP, but plumbers and builders who previously relied on answering machines."[37] In so saying, he modestly ignores the fact that thousands of competitors stumbled on the same idea at the same time, but only he and John Caudwell of rival Phones4u turned their small businesses into enduring corporations.

7

CORPORATE AMBASSADORS

Corporate ambassadors have a global vision that has a broader societal impact. They operate at the geopolitical level and deliver transactions that transform industries. They almost exclusively lead long-established businesses with global footprints and are most frequently found in resource businesses, such as oil and minerals, or global banking groups. Much like their diplomatic brethren, they have a calm and measured management style. They're most effective in situations where interaction with regulators, governments, and other authorities is critical. They thrive on solving high-profile problems and possess the vision to see how their companies have to change to maintain and enhance their roles in the future.

John Varley at Barclays is an example of a corporate ambassador who realizes the importance of how he is seen to lead. "I am clear that a chief executive who is wild and unpredictable is a menace," he says. "A CEO must be balanced. You cannot have an organization which is twisting in the wind of the chief executive's mood swings. People have to be able to predict me; I cannot be moody. Moodiness is something I am very suspicious of."

Corporate ambassadors lead by example. Sir John Bond, the Vodafone chairman, famously refused to fly in first class on short-haul flights when he was chief executive and then chairman of banking group HSBC. He was renowned at the bank for his smooth, affable style. He always took time to talk to even the lowliest staffer on his tours around operations, checking the temperature of the organization and boosting morale. Even trade unions found it hard to dent his measured ambassadorial style. At one stormy annual meeting, unions arranged for the immigrant worker who cleaned the windows in Sir John's office at the bank to ask a question about the difference between his pay and that of the chairman. "You probably don't know who I am, but I get up at 5 a.m. to clean your windows," the cleaner told Sir John. "Of course I know who you are," came the friendly retort. "I've often seen you and wanted to have a chat. Next time you do the windows, why don't you stop by for a cup of tea?"

Stylistically, corporate ambassadors tend to be traditional in their bearing, fastidious about their appearance, and fiercely protective of their reputations. Varley is known for his braces and formal dress sense, while BP public relations advisers always took great care to ensure that the diminutive Lord Browne was pictured from below, for example on a staircase, to boost his stature.

Corporate ambassadors possess the leadership talent necessary to cope with the transforming changes of globalization, sustainability, technology, alternative capital, and the war for talent. They not only possess great vision for the future of their industries, but are also personally engaging and able to generate support from a range of stakeholders, allowing them to follow an ambitious path.

They have an ability to see change coming and prepare their people and organizations for change. They also tend to run their companies according to strict moral codes.

Profile of a corporate ambassador:
Lord Browne, managing partner, Riverstone Holdings

Corporate ambassadors are a comparatively rare breed, but a British business leader who illustrates the type well is one of the nation's highest-achieving chief executives in recent times. Corporate ambassadorial skills propelled John Browne to the top of BP, where as chief executive from 1995 to 2007, this son of an immigrant Auschwitz survivor turned a mid-ranking European firm into the third-largest oil company in the western world and Britain's biggest and most globalized company.

Lord Browne's business record speaks for itself. When he became the youngest chief executive in BP's history in 1995, the company's share price stood at 222p. When he resigned in 2007 it was 563p. During that period, BP returned an 8 percent annual average increase in share price – nearly double the average for the FTSE100 index.[38] He achieved such growth by wreaking major transformational change, leading oil industry consolidation with the takeovers of major US oil companies Amoco and Atlantic Richfield, and moving into Russia by taking a 50 percent stake in what became TNK-BP, which was, before its troubles in 2008, after Browne's departure, the largest and most profitable investment in Russia by a western oil company.[39] These moves demonstrated the assured handling of top-level government and corporate players that typifies a corporate ambassador.

Browne also reacted to low oil prices in the 1990s by waging a war on costs. Rival industry executives said that he was the toughest cost cutter in the business. The result was that in 12 years he turned BP into the third largest western oil company by market capitalization.[40] While driving BP's core businesses, he also exhibited the global vision and eye for societal impact required of a true corporate ambassador by launching a massive sustainability push by BP: "Beyond Petroleum". No wonder he was voted Britain's most admired leader for four years in succession from 1999–2002.[41]

Browne on being a corporate ambassador

"For me it was at the heart of the purpose of the firm. It was about whether I could help shape the business and influence the markets that it would operate in, such as Russia or the entire alternative energy sector. It was about why energy is important in terms of giving as many people as possible the light, heat, and mobility they wanted. And it was about new jobs for a diverse set of people in new places.

"Leaders need to have a view of the world. The very best leaders are able to pick and trust people. That is hard because people are trained to distrust and often appear to act in a way which destroys trust. Leaders must not be small-minded and must be capable of not being cynical. And they must not be people who want to get everything in place first before anything is done. Life is untidy. In all big things I did, I had to extemporize a bit."

Formative years

Browne was born in Hamburg, Germany, to a British Army officer father and a Hungarian Auschwitz survivor mother, the multilingual Paula Wesz, who had worked for the Allies as a translator and met and married Captain Edmund Browne in 1947. Capt Browne worked in civilian life for Anglo-Persian Oil, which later became British Petroleum. The family settled in Cambridge and the eight-year-old John Browne began his education at King's School in Ely. He says that his years there taught him the value of diversity and of not having to bow to "the tremendous pressure to conform". His mother, whom Browne would later regularly take along to BP social events, didn't conform either. Browne once recalled that she was "definitely different", adding: "She dressed in an elegant way and wore makeup, which was somewhat unusual in the fens in the 1960s. She spoke with an accent which she never lost. I'm sure she did this on purpose."[42]

In 1957 Capt Browne moved out to Iran and by 1959 he had persuaded John's mother to send their son to boarding school. His mother thought it was a deeply barbaric thing to do and never reconciled herself to it. Friends of Browne remember him constantly questioning formulae in science and maths classes at Ely. He at first considered an academic career and was offered a Cambridge research fellowship to study continental drift and the ocean bed, but his father persuaded him to take a wider view. "He knew me better than I did myself," Browne recalled. "He kept on saying, 'You need to see the world. Do you really want to live in England for the rest of your life?'"[43]

After initial postings, BP sent Browne to Stanford University in 1980. On rejoining the company, he was appointed commercial manager of the upstream business. The 1980s also saw changes in his personal life. He became closer to his mother after the death of his father at the beginning of the decade and moved her into a flat at the top of his house in London's Notting Hill.

Browne on his roots

"My father gave me the ability to be very comfortable in a world full of different people doing very different things. My mother, who was a foreign worker in the UK in the 1950s, which was very unusual at the time, gave me the confidence to be a little different. Living overseas also shaped me. It's only very recently that I've thought of Britain as my home. I've only really lived here since the late 1980s. I owned a house early for financial reasons, but I did not live in it.

"I didn't have a burning ambition in my 20s. I liked getting great things done and liked it when they were different. That was a purpose in itself. I didn't have a world mission in the early days, but I began to see interesting things as group treasurer at BP. Barriers, such as exchange rate controls, were coming down. Things were about to happen."

Career progression

It was appointment as worldwide chief of exploration and production in 1989 that set Browne up for the chief executive's position. At 41, he was responsible for more than half the company's earnings and expenditure. From this role, he set off on two critical paths that he continued to pursue as CEO. First, he took BP beyond Alaska and the North Sea and saw it become successful in the Gulf of Mexico, Azerbaijan, and Angola. Second, he enforced rigorous discipline and set stretching targets for the division.

As chief executive, he became the company's deal maker. From being a relatively small European oil firm that looked like a target for US consolidation, BP became a major global player in the oil industry. Browne first paid $55 billion for Amoco and three months later another $27 billion for its fellow US oil company Atlantic Richfield. That put BP just behind what was soon to be ExxonMobil and neck and neck with the Royal Dutch/Shell Group.

"Some CEOs will endeavor to outperform the competition," Browne says. "Other CEOs will look at the industry as a whole and decide whether to change the game, for example through consolidation. My idea of what to do only really came in the late 1980s when the Berlin Wall came down and ultra-high-speed computing opened everything up."

But Browne's vision wasn't restricted to mergers and acquisitions. It also included an early understanding of how sustainability and environmental issues would become a pivotal part of business. Back in the late 1990s when green measures were still regarded as somewhat peripheral, he gave a speech at Stanford University committing BP to reducing greenhouse gases. He changed the company's slogan to Beyond Petroleum and used it as the clarion call for a series of alternative and renewable energy initiatives. "For those of us who have long been advocates of a greener economy, the change of British Petroleum to Beyond Petroleum was a single moment that marked the mainstream business world's adoption of sustainable development," wrote the *Sydney Morning Herald.*

It wasn't just the corporate logo that turned green. Browne was convinced that the company had to lower its impact on the environment and began positioning the group to succeed in the post-hydrocarbon world. Today BP is the world's largest producer of solar panels. It has also invested heavily in alternative and renewable energy projects and has reduced its greenhouse gas emissions while raising its energy output every year for the past decade.

Management style

Browne's management style is characterized by attention to problem solving, recruiting and managing the best talent of his generation to work for him, and wielding the power that he possessed as chief executive with a comparatively light touch.

His friend Peter Hennessy argued that Browne ran BP "like a research scientist" and Browne himself admitted as much. "I have great satisfaction in solving problems," he once said. "I have great satisfaction in exciting, different and new things. And that's why, at the beginning, I tried to find exciting things to do, challenging problems, things which were a bit more difficult to solve. If driving for that sort of thing is ambition, then that's a definition of ambition."[44]

One of Browne's most impressive characteristics as a leader, and one that was evident when we interviewed him, is his tremendous clarity of thought. He is able crisply and persuasively to frame complex geopolitical and business issues at will.

His success at recruiting and managing talent, moreover, is evidenced by the fact that his succession was always an internal issue, despite the troubles that BP encountered after the Texas refinery explosion toward the end of his tenure as chief executive. It was also probably not a coincidence that his successor, Tony Hayward, came from the same exploration and production path that Browne had himself taken at BP. Browne maintains the intense interest in developing the next generation of talent that he exhibited at BP; he continues to be active in addressing people early in their careers. His clarity of thought is matched by an impressive ability to inspire people at these events.

Browne's views on how power should be wielded epitomize the views of corporate ambassadors, who do not tend to develop huge egos. "Power is something that has to be used very, very carefully," he says. "It's much better to think you have none, rather than to think you have a lot. That is the way, I hope, you can make more sensible decisions. I have the sense that power – the ability to get things done, to make changes – is limited. And perhaps it's most effectively used from a position of humility rather than strength."

Browne on his management style

"I found that effective business leadership required a tight focus on the plot. Set a clear strategy and organize your resources behind it. Strong values and careful delegation are essential, but above all, keep clear where you're driving for.

"Make sure you have enough time to get out there and develop people and markets. You need a great chief operating officer because the job is changing a lot. It's a little team approach. It can be two or three people but not four.

"There are too many things for one person now because the nature of competition has changed. Competition is not in your backyard; it's everywhere. You need a radar, but there's always too much information, so you need people with experience to help you pick places to go.

"No company can survive without reinventing itself. Go and expose yourself to new ideas. Search, listen to people, and train yourself to be interested in things. Then you assemble a pattern of the world. Sometimes you get a good idea, but they don't arrive every day."

Browne's downfall and the risks of the corporate ambassador model

Browne's reputation suffered a blow in 2007 when he resigned, after misleading a court during an action aimed at preventing a newspaper revealing personal details given to them by a former boyfriend. However, since Browne has left there has been comment on suggestions that he became too distant from the daily workings of BP and that he allowed some business processes to weaken.

There were rumblings about Browne's "huge power" from early in the new century. For example, one former director told the press anonymously in 2002 that "the longer he is there, the more a feeling of a court develops".[45] More damagingly, Tony Hayward, then BP's five-year veteran chief executive of exploration and production, wrote on the company's internal website in 2006 that "the top of the organisation doesn't listen hard enough to what the bottom of the organisation is saying" – a posting that rapidly made the newspapers and was widely viewed as a criticism of Browne's management style.[46] Browne had long been a media figure, nicknamed "the sun king", and this cultured, successful, Renaissance man was increasingly portrayed in the press as appearing and acting rather like a monarch.

The accusation of a weakness in process control came to the fore with the results of an investigation into the series of tragic explosions at BP's Texas City refinery, which killed 15 people and injured 180 others in 2005.[47] Led by former US Secretary of State James A Baker, a panel found "material deficiencies" in BP's safety procedures at its American oil refineries. The report found that prior to the Texas City tragedy, BP had emphasized personal safety over process safety. Indeed, at that time BP was proud of its achievements in personal safety, which it believed probably saved hundreds of lives. Although the report stressed that it did not find any deliberate or conscious efforts on BP's part to short-circuit safety, the panel said that the company mistakenly interpreted improving personal injury rates as an indication of acceptable process safety performance at its US refineries. It found instances of "a lack of operating discipline, toleration of serious deviations from safe operating practices, and apparent complacency toward serious safety risks" at each US refinery, albeit adding, "we are under no illusion that deficiencies in process safety culture, management, or corporate oversight are limited to BP". In addition, in 2006 BP suffered further fallout from a spill caused by poor maintenance of a key oil pipeline in the Alaskan exploration and production division. Critics put these two high-profile incidents together and alleged a systematic failure by Browne and his top management to monitor process controls adequately.

These criticisms highlight the key risk in the ambassadorial model, but need nuancing and pegging back. Corporate ambassadors are by their nature outward looking, so great ambassadors build a team around them to keep tight control over the internal operations of their business. Browne made a conscious effort to do this by appointing a very strong deputy chief executive in Rodney Chase in 1998 and building a set of highly trusted personal advisers around him. This model worked phenomenally well for five years. However, Chase retired in 2003 after 38 years at BP.[48] It is from this point that concerns about BP seem to mount. "I could not get approval to keep Rodney beyond 60, he left and left a big hole," admits Browne. "It was a tremendous partnership, which allowed us to achieve a huge amount."

Browne had been trying to bring on a fresh generation of talent, a move that was undoubtedly one cause of concern by some that he was sidelining some of the old guard. In response to Chase's departure, Browne moved some of these younger executives up and added additional processes at the center. In one sense this worked: Tony Hayward, after all, flourished under Browne. However, the transition was not competely successful and the problems discussed above developed. While the Texas explosion was a tragedy, Browne's misfortune lay not in a deep failing as a leader, but in not transitioning his management team.

Browne on his support network

"Being single doesn't mean you don't have a family life. It's actually just a little bit more difficult. I always think of my closest friends as my surrogate family. When my mother died – she was the last member of my family – that became even more important to me. There's a deep loyalty that you might find in a family in the people I am closest to. They do actually behave as members of my family. They're just not related by blood or by marriage."

Life after BP

Browne has continued with his vision in his life since BP. His principal commitment is as managing partner (Europe) of Riverstone Holdings, an energy specialist private equity house that has about $17 billion under management and is investing a $6 billion conventional energy fund and a $3.4 billion renewable energy fund, believed to be the biggest in the world.[49]

Browne also stays involved in the energy sector in his other roles, including being president of the Royal Academy of Engineering. He observed in 2009 that "the move to renewable energy is probably the biggest shift I have seen in my time in the industry. I don't think we should rely on the big oil companies as being the renewable energy people of the future, much as we never should have relied on the fixed-line phone operators being the mobile operators of the future. They weren't."

As ever, Browne sees a systemic solution requiring a balance of governmental and market measures: "The shift to a broader energy supply will have to have all forms of energy to satisfy demand, and it requires the right incentives to be in place. There are clear incentives for producing oil and gas at the moment, and they're called high profits, appropriate taxes, and low penalties for producing carbon products."

True to his ambassadorial colours, Browne also continues to influence formally and informally at the highest levels of government. He is a member of the UK's "Business Ambassador" network, responsible for promoting UK trade abroad, and in 2009 it was announced that he would chair a very high-profile inquiry into university tuition fees. With global climate change at the forefront of everyone's minds and "plenty of oil around", Browne's dual interests and ambassadorial skills seem set to remain firmly in demand.

PROFILE OF A GLOBAL AMBASSADOR: SIR JOHN PARKER, CHAIRMAN, ANGLO AMERICAN AND NATIONAL GRID

Global ambassadors operate at the geopolitical level and in his long industrial career Sir John Parker has crossed more divides than most. Over 28 years, he has sat on 13 quoted company boards, nine of which he has chaired, and he is still very much in demand, adding the chairmanship of mining group Anglo American in 2009 to his continuing chair at National Grid. His list of positions includes three dual-listed companies in cruise ship operator Carnival (London and New York), pallets giant Brambles (London and Sydney), and paper group Mondi (London and Johannesburg). In addition, he has presided over two major demergers (Lattice Group from BG Group and P&O Princess from P&O), two sales to foreign companies (P&O to DP World of Dubai and concrete group RMC to Mexico's Cemex), and two major mergers (Lattice with National Grid and P&O Princess with Carnival).

As well as chairing Anglo American and National Grid, his portfolio of nonexecutive jobs includes companies in the Middle East (DP World), continental Europe (aircraft maker EADS Airbus), South Africa (Mondi), and the US, where Carnival is also the only company to be a member of both the FTSE100 and America's benchmark S&P500 index. Somehow Sir John, knighted in 2001 for services to defense and shipbuilding, until recently found time to also be a senior nonexecutive director of the Court of the Bank of England. He's still a member of the Prime Minister's Business Council for Britain and Chancellor of Southampton University.

Sir John as a corporate ambassador

Sir John's breadth of experience has enabled him to be early to spot important macroeconomic trends. As chairman of shipping group P&O, for example, he foresaw long before globalization became a corporate buzzword how the rapid development of container shipping would drive world trade. Like other corporate ambassadors, he is calm and has a measured management style, but he is also methodical and highly structured.

When he took over as chairman of Anglo American in 2009, at a time when the company was the subject of a hostile takeover bid from rival Xstrata and its chief executive Cynthia Carroll was under pressure from shareholders, he reverted to his tried-and-tested practice of taking a single sheet of A4 paper. On it, he wrote down the changes that he thought would be required both at board and at operational level to deliver the value in Anglo American that he did not believe Xstrata's bid reflected. After eight weeks, of which three were spent on investor roadshows, Sir John was still using the same piece of paper.

He is similarly robust in his firm belief that there are five pillars around which to run a company; the first one – leading governance – is part of the reason he didn't add two other companies to his list of appointments. One turned out to be a blessing in disguise when he managed to extricate himself from what turned out to be the poisoned chalice of chairing Railtrack, the now nationalized UK rail infrastructure group. The other time was when he turned down the chair of aerospace group BAE Systems not that long after National Grid had merged with Lattice Group. "I had a big commitment at National Grid and I wasn't going to risk it at that time," he recalls. "It was sensitive to chair two FTSE100 companies."

Sir John did end up twice having double FTSE100 chairs, taking on those of aggregates group RMC and P&O when they were outside the index and presiding over an increase in value that took them into it. However, he took a characteristically pragmatic view of those corporate governance transgressions.

He laughs: "Chaps in the media would say: 'Aren't you worried that it could get into the FTSE?' I would say: 'Actually I'm worried what happens if they don't get in.' Wouldn't it be a very strange governance system if a new chairman said: 'Well, I'm not running this company in such a way that it risks getting into the FTSE100'? I never agreed with that rule but I was never going to abuse it. I was not going to blatantly go out and flout it."

His other pillars are strong financial control, sound administration, strategy and accountability, and good corporate citizenship. However, this high-level approach does not mean that he flinches from conflict. Firing chief executives and nonexecutives is one example. "Unfortunately, if you're turning companies around, you normally find that the old adage that fish rot from the head is normally true," he says.

"If a company really jumps off the rails at any point in time, you can be sure that you have to start with change in the boardroom. I don't enjoy sacking anyone, but any leader has to bite the bullet on difficult issues with people, because you're doing it for the majority in that organization. If you don't do it, it's going to weaken the organization and damage a lot of people and therefore you have to do it."

Sir John on being a corporate ambassador

"Whether you are a big company or a small company, whether you're in one country or in 30, the same principles apply. You create one company in terms of values and ethics and you have to make sure that the standards by which you deliver customer service, safety management, and everything else are exactly the same wherever you go in the company. A quality board that acts cohesively and has open, transparent discussion sets the tone; it really sets the drumbeat for the organization as a whole. You take learning from one company to another, which is very important, and you can issue challenges in the boardroom to management's proposals.

"I believe that you have to install great leadership that takes ownership at every level. Leadership is a privilege, so it's vital that you leave things in a better condition than you found them. My philosophy is that if an organization is not on a journey, don't bother about leadership. Just settle for management."

Formative years

Born in County Down, Northern Ireland, Sir John served a tough apprenticeship in management, joining the ship design team at Belfast shipbuilder Harland & Wolff after university. He then became managing director at Sunderland shipbuilders Austin & Pickersgill, before returning to Harland & Wolff as chairman and chief executive, later moving on to become chairman and chief executive of Babcock International.

He remains true to his shipping roots as governor of the Royal National Lifeboat Institution and a member of the General Committee of Lloyd's Register of Shipping. He also leads the Young Offenders into Work program, serves on the Defence Academy Advisory Board, and is a member of the UK government's Asia Task Force and the international advisory board of CitiGroup.

Sir John on his formative years

"In an interview I gave about 20 years ago, I was asked if I had any regrets about the career I ventured out on. I said then: 'I have never doubted the wisdom or the great privilege to have studied naval architecture and engineering for the years of my student apprenticeship at Harland & Wolff's famous Belfast Queen's Island shipyard, that great university of life where I experienced not just the design and construction of great ships, but where I first learnt about human engineering and the management and challenges of leading teams of people.' Today, the response would be no different. I look back with a degree of wonderment at all the great experiences I've had. My life has been enriched, not only from all the challenges – some of them fairly daunting at the time – but from all the great people I've worked with, known, and learnt from over the years. I'm also glad to say I'm still learning."

Life after Anglo American and National Grid

At the age of 68, Sir John's current major board chairs are likely to be his last, but he will no doubt continue his plural life, bringing his corporate ambassadorial skills to bear on behalf of portfolio companies. The wise head that has helped him steer his course is unlikely to allow him to venture into unfamiliar waters, however. "One is lucky in life when people seem to want you," he says, "but I wouldn't be interested in the gaming industry or cigarette industry, and insurance isn't an industry I would feel particularly comfortable in.

"I'm an industrial guy. You have to choose your company wisely, as carefully as you choose your friends. It's so important. I would say that my weeks are full, but that's the way I happen to like to run my life. And, while I have a number of roles, none of them ever gets neglected. The day I thought I was neglecting any of them, I would be off."

Pitfalls of the corporate ambassador model

Lord Browne's premature departure from BP is a perfect illustration of the risks of the corporate ambassador model. The distance that some corporate ambassadors tend to cultivate makes them an easy target for the media and can be damaging for businesses with a strong consumer presence.

It's not only Browne who suffers from this, though his fall from grace was the most dramatic in recent years. Take this commentary on John Varley, from an interview in *The Sunday Times* by Andrew Davidson: "With his high-cut trousers, stiff-collared shirt, blue braces and monogrammed cufflinks, he looks at times like a man who might not even know who David Beckham is."[50]

Corporate ambassadors risk becoming so distant from their business's operations that they are not able to dive deep into detail if a crisis blows up. In addition, the media profile that their high-visibility leadership attracts means that their personal reputations can become so inextricably linked to that of their employer that they can inflict collateral damage on their company if they do fall from grace.

8
GLOBAL MISSIONARIES

Global missionaries are on a personal mission to make a significant difference and a corporate mission to make their company great. They are typically customer champions, and lead by inspiring people and energizing them to tap into their full potential.

They possess strong beliefs and values that drive them to bring transformational change to the companies they lead. They're passionate in their belief that changing and revitalizing people is the key to refreshing businesses that have lost their way and need renewal. And they have the personal and leadership skills to inspire their workforces to attack the change agenda with similar zeal.

Global missionaries are most commonly found in established businesses that have struggled and need to be reinvigorated; they're not overawed by the prospect of doing this with large numbers of people. They can bring their value-rich approach to bear on any industry.

They measure their own success by the success or failure of their mission, so what resonates with them most are their achievements according to holistic management measures, rather than purely financial metrics. This might be redirecting a traditional company to focus on sustainability issues and the environment as a way of appealing to customers and motivating employees. Or it could be a greater company-wide vision of engaging with customers in a more tailored and personal fashion, with the aim of not simply bringing in more business but achieving a total transformation of a company's brand image and culture.

Culture and values are particularly important to global missionaries, whether they be living inside the company or on prominent display in its advertisements. But most importantly of all, the global missionary is on a mission for hearts and minds. He or she seeks believers and, in that quest, welcomes open discussion and even disruptive opposition as a necessary process through which to convert followers.

The ranks of global missionaries include Alcatel-Lucent chief executive Ben Verwaayen; Thomson Reuters CEO Tom Glocer; Ruben Vardanian, CEO of Troika Dialog, Russia's largest investment bank; Narayana Murthy of Infosys; James Murdoch of News Corporation; Philip Green of United Utilities; and John Neill, chief executive of logistics group Unipart. However, two of the best examples are Zhang Ruimin, CEO of Chinese conglomerate Haier, and John Chambers, chief executive of US technology giant Cisco Systems.

PROFILE OF A GLOBAL MISSIONARY: ZHANG RUIMIN, CHIEF EXECUTIVE, HAIER

Global missionaries are flourishing in the high-growth Asian economies. In China, few companies have yet gone beyond their own borders to attack global markets in earnest. A standout exception is Haier. With turnover of more than $15 billion, Haier manufactures home appliances in more than 15,000 specifications and in 96 categories. Market shares of more than 30 percent in Chinese refrigerators, refrigerating cabinets, air conditioners, and washing machines are balanced by strong positions in several European and US categories. Euromonitor reports that the net result is that Haier holds 10 percent of the global market for refrigerators and 8 percent of the market for washing machines. Haier is the subject of a book, *The Haier Way*, and 30 business school case studies, so the world is taking notice of the company and its CEO, Zhang Ruimin, who exemplifies the power of the corporate missionary model in underpinning fast global growth.

Zhang as a global missionary

Deep care for people, dedication to quality, a drive to go global, and a steady focus on innovation are at the core of Zhang's leadership style.

While Haier's motto is "Great managers make great people; great people make great products", as with all true missionaries, Zhang pays more than lip service to people care. Evidence is all around that Zhang and his team genuinely want Haier to be a platform on which its employees can realize better futures for themselves and can live by their true values. For example, while it's clear that Zhang is venerated by his teams, there's no sense that they fear him, as many CEOs' direct reports so clearly do.

Quality has been a cornerstone of Haier from its early days. In 1984, around the time Zhang took the reins at the then Qingdao General Refrigerator Factory, there were 300 refrigerator factories in China, mostly turning out poor-quality products. Zhang decided that the firm had to differentiate on quality. In 1985, a customer complaint provided the catalyst. On auditing the warehouse, Zhang identified 76 "Auspicious Snow" refrigerators which did not quite meet standards. Costing the equivalent of a worker's monthly salary, these were valuable items but, rather than use them as gifts for party officials or rewards for high performers, Zhang personally started breaking them with a sledgehammer – and insisted that the workers who had made them help, in front of the factory's whole workforce.

Alongside attention to detail and high standards, Zhang also has a restless, burning commercial ambition for the company. He's determined that Haier become the undisputed number one in its markets around the world. Frustrated that "China had no brand names", from the early 1990s Zhang tried to localize the Haier brand in the main global markets. Indeed, in 1999 the Haier US industrial park became the first Chinese home appliance industrial park to be established abroad. He drives himself and his fellow leaders to track the latest global developments – he spends several hours a week on the internet sponging up the most recent events – and has institutionalized innovation right at the top of the business. His top 30 team members meet weekly on a Saturday and each of them is expected to have a new idea for discussion. Zhang keeps driving home the need for urgency in product development and the need to invent the future. As one of this close team puts it: "He does not want to look at yesterday – he only wants to look forward for tomorrow."

Zhang is extremely sensitive toward the changes in business caused by the internet era. He believes there is a big difference between brand building now and before the web. In the past, the growth of a brand took decades to accomplish; the internet has broken down the barriers. Customers are always curious, and they like and accept reliance on the internet for convenient services and brands. Thus, Zhang believes that the internet era has allowed Chinese and international brands to stand at the same starting line, challenging Haier to grasp quickly the barriers and opportunities that the internet era brings.

Zhang on being a global missionary

"For most western firms, the purpose is money for Wall Street. Our purpose is to set up a platform for all the employees. For Haier, the most important things are employees, customers, and shareholders. If employees can realize their own values, they can create value for customers. So the key is for the company to set up a platform for employees to create their own values.

"A company without a culture is like a person without a soul. The company is always close to bankruptcy, so the company must always adapt to the changes outside it. Who can drive the company to change? It is me. So I must change myself every day so the company can change itself to keep up with the changing world. If you're a super leader, the regular employees do not know you exist.

"It is not that Haier has done something extraordinary – it is that China has produced nothing we can boast to the world about since the opium war. Nothing!"

Formative years and early career

Like the People's Republic of China, Zhang was born in 1949. His father was a textile worker living in Laizhou in Shandong. Like some other successful CEOs, Zhang underwent great hardship as a child. He survived the great famine of 1960–63 and was in high school when the Cultural Revolution began in 1966. Escaping being sent for "reeducation" in the fields by dint of being an only child, he was fortunate to become an apprentice in a collectively owned metal processing factory in Qingdao in 1968.

He worked his way up through the factory and, aware of his interrupted education, shunned a love of literature to take night classes in management through the first four years of his career. He was eventually made deputy director of the factory before being promoted to Deputy Manager of the Household Appliance Division of the Qingdao Municipal Government.

In 1984, Zhang was appointed to turn around the near-bankrupt Qingdao General Refrigerator Factory. He was the fourth manager parachuted in by the government to try to save the company. The early years were a struggle, with the factory hemorrhaging cash, ill-disciplined and disillusioned workers, and very scarce credit. Stories have entered corporate folklore of the lengths Zhang would go to to support his employees through the hard times. For example, it's said he would drive into the surrounding mountains in a rickety three-wheeler in bitter weather to track down a lender who would stump up cash for a small bonus for his workers despite the factory's parlous finances. When he'd travel to Jinan to petition for foreign exchange certificates, he'd stay in a hostel costing one fifth of the price of a hotel, in a room too stiflingly hot to sleep, cycle around the city to save on taxi fares, and patiently stand all the way there and back on the sleeper train.

But personal hardship aside, Zhang's determination to crack the quality code was evident. Less than a year after joining the firm, he entered into a joint venture with the German firm Liebherr, gaining access to technology and the cachet that quality German engineering then carried in China. In 1992, the group was renamed Haier, a corruption of Liebherr's "Herr" and a pun on the company's logo at the time (a western and a Chinese boy – "boys" being pronounced "hai-er" in Chinese). Zhang has since led the business as CEO and chairman into over 100 end markets around the world.

It is clear that Zhang's thirst for new knowledge, total commitment to quality, deep respect and care for people, and impatience with obstacles to growth developed with him as he worked up from the factory floor to the ultimate transformation of Qingdao's basket-case business.

Zhang on the importance of his roots

"Perhaps I am different from other CEOs. I started as a worker. For the 10 years I was a worker, all I wanted was for the managers to know about my existence and what value and innovation I did for the company. The goal of living is to achieve harmony and enjoyment for oneself and others through acting appropriately. You must have sharp discipline but be ruled by your heart. You have to create a family environment through genuine care and consideration, a sense of belonging, like a home.

"In the past I only needed to take care of about 800 workers. Now I have to think about more than 60,000 employees. This is a very big pressure which leaves me little time for my family."

Zhang's management style

The powerful culture of contribution at Haier is in part a direct result of Zhang's own personality. Though he is unusually big and highly energetic, which mean he has a very imposing presence, like most of his fellow missionaries Zhang is a very humble man, self-effacing and respectful, creating space for his teams to innovate and contribute. It's a powerful approach – as one team member told us, "I don't work for Haier for the money, I work for it from my heart." Equally, Zhang does not take a back seat to his team: once he has listened attentively, he eagerly seizes on the opportunity to debate, probe, and open a question up for closer scrutiny.

Zhang has also thought very deeply about how to structure Haier to put both its people and its customers at the center. Although a practical and outcome-focused CEO, he has also eagerly embraced new ideas on leadership from western management thinkers, notably Peter Drucker and Michael Porter.

Zhang believes the biggest challenge now is how to create customers. "Before the internet era, companies had market appeal if they had good products. Today the situation has changed because there are so many good products on the market, and now companies have to provide great service as well. Zhang emphasizes an insight from Drucker: "The internet's biggest impact is that it eliminated distance."

And the results are bold. Haier today is run in an extremely devolved fashion. Each employee is treated as an individual profit-and-loss account. The "market" – customer-facing – teams determine what is produced and by when. Working from their day-to-day interactions with customers, they instruct the rest of the matrix on what innovation, time to develop, price point, and execution are required. Leaders all the way up to Zhang are taught that their role is to clear any obstructions the system raises in order to deliver on the market teams' demands and manage the company's incentives effectively. Where many CEOs preach their support role, Zhang's claim to be at the apex of an inverted triangle simply supporting the customer and customer-service team appears to be an accurate description of the way Haier operates. The result, as Zhang puts it, is that "the traditional financial report is oriented toward financial capital, but Haier's model is oriented toward employee resources." Haier reports very high employee efficiency, high value additions, and an ability to pay higher salaries.

Zhang on his management style

"We operate three principles at Haier. First, we are end to end. The market-facing team decides how to deliver the right solution to customers. Secondly, each person has one target. They specify the target and that then becomes the whole team's target. Because we operate in a matrix, the relevant research and development and other matrix teams report to the market-facing team too. Thirdly, the system is a push. If the customer-facing team say there's a 36-month target, then research and development must deliver in six months so that can be achieved. This means the market gives the orders.

"Each employee should be a unit of innovation. Everyone in Haier has their own targets and own customers so it's a 'win–win': if the customer wins, the employee will win.

"Our teams are self-governing through three systems. The first system is: Can the team verify their ideas with the customer? The second system: If someone is doing better than the team leader, he may become the team leader. The third system: Everyone may contribute to improvements, so it's the team itself that considers the team's efficiency and improves.

"As CEO, two things are most important: to set up the right systems and the right incentive plans. Today, buying the product is just the start – we are trying to become the trusted friend of the customer. Each employee's bonus depends on the profit in his personal profit and loss. But the most important thing is values – if someone does not understand the values, even if he's performing well, he will leave the company."

Life after Haier

Zhang created Haier and grew it from scratch into a globally leading business, so his life and achievements are inextricably bound up in the company. However, it's clear that Zhang will give up control of Haier in due course and, with professional management and a distributed system, his exit need not necessarily cause the business to falter. He says: "One day I will retire and at that moment I think, if the company is running as it is today, for regular operations you'll not notice a change. The only issue is whether the working style of the new CEO will be the same." We might add – and if his successor has the same clarity and drive for growth. In further contrast to many Chinese businesses today, Zhang is insistent that his son, currently studying at Wharton, will not "inherit" the business; no dynasty building here.

Zhang on the risks of global missionaries

Haier's model of the market "pushing" innovations through the firm to the CEO, rather than the CEO directing a command-and-control process, is an excellent way of driving evolutionary changes. However, Zhang admits it is open to the "Kodak" risk: that a new technology or approach takes the market and hence customer expectations to a place the customers themselves did not envisage or demand. There is a risk that Haier develops a cadre of managers who are fantastic at driving effective daily business performance, but are not well equipped to innovate and drive long-term growth. Haier is guarded against that by the vigilance of its CEO, but other great companies today are building systematic radars and innovation teams to flag disruptive opportunities early and drive commercial returns from them earlier still.

Another risk is that missionaries become crucial to their business. While Haier has robust succession planning in place, there's no doubt that Zhang is revered within the business and remains not only the figurehead but the source of renewal for the values, strategy, and mission. Haier must "bottle" his contribution so that the company can grow uninterrupted when he leaves.

Finally, like so many missionaries, Zhang's total dedication to the mission means that he drives himself to the point of exhaustion – and also often to the exhaustion of those around him. "If you have commitment to the company, you may not have commitment to your wife," he told us. It's said that Zhang's wife was once so surprised to be sharing a bank holiday with him at home that she cried with surprise and relief. A selfless dedication to your employees and building the best company in the world can come at great cost.

Profile of a global missionary: John Chambers, chief executive, Cisco Systems

It's hard to believe that John Chambers is not a technocrat by background. After all, the highly charismatic chief executive of Cisco Systems seems to have been at the forefront of the internet revolution for almost as long as it's been taking place. He was one of the first technology bosses to gain wide acceptance for the forecast that data volumes on phones would exceed voice traffic – something achieved a decade ago in most western markets. And he has been a pioneer of the internet's incursion into virtually all areas of modern life, ranging from the NetAid web-linked charity rock concerts that Cisco sponsored in 1999, to the company's giant Telepresence monitors that seek to reduce the need for a lot of corporate travel by enabling life-size eye-to-eye contact by videoconference.

Chambers has never developed software like Bill Gates or designed technology gadgets like Steve Jobs, but he has long transcended his law and business degree qualifications to demonstrate a visionary understanding of the way the infrastructure of the internet – something that Cisco's networking equipment has a dominant share in providing – can transform people's lives and possibilities.

Founded in a Californian garage in 1984 to link a Stanford University academic's office computer with his wife's, Cisco was a little-known firm with 300 employees and $70 million revenues when Chambers joined it in 1992. By the time he was promoted to chief executive in 1995, sales had jumped to $1.3 billion, but by 1998 it was making $2 billion profit on $12.2 billion revenues. In his first five years as chief executive he made 40 acquisitions, leading Cisco to become the first US computer company to obtain the same market share in Japan as on its home turf.

Overall, Chambers has brought Cisco Systems enormous success, growing the group's revenues from $1.2 billion to $39 billion in 16 years as chief executive. During his tenure, the company has been named America's most admired company seven times by *Fortune* magazine, while Chambers has featured in dozens of global CEO awards. In 2000, at the height of the dot-com boom, Cisco was the most valuable company in the world, with a market capitalization of more than $500 billion, while the company's shares were voted stock of the decade on the Nasdaq stock exchange.

Chambers' transforming mission

Born in 1949 in Cleveland, Ohio to doctor parents, Chambers suffered from dyslexia in his youth – one reason he says he still doesn't read many books – but this didn't prevent him graduating in business studies from West Virginia University and later gaining a MBA from Indiana University. He also attended the School of Engineering at Duke University before spending six years at IBM and eight at Wang Laboratories.

When he arrived at Cisco, the company was already growing extremely rapidly but it had been riven by internal strife. Sandy Lerner, one half of the couple who had founded the company, was fired in 1990, with her partner Len Bosack quitting as a result. The company's direction was then forged in the early 1990s recession when it was under the direction of CEO John Morgridge. Cisco was a router company going into that downturn, but it bought three telecoms switching companies and emerged as number one in switching technology. That business now has revenues of $10 billion a year.

Chambers says he learnt from being involved in that approach and replicated it later. In 1997, during the Asian financial crisis, Cisco expanded in the region, moving many of its top executives to China and India. Within nine months it was number one in every major Asian market – a position it retains.

Chambers also sustained and developed Cisco's reputation as a rapacious acquirer of businesses. During the internet boom from 1998 to 2001, Cisco made several major acquisitions, including Stratacom and Cerent, to bring in products and talent. Although not every one was successful, Cisco has succeeded more frequently than most of its competitors in integrating and growing revenues at acquired companies. By 2001, Cisco had grown to represent 35 percent of the stock market capitalization of all the companies in its sector. Today, that proportion has grown to 85 percent.

Missionaries also have to be tough and resilient and capable of surviving crises, however. Cisco's came in 2001 when Chambers admits the company was "blindsided" by the dot-com bust. Even then, his response, while drastic, ensured its survival and a pathway to the future success of its mission. "In 2001, it was about survival," he says. "We took out 25 percent of our expenses, including a quarter of our headcount, in 51 days. On day 52 we gained market share. Our peers, who had a combined market capitalization of about $1 trillion at that time, now have a combined market capitalization of about $14 billion."

Chambers had learnt a painful lesson about retrenching in his days at Wang, when he was deputed to help sort out the mess made by senior management. "Nothing hurts you more than laying someone off," he says. "At Wang, it was mismanagement, misexecuting. I had to fire 5,000 people. That hurts. It was unbelievable. A healthy paranoia is the realization that if your company does not keep up, if you don't keep up as a leader, you hurt everyone: your customers, your shareholders, your employees, and your partners."

Chambers as a global missionary

Chambers' 14 years at other technology companies prior to joining Cisco were clearly instructive in his development as a technologist.

However, technology is almost incidental to how he operates. His passion for people and desire to win their hearts and minds could equally have been channeled through leadership of a media or retail company. In the internet age, what he cares about most is using the power of the net to change people's lives. In so doing, Cisco, whose routers and hubs are integral to the running of large parts of the web, makes a very profitable living.

It's easy in retrospect to underestimate the size of Chambers' evangelistic mission in its early days when there was widespread cynicism about the internet, which many critics thought was something just for technology geeks that could never be effectively monetized. Chambers begged to differ.

In the early days, this involved physically touring the world and evangelizing the possibilities of the net to virtually every world leader – at one stage, he claimed he had met all major national leaders except the heads of state in France and Germany. His converts included Tony Blair, Bill Clinton, Nelson Mandela, and pop stars from Bono to David Bowie and rap artist P Diddy. Chambers' passion for people and desire to use the internet to bring about positive world change have led him to front ambitious projects aimed at doing just that, ranging from anti-poverty initiatives to moves to mitigate climate change.

In 1999, the NetAid web-linked charity rock concerts that Cisco sponsored in London, New York, and Geneva were widely perceived as a flop, but Chambers was in no doubt that the experiment, though ahead of its time, was pioneering something very big. Indeed, it can now be seen as an early social media initiative. "When Live Aid got $200 million, it was a huge amount," Chambers said at the time, "until you realize that the African countries pay that amount in debt relief every week. It didn't even make a dent. The power to end extreme poverty is now online. The internet already has made a difference in the way business is done around the world. Now the world's most powerful website can help make the difference in eliminating one of the globe's most pressing problems."

Today, Chambers is putting equal effort into mitigating climate change, becoming the US CEO arguably most associated with such efforts. Again, the agenda is not wholly altruistic, with Cisco bene-fiting, for example, when business executives give into the pres-sure to hold internet rather than physical meetings, in order to cut carbon emissions and be more planet friendly. Cisco itself encour-ages use of the internet where possible for both internal and exter-nal meetings, and in 2008 it held its biggest ever virtual meeting of employees, with 14,700 tuning in through various media. Cisco claims to hold more than 200,000 internal Telepresence meetings a year, bringing together its staff all around the world without the need for them to step on a plane.

Like all effective missionaries, Chambers seeks to practice what he preaches. Indeed, one of the interviews he gave us for this book was carried out over Telepresence at 12 noon in London – an unearthly 4 a.m. in his Californian office. "In the last two and half weeks, I've been around the globe twice," he declared, describing trips to Kazakhstan, Spain, Switzerland, and India. "Today I'm going around the globe in 12 hours through the meetings I'm hav-ing and I like this better. It's helped cut our annual travel budget from $750 million a year to $350 million and is much more effec-tive in terms of leadership time. I'll be having 14 meetings today, including several in Spain, two in Italy, two in the UK, one in Atlanta, one in Mexico, and two others that I can't talk about. I reg-ularly do sessions with as many as 20 locations at any one time."

Chambers carries out 100 such video meetings every quarter and says he's seeing three or four times as many customers than before, though he's only cut down on about 20 percent of his phys-ical business traveling. He is also unfazed by working through the night, regularly holding all-nighter Telepresence sessions as a way of dispatching a month's travel in 12 hours. Before settling down for the stint that included our interview he ran four miles; when we asked where he gets his energy, he simply laughed, while the team that was supporting his unconventional work style groaned with exhaustion. Chambers says he regularly goes weeks without much sleep and admits that he once bounced off an overnight flight from India and "drove the team crazy" with eight new ideas for the company. Fittingly, Cisco's company vision reads: "Changing the Way We Work, Live, Play, and Learn."

Chambers' evangelism goes far beyond well-timed stunts, however. His current mission is for Cisco to use the next phase of internet technology to facilitate a new collaborative way of working. Cisco's 26 priorities for the next five years – described in Chapter 2 as the key to boosting revenues by a further 25 percent – also envisage the company mushrooming its use of collaborative tools such as YouTube, Facebook, Twitter, and Second Life, and pods, blogs, and wikis.

Despite the mind-boggling size and scale of this Dow Jones powerhouse, Chambers exhibits another characteristic of the global missionary model when he maintains that Cisco is still a "family business" and that he prides himself on a personal approach to the group's 65,000 staff. Like Ben Verwaayen, he is aided in this by a photographic memory.

Chambers is also a noted philanthropist. He is involved in healthcare and education initiatives in Sichuan, China, the Jordan Education Initiative and the Partnership for Lebanon, and has received the Clinton Global Citizen Award from former US President Clinton and the Woodrow Wilson Award for Corporate Citizenship. He is particularly known for leading numerous corporate social responsibility initiatives around the world focused on improving access to education. The ultimate mission, he says, is for Cisco to become "one of the most influential companies in history".

Chambers on being a global missionary

"Make no mistake. Anything that helps the growth of the internet helps Cisco, so we absolutely are evangelists for the internet. And if you watch what we have evangelized, it has always come true.

"The hardest thing when you get new technology isn't whether the technology works. It's about people. It's about how you change from the old to the new in terms of the way you spend your time.

"We are the fastest-growing and most profitable computer company in history and with that success comes an obligation to give back something. But we do things in ways that are different; new world, not old world. I know every illness of every employee in the company that's serious for themselves, their spouse, or their children. It's a huge issue for us to do that, but it's part of our culture."

Life after Cisco

Like other global missionaries, Chambers' mission transcends the corporate parameters of his current employer. Despite having made his name, fortune, and reputation at Cisco, it's quite possible that Chambers has a future elsewhere, whether in politics, philanthropy, or global enterprise. Indeed, he has a strong political bent, having served as co-chair in republican John McCain's 2008 US presidential bid. Like religious missionaries who move territories, sometimes spanning whole continents to spread the word, global business missionaries are focused on the mission, not the territory. For the time being, however, Cisco will continue to benefit from Chambers' evangelical zeal.

"I love what I am doing," he says. "Is there a higher purpose than perhaps changing the world? I realize it's an aspirational goal and almost unobtainable. But to attempt to be the best company *in* the world and the best company *for* the world: that's something that has to motivate anyone."

Pitfalls of the global missionary model

It is their fervor that makes global missionaries stand out from the crowd as chief executives. Sometimes their missions can make them appear so single-minded and focused that they become controversial figures, evoking opposition in the workforce.

The strengths of global missionaries can also become their weaknesses. If it is not carefully controlled by a company's board, the strength of character of a global missionary chief executive can develop into almost a cult of personality, leading to a situation where a dynamic leader and his or her personal whims become too important to the organization. People may identify too strongly with such leaders and be unable to function properly without them, so that decision making suffers lower down the chain, succession planning is inadequate, and a vacuum is left when they depart. The global missionary may be in effect the glue that holds the company together.

LEADING AT THE TOP TODAY

You have now seen the main categories that most of the top CEOs we interviewed fall into, when each type of leadership typically comes into its own, and how some outstanding examples of these CEO types actually do the job of leading today. At the highest level, the types compare as in the table opposite.

There are clear similarities, but also stark differences. For example, corporate entrepreneurs' drive and focus echo those of value-driving CEOs, but their personal attachment to the business they started could not be further from the cold-blooded detachment of the shareholder value-focused value driver. Equally, commercial executors share a metric-driven style with value drivers, but these leaders focus on different priorities. Similarly, although corporate ambassadors resemble global missionaries in valuing a societal purpose very highly, the typical personal leadership approaches of each type differ markedly.

As with any categorization, much information about the individual can be lost in the act of characterization, and we would not suggest that the leaders profiled are either fault free or only capable in the ways we've described when illustrating the leadership type. Equally, the leaders profiled may in the future develop their style, for example from a corporate executor focus to a missionary focus, if circumstances demand. On the other hand, we think that these categories highlight striking similarities across the CEO population, and allow illuminating conclusions to be drawn about the leaders we have today and which of them may be better placed for success in the future.

One interesting illustration of how this categorization can be applied is to examine which leadership types are typically favored by private equity and public equity owners respectively. Although examples of each type are currently found in both settings, at present most private equity firms tend to prefer commercial executors and value drivers for their focus on driving financial and operational results. Equally, most public companies tend to prefer

	COMMERCIAL EXECUTOR	FINANCIAL VALUE DRIVER	CORPORATE ENTREPRENEUR	CORPORATE AMBASSADOR	GLOBAL MISSIONARY
CASE STUDY	Sir Terry Leahy	Mick Davis	Sir Martin Sorrell	Lord Browne	John Chambers
FOCUS	Results	Shareholder value	Personal mission	Society	Corporate potential
MEASURE OF SUCCESS	Business metrics	EPS	Cash	Market capitalization	Holistic management
DEFINITION	• Driving focus on achieving best results in industry • Relentless focus and attention to detail to ensure operational and strategic ambitions become reality	• Relentless focus on shareholder value • Understand value metrics of industry and often highly skilled in identifying value-enhancing corporate transactions or realizing value from portfolio disposals	• Have something to prove • Disrupt industries because believe in better way of doing things • Excel in spotting breakthrough opportunities and making them reality • Their vision for companies is their life vision	• Have a global vision with broader societal impact • Operate at geopolitical level and deliver transactions that transform industries	• On personal mission to make significant difference, as well as corporate mission to make company great • Typically customer champions, lead by inspiring people and energizing them to tap into their potential
SITUATIONS BEST AT SOLVING	Businesses that need to be taken from average to great	Complex businesses requiring portfolio rationalization, or buy-and-build strategies where transaction-based growth needed	Young businesses and those where industry-changing opportunity exists	Where interaction with regulators, governments, and other authorities is critical. Thrive on high-profile problems. Almost certainly established businesses	Established businesses that have lost their way and need to be renewed. Dealing with large workforces a particular strength
TYPE OF INDUSTRY MOST OFTEN SEEN IN	Can operate in any industry but not usually effective in professional services	Diversified industrial businesses, financial services	Technology, biotech, consumer, professional services	Global resource businesses, global banks, industrials	Broad range
RISKS OF MODEL	• Taking on too much and burning out • Organization risks being political • Risk if corporate entrepreneur changes industry game • Not attracting very best talent	• Managing economic downturns • Being blinkered, not seeing industry shifts • Lack of people glue beyond wealth generation • Loss of successful executives when become independently wealthy	• People burn-out • Succession • Getting right people to scale business • Weak at managing steady-state businesses • Chaotic processes • Shareholder heartache as may "bet the company"	• Getting distant from business's operations • Not being able to dive deep into detail if crisis blows up	• Succession • Personality of CEO may be too important to company, people may identify too strongly with him or her

corporate ambassadors and global missionaries. Corporate entrepreneurs sit a little uneasily with both sets of owners. Because private equity firms are increasingly taking note of their wider
societal impact and public company leadership is fast taking lessons from private equity, the distinction laid out in our illustration
may erode over the coming decade, although it remains in active
play today.

There is another application of the categorization: self-analysis.
We hope that these chapters will have assisted you in identifying
your own leadership type. Most people are clear by the middle of
their career what their dominant leadership style is. However,
beware – a substantial minority find that they have only a weakly
dominant primary type alongside an important secondary type. For
example, you might find that you've spent a long time thriving on
the freedom to act in entrepreneurial businesses, but that in reality you are a global missionary who needs a corporate platform and
a mission to be properly fulfilled and have the full impact of which
you are capable. The trick to using these insights to plan your
career is to consider where you are now and where you want to be
in the future, and in so doing to balance what situations you thrive
in, where your leadership type is best suited to being used, your
personal strengths and weaknesses, and whether each concrete
opportunity that presents itself matches your values and personal
mission.

Having examined how some of the world's best CEOs lead
today and perhaps what you can learn from them, read on to discover how CEOs expect they will have to reshape their leadership
styles and the companies they lead in the coming years, the advice
they give for getting to the top, and, once there, how to have a successful career and a happy life.

PART III

LEADING INTO THE FUTURE

In Part I we showed you the five critical shaping themes for the next decade and top CEOs' tips on how to respond to them. In Part II we explored the way in which some of the world's best CEOs run their businesses today.

In this final part of the book, we set out:

❑ CEOs' secrets on how to organize and lead tomorrow's businesses.
❑ CEOs' guidance to ambitious young people on how to get the apprenticeship you need to set you up for a fulfilling career, to succeed, and to get to the top.
❑ Tips from leading CEOs on how to stop the role dominating your existence and forcing your personal life to one side.

9

DITCHING COMMAND AND CONTROL

"Command and control is dead. Management in the classical sense is dead. That will be scary, very scary, to boards."

Ben Verwaayen, chief executive, Alcatel-Lucent

"To me, leadership is primarily about raising the aspirations of people, making people say that they will walk on water."

Narayana Murthy, chairman, Infosys

CEOs in this reset world will face two fundamental challenges over the coming decade. Regardless of whether they are domiciled in the West or the East, all domestically focused international businesses will have to shift to truly global businesses. Secondly, all businesses, faced by governments and consumers made more skeptical by the global recession, a changing climate, and tighter public finances, will need to work ever harder to earn and retain a license to operate.

World-beating companies will also have the consumer and the needs of their talent at the heart of their businesses. They will have to respond swiftly and innovatively to shifts in their environment, exploit the power of the web, form close partnerships, develop best-in-world solutions to local problems, and take a broader view of success than simple financial profits, so becoming welcome neighbors in communities around the world.

Most longstanding role-model companies have had their reputations damaged by the recession, so we no longer have clear role models to emulate. This chapter sets out how CEOs can create a new generation of sustainable, world-class companies.

COMMAND AND CONTROL IS DEAD

Most western businesses operate a command-and-control system: a 200-year-old manufacturing-derived model of efficiency driving. Command-and-control firms tend to be underpinned by rules-dependent management, which often reduces decisions to formulaic approval processes operated through ponderous, often bureaucratic decision gates. This deprives junior staff of opportunities to exercise their initiative; issues are funneled to the top and decisions are handed down through the layers from on high. That is not empowering. Lord Davies recalls businesses where "memos came from the autocratic boss and people were scared". Severe hierarchies of this sort also find it hard or impossible to accommodate exceptions or innovations, and make for incremental and linear career progression. So, they waste human potential and block individuals' fulfillment. Top talent then leaves – so we agree with Mukesh Ambani that "you cannot run an organization of intelligent people with the big 'Boss' or a 'feudal' system".

Command-and-control management was found wanting again and again through the recession. Conventional CEOs saw the problems late, waiting for the inevitable plunge in performance to show up in their numbers, and their traditional budgeting and management reporting left them far too slow to respond. Consequently, many had to issue profit warnings, suffered a loss of confidence and a share price cliff-drop, and had to move on. Such systems simply can't cope in crisis conditions.

Command and control will continue to be useful from time to time, mostly in turnaround situations requiring tight control, but it will not be adequate in most mainstream businesses most of the time. Worse, command and control is also simply not flexible enough for settings requiring long-term decisions and multi-constituency considerations that are as yet hard to quantify in financial terms – the kind of decisions that companies will increasingly have to take.

THE ALTERNATIVE: UNLEASH THE TALENT WITHIN

"I think command and control is dead," agrees Ben Verwaayen. "Location and time is dead. Management in the classical sense is dead. It has to be on different notions. That will be appealing to many people but also scary, very scary, to boards." However, what is the replacement?

The central problem with command and control is its failure to engage people by offering them meaningful work and freedom to innovate. John Weston, former CEO of BAE Systems, explains: "Throwing tablets of stone from the top just does not work. But getting people fired up about what they can achieve and giving them the freedom to be masters of their own destiny is a better way – and they appreciate it."

Great businesses will provide employees with space to think and a global meritocracy to grow within. A good example is Google, which claims to be committed to making itself a natural home for a diverse group of the most talented people in its industry. The company states: "We believe we have created a work environment that attracts exceptional people. We know that people value meaning in their work; they want to be involved with things that are important and that are going to make a difference. Talented people are attracted to Google because we empower them to change the world."[51]

If providing fulfillment to employees is the central challenge, we need briefly to consider what people want out of their work. As Todd Stitzer states: "People want meaning in their work experience; they don't want merely to be a wage earner. They're searching for several levels of meaning – for themselves, their families, and society."

Tony Robbins is the world's best-known personal development coach and has worked with several US Presidents, including Bill Clinton, and a number of leading CEOs.[52] Through his research, he has concluded that humans have six core needs. The more needs that are met more fully, the more fulfilling the work experience will be for the employee. While command and control gives people a high degree of a very narrow form of certainty in their lives, it cannot satisfy any of the other needs adequately. Furthermore, the critical shift in the talent that businesses will rely on in coming years is the rise to prominence of Generations X and Y; these generations have significantly different parameters for needs fulfillment than the baby boomers who are typically managing them. The table below summarizes the core needs and the differences.

HUMAN NEEDS (Robbins)	THRESHOLD CRITERION FOR FULFILLMENT THROUGH WORK	PARTICULAR NEEDS OF GEN X/GEN Y IN CONTRAST TO BABY BOOMERS
Certainty	Feel secure that I will continue to have a job and be paid for a living	Lower need for job security than baby boomers, higher propensity to move
Variety	Require a variety of responsibilities to avoid monotony	Higher need for job moves or internal progression and for variety while in role
Significance	Feel that I have the opportunity to make a difference professionally both as an individual and through the company's actions	Not willing to be micro-managed, deep desire to make a personal difference to company and industry
Connection	Sense a personal connection with peers, management, and leaders	Expect to connect deeply both at work and at home and so less likely to accept work–life imbalance
Growth	See opportunities to learn and develop capabilities	Expect to grow faster and demand focused personal development
Contribution	Confident that through work I am able to contribute to society beyond simple commercial success	Higher expectations that company will be responsible and make a significant contribution to society as a matter of course

As Generation Y expert Bruce Morton underlined to us, "Gen Y demand more from their employers than their predecessors. Though it may have an effect, more money is not the answer to making your Gen Y employees more passionate. Above all it is the leader's passion that will make the difference, and that passion needs to be embedded in a cause that the people can buy into – something they can be known for."

Command and control is not only too slow and cumbersome for the next decade, but is also likely to be rejected by the younger generations.

Replacing the command-and-control zoo

Command-and-control businesses use military metaphors and rely on vertical and rigid structures. But today's fast-moving world breaks inflexible structures. From our research, we believe that a better metaphor for a global business is a human cell. At ICICI, KV Kamath agrees: "An organization's structure is a living cell. The boxes in organization charts quickly become cages. An organization full of cages – that's a zoo."

Cells have elastic edges that can dynamically expand and contract and are porous; a central nucleus that regulates semi-independent processes; and a fluid body that allows the free circulation of critical nutrients and energy. And cells are alive! Visualizing the corporation as a cell allows leaders to make the most of three critical insights.

Soften the corporate boundaries

The CEOs we interviewed believe that most tangible and intangible assets will increasingly be shared through partnerships, joint ventures, and the further fragmentation of the supply chain in the coming decade. To keep up with the fast-changing environment, businesses will need new rules of engagement allowing quicker, more flexible, and deeper collaboration with external parties. They will have to assimilate information quickly; form technical and business partnerships speedily in response to market change – and dissolve them as rapidly; foster proprietary innovation as extensively as possible; and be open to working with communities and governments more closely than ever before. Liu Jiren states, "To be a leading global player, competing with firms with a 100-year history, we need to create a new business model. We need to know how to make innovation happen through open collaboration."

Change the role of the CEO

To unleash the inventiveness of their employees, CEOs cannot be generals directing every action of their team members. Rather, they must be facilitators for the talent and energy of their teams, removing critical roadblocks to brilliant execution.

Cris Conde, CEO of Sungard, urges, "Redefine the role of the CEO. If different employees can share information with each other, they do not need to rely on bosses to do that. Therefore, one of the major roles of old-world bosses (being an information conduit) disappears. The imperial CEO has to disappear – the CEO now has to ensure that everyone can play their part to the full. The CEO is like a conductor – he creates and orchestrates a system. It is very arrogant to think you can make better decisions than the thousands of people below you. This may be true if you have more information. But in the last five years I have maybe made one decision (to take the company private) that no one else could make. The role of the boss is to make the handful of decisions that cannot be made by anyone else and to maintain the collaboration systems. I really think that the rise of these collaborative systems is redefining organizational structures and the role of the CEO; they are the last nail in the coffin of the imperial CEO."

> The imperial CEO has to disappear – the CEO now has to ensure everyone can play their part to the full

Nikesh Arora adds: "The real engine of Google's success is innovation. Consequently, we look to our managers to encourage innovation and guide it to scale, so that it can make a global impact. Google's success has been built squarely on the shoulders of our amazing employees. Google has done well because we've provided a great work environment where people can literally change the world. As Google grows, we're still committed to this culture that fosters rapid innovation."

It's not just technology businesses who believe this. Thras Moraitis is on the same wavelength. "It's impossible for people at the center to have more information than guys on the ground," he says.

To unleash your teams, you have to face up to another truth: that the bureaucracy of command-and-control businesses avoids, rather than rewards, risk taking. Lenovo has recognized this. Says Bill Amelio: "We try to eliminate organizational obstacles that might hinder idea development, such as functional silos and hierarchical decision making. How well we foster such a mindset internally dictates our success globally. It directly impacts our flexibility in adapting quickly to changing market conditions and fast-changing customer tastes. Our approach of organizing around hubs in diverse regions to specialize in major functions, rather than having a single headquarters for all significant decisions, is an innovative departure from the traditional, single hub-and-spoke management approach of most other 'global' companies.

"With no designated headquarters office, our multicultural management team is free to convene wherever and whenever it makes the most sense. Similarly, world-sourced business functions are located solely on the basis of concentrations of specific talent, skills, proximity to key markets, infrastructure, language proficiency, IT capabilities, costs, and facilities."

Give the center a fundamentally different role: The nucleus

The final insight on organizational design from our research requires greater discussion than the first two. The cell approach depends on the center orchestrating rather than rigidly controlling the global business by focusing on a few critical areas, while providing soft leadership that releases the latent energy in the operating units and results in better performance across the entire organization. Let's look at what this model means in terms of both business and personal leadership.

Business leadership requirements

The CEO remains guardian of purpose and strategy

Day-to-day pressures mean that some big, developed companies are distracted from their underlying purpose by fire-fighting and short-term priorities. This problem needs to be addressed, but many professional managers find it hard to make the changes necessary to bring soulless companies back to life.

The CEO must make clear the company's purpose ("What is our company here to do?") and its strategy ("How do we beat the competition?"). A company's purpose has to inspire it to outperform, capturing the imagination of all stakeholders and instilling a sense of pride in employees that they are part of the company. And clearly, the strategy needs to be dovetailed to this, because if a company does not have an effective strategy, it will not succeed in its purpose.

Ian Coull says: "This is probably the message that I talk to my people about most often, because if we are going to have a business that we are going to persuade shareholders to invest in, they have to know and understand what the company is about and how it's going to behave. If we don't have the right purpose and values, we're going to lose some of the potential appeal to these investors."

Archie Norman has observed a distinct shift in people's aspirations and a concomitant increase in the importance of purpose and strategy in recent years. "In my view," he says, "what's really changed is at most western developed companies, the way you attract people and employ people, and the way you obtain performance from them, has become so much more demanding because people have so many options. They're much more transactional. Good people can go and get a job somewhere else tomorrow. Therefore, enlisting from them some loyalty that goes beyond the salary you are paying has become a much more challenging task. That's why creating something they feel they can be loyal to – a sense of belief, purpose, a project we're all on – has become so much more important for people, and it requires a very different style of leadership."

> Enlisting loyalty beyond the salary has become much more challenging

The CEO must also make sure that the organization lives out its goals. Too many company mission statements are not compelling and too many business strategies do not properly set out how the company intends to outcompete its rivals and succeed across sectoral, industrial, and national boundaries. Philip Green states: "In my experience, we get the best from people when they derive a sense of meaning from their work activity; few are driven solely by the promise of material reward. At P&O, our vision was concise, short enough to be remembered by all in the company, specific so progress and achievement could be measured, and ambitious.

Visions are of little value if they are not stretching and carry with them the possibility of failure."

The CEO must therefore ensure that every employee understands what the company is there to do and how it will win against the competition through communicating purpose and values clearly, consistently, and with great impact.

The CEO lives and celebrates the company's universal values
Values answer the question: "What do we stand for?" They stem from a company's history, its market proposition, the values of its leader and employees, and the external environment in which it operates. In global businesses values need to be universal, setting the framework for how the company should act at every level, wherever its people are and whatever the context.

Universal values do not trample over or ignore local cultures in global organizations. In contrast, they act as a golden thread that can hold the company together, while recognizing the importance of local traditions. Says Narayana Murthy: "You need to have universal values that are celebrated in every culture and are modeled on every culture, while still leveraging local norms. You need to be very open-minded to adapt to and leverage other cultures."

The trick to formulating values, however, lies in making them granular enough that they can guide action. As Whitbread CEO Alan Parker states: "Too many companies' values are just words, rather than actual beliefs of the organization." A recent study concluded that six universal moral values could be identified in companies' codes of ethics and associated literature: trustworthiness, respect, responsibility, fairness, caring, and citizenship.[53] Although some bad businesses struggle even with these, who would not want their business to observe them?

Great businesses go beyond these level one values and create level two values that, with some basic principles of human interaction taken for granted, are more specific to what the business is trying to achieve and, as such, provide stronger guidance to the business's employees in their daily lives. Where level one values secure a sound footing for business, level two values describe the qualities that tomorrow's business requires to win. For example,

Standard Chartered has "courage" as a really meaningful, strong value.

If you cannot create level two values, your company will struggle to maintain itself. Infosys is a good example of a company with level two values, which are expressed succinctly in an acronym – C-LIFE, standing for Customer delight, Leadership by example, Integrity and transparency, Fairness, and pursuit of Excellence. Samir Brikho at AMEC observes that "values need to go beyond the superficial and standard – you need level one, two, three, four values. For example, saying you believe in people is one thing, but really a modern company must ask: 'What more can we do to develop our people?' That's when people are really a value."

What more can we do to develop our people?

Values must also be actionable: people need to see how they fit into their daily activities. To this end, the CEO of General Healthcare Group, Adrian Fawcett, has gone so far as to draw a "pictorial values map which reminds us where we came from and how we serve our customer base today, our aspirations for the customer and company and the journey for tomorrow". To be actionable, values must be rooted in the business as it is now, rather than the board's vision of how it will be. Archie Norman says: "Values have to come from the people you're employing, not from the boardroom. You may be changing and reshaping the company so they don't want the old values, they want the new ones, but it's still got to be their language to ring true. They've got to say: 'Yes, that's what we believe in.' Sometimes the values that are expressed are boardroom pontification."

Values must be embedded deep into the business's culture so that they guide action. This takes a long time and concerted effort at a senior level. BT chairman Sir Michael Rake says: "We've put our values at the heart of our business. We've engaged over 3,000 people from around the world, from different countries, levels of seniority, gender, and so forth, which allowed us to build a set of global values which now underpin how we conduct day-to-day business and how we treat each other and our clients. It's taken seven years to embed them. They help our recruitment enormously and also our retention."

Values take a tremendous effort to distill and it requires yet more energy to embed them and make the business breathe them daily. However, they're both extremely powerful profit drivers and key to sustainable success once established.

The CEO gives wide freedom to act and ensures innovation is rewarded
The key advantage of the cell model of governance lies in the way it allows the smart devolution of power, with the objective to trust and empower staff so that the right decisions are made as close to the front line as possible. The energy will increasingly flow up from knowledge workers close to or on the front line, rather than being forced down from on high.

Ben Verwaayen wants "a culture in which people take the right decision as close to the problem as possible in a collective perspective that you have developed in which they know it's the right decision". He adds: "So, first of all, they have to ask less. Second, they know in the culture and in the values and in the targets that you have set, what the right decisions are, and therefore, because they own it, it's their decision, it's a much easier sell."

Shiv Nadar, chairman and chief strategy officer of India's HCL Technologies, focuses on making sure the entrepreneurs in his business are unbound. "You can see entrepreneurs: it's screaming on their foreheads," he says. "So we actively look for entrepreneurs. Real stars join HCL every day and it's on their foreheads. If it's not, they are not stars. We give them the tools and empower them to drive the business from the bottom." Nadar recognizes that "once you grow to a certain size, you need processes to manage the business", but emphasizes that "you also need to ensure that the entrepreneurship emanates from the bottom of the business".

The same applies online. Mitch Garber, former CEO of PartyGaming, believes: "In twenty-first-century companies, it is important to hire great people and to give them flexibility and have confidence in their decision making. As CEO, you can't take decisions in India, Israel, or America, but you can create a business framework whereby the big decisions come up to the top and you can make the right call."

To release the talents you have in the business does not require a mere change in tone. As a CEO, you must fundamentally reassess how you see your role. You must learn, as Sir Bill Castell puts it, "to suppress your ego so that you can then be a champion and help others learn, like you do your children". He adds, "CEOs are going to have to get used to being at the bottom of the hierarchy, supporting the 460 managers above them."

CEOs have to get used to being at the bottom of the hierarchy

At Alcatel Lucent's Chinese business, president Liu Jiangnan agrees: "It is clear that whenever decision-making is empowered with local management, we make the right decisions and do very well. But if we do not take inputs from local management, we suffer setbacks; you have to empower."[54]

You must also ensure that your incentive system encourages employees to experiment and be innovative. Google is a good example here. Its aim is to provide "an environment where talented, hard-working people are rewarded for their contributions to Google and for making the world a better place". And it has flexible rewards to make this happen. For example, its "founders' award" is designed to give "extraordinary rewards for extraordinary team accomplishments". While there's no single yardstick for measuring achievement, a general rule of thumb is that the team accomplished something that created tremendous value for the company. The awards pay out in the form of Google stock units that vest over time. Team members receive awards based on their level of involvement and contribution, and the largest awards can reach several million dollars. In 2005 Google awarded about $45 million in restricted stock to 11 different projects, citing the recipients for creating "tremendous value" for the company. Cynics question whether Google sees a profitable return from the awards. However, these initiatives have been at least a key factor in attracting and motivating the top talent to the business, and there can be no doubt that Google developers turn out a large number of innovative products.[55]

Indeed, companies like £35 billion revenue Haier, where the mindset is that every employee is treated as an individual P&L, and Linden Lab are starting to experiment with overtly market-based systems for allocating resources and talent. Promising results mean that this could be a signpost for how the best businesses organize and account for their businesses.

The ability to give individuals the space and incentives to act innovatively while still delivering results will distinguish leading CEOs from the rest of the field over the next ten years.

The CEO is primarily responsible for talent

As we saw in Chapter 3, talent-magnet companies will build talent development partnerships between the chief executive, human resources department, and the search industry. The CEO will have to be the talent champion and ensure that talent stays at the top of the business's agenda and that talent development is driven down into all line managers' performance metrics.

Top CEOs will make sure that their key executives are drawn from the top 1 percent of global talent and that attracting the top talent is as high a priority as serving customers. These CEOs will be committed to investing money and at least 25 percent of their time to talent development. Not satisfied with a process-based approach to HR, these CEOs will push their HR teams to become true internal talent champions and to find a global search partner who knows the top 1 percent of global talent.

The CEO monitors the company radar and future-proofs the business

Chief executives don't read enough, states Val Gooding. "They need a political, social, and economic view on the world." Tomorrow's leaders need to have a great feel for what's happening in and around their companies and then have flexible resources with which to reshape their core businesses and to develop novel businesses to capture value from shifts in the environment. Too many twentieth-century companies were caught out by swift changes in technology or the entry into their core markets of new foreign competitors. The quickening pace of globalization makes these dangers all the more prevalent.

A FTSE100 CEO told us: "Countries and companies have wonderful assets but also carry baggage. You need a radar to understand what's coming up across the different regions in your business. For example, Europe's outlook, with social costs rising and labor inflexibility, is very different to what's happening in Asia." Meanwhile, Sir Bill Castell has some practical advice. "CEOs must get out there and test their vision," he says. "CEOs should use universities to help with their radar. For example, I had Massachusetts Institute of Technology help me to understand the future of world energy." Finally, as Compass Group chairman Sir Roy Gardner emphasizes, "It is important that the center does not delegate away the radar – it needs to keep an eye on the future of the customer."

Inside their organizations, CEOs need to discern what's going well and badly in regard to customers, competitors, and talent. Archie Norman says, "You've got to understand what's happening on the front line, and you've got to understand in some cases more about that than the line manager. The good leader today in business is complex and fast moving, and there are ways of informing the inner circle. You have a grapevine. So, you walk the stores or you walk the customers, you have people who pick up the phone and tell you things. You have an internet blog with suggestions; you have lots of different ways which tell you what's really happening. The line never tells the truth, never, even in great organizations. Good news travels fast, bad news travels slowly, and so you've got to know."

Good news travels fast, bad news travels slowly, and so you've got to know

These insights are no use if they are not actionable. The radar has to drive CEOs' efforts to prevent themselves being wrong-footed by shifts in the future. Brent Hoberman comments: "The best corporates will have a team focused on future-proofing their own business, spending time bettering and breaking their own processes. These groups should not worry about existing investment cases; their mission is to create the next generation and to avoid the company betting its future on what it does today."

Such teams will be available to CEOs to work on growth initiatives, scope major strategic moves and mergers and acquisitions, and continually reexamine how to use corporate assets to create disruptive new businesses. CEOs should therefore consciously build teams to create wide-ranging insights about the world and to incubate significant new ventures.

The net result of an active radar is that the CEO gets insight early enough to future-proof his business effectively. That's critical. As Jacob Hsu, CEO of Symbio, told us: "A successful leader today needs to be constantly thinking about how to break their business model. If I look back at business plans from five years ago, very few of those assumptions hold today."

The CEO polices business performance and ensures global minimum acceptable standards are met

Freedom to act does not mean that the business units and employees are unregulated and totally unconstrained by the center – far from it. Great businesses regulate themselves along two axes. First, to drive value there is rigorous transparency on performance; these businesses compile financial and nonfinancial data that is comparable and timely. And they monitor the security of their corporate assets – financial, tangible, or intangible.

Xstrata provides a good example. The center sets very demanding targets and executives are rewarded lavishly for meeting them but, equally, failure to meet targets is investigated very carefully and consistent failure is not tolerated. That's performance policing: the question of whether people are reaching high enough.

However, to guarantee the integrity of your business you also need to ensure that all operations meet quality and sustainability standards. Therefore, great businesses set and monitor minimum acceptable standards – they ensure that people are standing on the right foundations. Bernd Scheifele, chairman of Heidelberg Cement, says: "The challenge is in reaching technical standards globally, principally in production and sustainability. Whereas sales and marketing are managed locally because cement is a local market business, we use global best practices for production and sustainability."

Sir John Parker wraps performance policing and minimum acceptable standards together neatly. "At National Grid, the model is very simple," he says. "We have to have leading governance practices, visibility on accountability, and transparency, because governance at the end of the day is about discipline. You need to decentralize management decision taking

Governance at the end of the day is about discipline

to the lowest possible level, but with well-defined responsibility and accountability all the way down the line. You need strong audit control with a solid line from the board to every audit controller, sound administration, strong compliance, and very strong legal teams ensuring you are conducting your business correctly. Whether you are a big company or a small company and whether you're in one country or 30, the same principles apply."

The risk in a company with a command-and-control legacy is that minimum acceptable standards and policing are used as excuses for a return to the old system. It's worth remembering Feng Jun's advice to focus on empowering the front line: "Small failures are better than doing nothing. After you grow to maybe 200 people, there is a risk of disempowerment and that the board/management may be the company's biggest obstacle." There's risk in both a lack of policing and in overzealous policing.

People leadership requirements

The CEO inspires

Ketan Patel, founder of investment firm Greater Pacific Capital, states: "Big adventures require visionaries, charismatic leaders, and controversial thinkers. Such qualities are rare. So instead, many leaders focus on those things that do not require vision (we call them pragmatism), do not require personality (we call them reliable)."[56]

"Hold on," you may be thinking, "I thought the era of the inspirational, big-ego CEO was dead?" Absolutely right. However, the current generation of professional managers are not going to be able to provide the personal leadership that companies will require either. Fresh role models are needed for global companies. Great CEOs find inspiration for themselves and their team in their passion for the company, what everyone can do together, and their personal purpose. Inspirational leaders don't have to jump up and down frantically and be on the front cover of *Time* magazine. Great examples are often found in the emerging champion companies.

Samir Brikho contrasts leadership with managing. "You give a manager targets and he is determined to meet them, you coach him to meet them, and he meets them," he says. "A leader inspires. He articulates a compelling vision, has certain values and lives according to them and, when you think you can only jump 2 meters, he can get you to jump 2.5 meters."

In the new world of work, chief executives need to be able to lift their people to go beyond themselves. Comments Narayana Murthy: "To me, leadership is primarily about raising the aspirations of people, making people say that they will walk on water. A plausible impossibility is better than a convincing possibility."

Mukesh Ambani is another remarkable Indian leader. By his own admission, he doesn't "force anybody to work six-day weeks and 18-hour days". But he inspires such pas-

Leadership is about soul, heart, and mind   sion for the work that his teams do it anyway. Despite being a self-effacing man, he actually has a very clear understanding of how he inspires such determination. For him, "leadership is about soul, heart, and mind. 'Soul' is what you believe in – your values. Everyone's values are different; it's not necessary to converge on them. 'Heart' is your passion – it gives you the courage to build something and compassion and the other qualities that define who you are. The last and least is 'mind' – your competences."

Great leaders get remarkable results from ordinary people. Says Sir David Bell, chairman and former CEO of the Financial Times: "When you assume that people don't have ambition, can't do more than they are already doing, and really therefore they don't matter very much – you're almost always wrong."

Inspiring leaders bring to life for every employee or partner what they, their team, and the company can do. Inspiration is about raising the aspirations of the group for the group.

The CEO elicits trust and belief

People need to be inspired by a compelling vision to make them want to go somewhere. However, the leader also has to get them to step out on the journey and then sustain them along the way. Getting them to cross the starting line requires that they believe that you, the leader, and they, the team, can get there together. They need to believe in you as an authentic person with the ability to help them overcome the roadblocks on the way; they need to trust that you are leading them toward a meaningful and decent future. In other words, where inspiration establishes a high bar as a worthwhile and achievable goal, trust and belief keep your team going through the hard times. In Narayana Murthy's words: "Achieving dreams means making sacrifices in the short term to achieve in the long term. It means that one of the most important attributes of a leader is trust. Trust means people will give their lives for you because people see that 'if it is good for him it is good for me'."

Achieving dreams means making sacrifices in the short term to achieve in the long term

Trust and belief are built through the decisions you make and the way you are seen to be with people. You have to ask whether people think you are a decent person trying to do the right thing. John Neill emphasizes the personal element: "The people in the front line of the company need to know you. They need to know that you care about them and all the company's stakeholders. They need to know that you know their business and care about their process problems and personal problems at work. You need to get onto the values level of all of the people at every level in the business and, while building respect for the past, clearly signpost the future." So too does Sir John Parker. "Good leaders walk the talk," he says. "They're consistent in their behavior. They live out the words. I can think of no higher risk to a leader's credibility than not living out the words." Murthy is blunter still. "Walking the talk is the most powerful instrument of adherence to a value system that our people adhere to," he says. "If you eat your own dog food, trust is automatically built."

Leadership does not have to involve the consumption of pet food. However, people's trust in you as a person is essential to their belief in their ability, with you, to reach the desired goal, so you must work to build that trust. If you manage to sustain trust and belief in you among your teams, you stand a good chance of getting the team across the finish line.

The CEO brings clarity

Errors made at the top are magnified as their implications spread through the business and the original instruction is reinterpreted.

As the lead delegator in the business, chief executives have to give the business clarity on strategy, objectives, tasks, values, and all other critical issues. It's very much easier if you are a natural communicator, though you can learn to improve your skills in this area. Being a great communicator means understanding what you're trying to say and how it's likely to be *Can you describe your vision of the* understood by the different audiences you're *future in two sentences?* addressing. Sir John Parker calls communication "the sister of leadership". "Can you describe your vision of the future in two sentences?" he asks. "Without being able to communicate effectively, a CEO can't instruct people."

Experts say that communicating is actually one of the most complicated things human beings do. Certainly, miscommunication, misunderstanding, and the subsequent confusion and lack of clarity are at the heart of many business difficulties. Although chief executives normally receive training in presentation skills, they are rarely trained in the art of communication, part of which involves being an effective *receiver* of information.

"The real art of communication is in understanding what message is received by the listener rather than what is transmitted by the speaker," says Alan Watkins. "Many CEOs make the mistake of believing that just because they said something or sent out a signal, they communicated. Rarely do leaders check what was received by the listener, but this simple discipline of checking what was received, when applied appropriately, can transform the quality of communication. The quality of communication can be significantly enhanced by understanding the type of person you are speaking to and how they see the world. The message has to be adjusted to fit the audience, not out of some manipulative Machiavellian intent, but simply because the message will fail to land or become distorted if such adjustment is not made."

Gifted communicators make this kind of adjustment naturally. Nevertheless, this flexibility is a skill worth developing, because it helps you ensure that listeners understand what you intend so that you can reduce the risk of them misunderstanding your guidance.

CEOs are role models in their dedication, consistency, and personal balance
Malon Wilkus, CEO of private equity group American Capital, insists that leaders "must have a passion, integrity, and personally work hard to make the business even better. If everyone can see and understand what you are about, then they in turn will be fired up to go the extra yard to do the same."

People will judge your dedication by your visibility to them. That means that you have to travel and meet with those in your distributed operations around the world. GE taught Sir Bill Castell that "the CEO needs to get around the world and see people face to face once a year. After that, he can do things by telephone." Indeed, when Philip Green became chief executive of P&O Nedlloyd, he set himself a target of seeing and being seen by 80 percent of the company's employees in his first 12 months. He achieved that goal and made sure he did it again when he moved on to become chief executive at United Utilities.

The CEO is always on display. John Weston believes that "on an average day, a senior manager has about 100 opportunities to provide leadership to the team. The problem is that they only take one and the team see the other 99."

For Sir John Parker, "the key to demonstrating personal dedication is consistency. Your people see you doing this day in day out and they start to trust and believe in you. Consistency is key to integrity, which for me is the most important value for a CEO."

Consistency is key to integrity, which is the most important value for a CEO

However, your actions will inform those of others, so you have to be smart in your balancing of travel and technology. Todd Stitzer sends his top 100 employees a monthly voicemail, communicates with his top 1,000 every two months, and sends a newsletter to the next 10,000 every quarter. Smart use of technology can protect your time and energy while still preserving your work–life balance. Remember that your working style and work–life balance will set the tone for the whole business, so by not looking after yourself and staying fresh you are indirectly reducing your business's energy, a point we'll come back to in Chapter 10.

The CEO judges and moderates organizational pace and energy

CEOs must make a judgment call on how much pace and change their company needs, and can handle, at this point in time. They then need to decide how well the business is achieving the necessary pace, increasing it if necessary or slowing the organization down before it overheats.

Sometimes the energy has to come from CEOs themselves. John Connelly, global managing director of accountants Deloitte Touche Tohmatsu, says: "Whatever the circumstances, optimism, giving people a degree of confidence, is the spine of leadership. At Davos 2008 the word of the moment was "gloomy" – everyone professed themselves "gloomy" at every opportunity. I wrote a report to my partners where my observation was that I didn't see any benefit to our business of being gloomy."

Equally, it's very unhealthy for the CEO to be the business's sole dynamo. John Neill says that Unipart has developed a vast number of carefully thought-out mechanisms by which management creates and spreads energy throughout the business. Every six weeks it has a glitzy "Mark in Action" awards event, where it celebrates significant achievements and recognizes the people who have made them. "Those who've been recognized then wear a hologram on their badge so it's clear that they've been celebrated," he says. "I have not missed a Mark in Action meeting in 20 years. So you do not have to bring all the energy. You get it from the groups you assemble and it's part of your job to transport that energy around the organization. You don't have to have the great idea, but you need to spot it and propagate it. All these events serve to identify and hold up exemplars within the organization and their stories get around the business. But they also help me to judge the pace the organization is moving at and where to speed it up and where to slow it down."

> You don't have to have the great idea, but you need to spot it and propagate it

Sir Terry Leahy has more cautionary words. "Energy and pace matter," he argues, "but you can be too energetic or frenetic. The bigger the organization, the bigger the ripple effect, and too much noise at the center can lead to chaos at the edge. Quiet leadership can be best. You still need lots of energy to be quiet. You have to cover the ground. Also remember that energy and freedom may conflict."

Finally, the level of pace and energy required will depend on the company you run. "You have to understand the pace and pulse of different organizations," says Philip Green, comparing life at the three companies he's led. "At DHL, you can't try to execute an order until you've received it. At Reuters, most of the revenues are through subscription and the concept of an order doesn't really exist. At United, we are a utility and there is no order book at all – it's a monopoly. The pace and pulse is very different."

As we warned you at the start of the book, being a CEO carries a health warning because of the amount of personal effort required in the role. However, the best CEOs channel the energy of the organization rather than trying to overcome sticking points and inertia single-handedly.

The CEO is flexible in the face of reality

The necessary flipside of clarity and the hard business output of performance policing is flexibility. Great CEOs have the unshake-able conviction that there's always a way. However, they must also be grounded in reality; there's no point leaving employees deflated by expecting them to do what really is impossible. Martina King underlines this, saying: "You have to paint an exciting future, but you must also face reality. You cannot be credible about the future unless you face reality." The CEO must recognize when brick walls are being confronted and the team needs to regroup and attack from another angle.

Flexibility is a key soft leadership element and a key distin-guisher from twentieth-century approaches, because it is funda-mental to the increased devolution of power and decentralization of authority that lies at the core of tomorrow's leadership. As Mick Davis showed in Chapter 5, the CEO has to distinguish "good" fail-ure and "bad" failure – the failure of anticipated returns to be reaped following the pursuit of an intelligent, carefully thought-through business risk is no failure at all. Deciding when to push and when to regroup is a classic leadership skill, but one on which a premium will continue to be placed.

The CEO develops and promotes the firm's personality

Personality is the character of a business; it is described whenever your employees are asked over dinner what it's like to work for your company. If it's a good personality for the employee, it will resonate with them and they will express it with pride and enthusiasm. On the other hand, in underperforming businesses personality can be flat or toxic. The CEO must then tune into the underlying energy of the business, such as it is, and create a new personality that feels authentic but energizing to the high-quality employees already in the firm and compelling to talents outside it. The CEO has a very direct influence on the personality of a business because he or she will typically be seen as personifying it.

A company without a culture is like a person without a soul

This is a task you can't avoid. As Zhang Ruimin tells us from Qingdao, "a company without a culture is like a person without a soul". Companies' personalities are as different as people's: at Haier, Ruimin thinks you have to "create a family environment through genuine care and consideration, a sense of belonging, like a home".[57] You mold the personality every day.

Many chief executives say that being a CEO is like being on television all the time. They are aware that whether they are in corporate headquarters or out in the field visiting operations, they are being continually observed. Even the most casual remark can change someone's day or get tongues wagging. "If you're a CEO, everyone in your company watches you all the time," says Leigh Clifford. "If you do something that's inconsistent with the values you espouse, it goes around the organization and everyone knows."

But there's a flipside to the high profile: every situation is an opportunity to evangelize the business's values and a chance to lead by personal example. John Neill once had to practice what he preaches when he was lecturing at Unipart's staff "university" and Jenny, the coffee lady, was struggling to serve 100 people in their 15-minute break. "She got overwhelmed and her broad smile faded as she became highly stressed, realizing she couldn't achieve the task," he recalls. "So I started serving coffee with her, but we still struggled. So when Jenny went home that day and her family asked what kind of day did you have, the answer was obvious and clearly she wasn't looking forward to the next course." Neill encouraged Jenny to learn the relevant components of the Unipart Way, the core of its business model, and apply them to her area of responsibility. The result was exactly the sort of continuous improvement exercise he was teaching about. "Now using the Unipart Way," he reports, "Jenny manages the system and uses her new-found skills to continuously improve the process. Today everyone gets served in less than two minutes and Jenny takes pride in chopping seconds off the process. Her family would get a very different answer now when asked, 'What kind of day did you have?'" Neill tells the story as part of the Philosophies and Principles course that he continues to teach at Unipart U.

And of course, businesses, like people, should not be entirely serious all the time. As the late Sir John Harvey-Jones, former chairman of ICI, once modestly explained his role: "Basically, I try to jolly things along."

Conclusion: The nature of the cell

The cell metaphor is designed to bring to life how the center of an organization should respond to the new business realities and the new world of work. Tom Peters, author of the bestselling *In Search of Excellence*, captures much of the essence of the cell when he says: "Passionate servant leaders, determined to create a legacy of earthshaking transformation in their domain... must necessarily create organizations which are... no less than cathedrals in which the full and awesome power of the imagination and spirit and native entrepreneurial flair of diverse individuals is unleashed... in passionate pursuit of jointly perceived soaring purpose and personal and community and client service excellence."[58] Peters' language is a bit over the top for us and for most CEOs, but its direction is definitely right.

THE FELLOWSHIP

So are we moving toward a breed of superhuman CEOs who can lead a complicated cell business while at the same time having a fulfilling life outside work? Probably not.

Step back for a second and try to imagine a new global powerhouse. Imagine a "dream team" of Lord Browne filling a global ambassadorial role, Sir Terry Leahy driving operational execution, Sir Martin Sorrell developing entrepreneurial new ventures and markets, Mick Davis pulling together massive value-adding deals, and John Chambers focusing on inspiring the troops. What a team that would be!

Clearly, in practice this would probably be a disaster, as each of these CEOs works in his own way and all are used to being the boss. Equally, however, it's clear from our interviews that top global companies, while on the surface operating as a conventional management group, are really run by a close-knit team of key executives with extraordinary and complementary skills. As D Shivkumar says, "It is better to build a bunch of leaders so if making a big move three or four people will come together and plan it."[59] We believe that the outstanding companies of the next decade will be led by a tightly bonded fellowship of remarkable leaders operating as one.

Arguably, the most well-documented fellowship is the so-called dream team that drove mobile phone manufacturer Nokia's phenomenal growth through the 1990s. Jorma Ollila worked in superclose partnership with Matti Alahuhta, Pekka Ala-Pietilä, Sari Baldauf, and his replacement as president and COO, Olli-Pekka Kallasvuo. A fellowship has also driven Infosys, as Deepak Satwalekar, lead independent director there, explained to us: "At the heart of Infosys is a fellowship which was formed over 20 years ago, based on a mission, strong values, and a firm commitment to doing the right thing and integrity." Indeed, a similarly close top team has led National Australia Bank through a fêted revitalization. CEO Australia Ahmed Fahour states, "Former CEO John Stewart ran the business more like a private equity business than a traditional corporate. John's really a managing partner and his reports are partners. This approach trickles a long way down the organization – for example, I run my business with 'partners' too.

"This is important because (1) in truth John doesn't have the same information we have about our businesses, so it's better that most decisions are taken where the most information is; and (2) because, frankly, we'd all leave if he micro-managed us! The partnership is based on mutual respect, clear principles and behavioral rules, and careful mentoring, which starts with John's expert mentoring of his business heads. At the end of the day, if you don't understand what you should do in the fellowship, you're not good enough to be in it." At Resolution, Paul Thompson also thought of his top team as "partners, not people run by command and control".

The truth is that fellowships feel radically different from a conventional leadership team in the closeness of their binding, the total openness between their members, the level of conflict and disagreement the members can tolerate with each other, and the high level of interchangeability of the fellowship members. Archie Norman fondly recalls his time at Asda, which spawned a generation of FTSE100 CEOs, including Richard Baker, Andy Hornby, Justin King, and Allan Leighton. "A real team is a rarity," he admits. "All chief executives tell you they've got a great team, but when you say who is the great team, 80 percent of them tell you it's these 20 people or these 12 people. I know what they're trying to say, but that's not a team. You very, very rarely find a team of 12 people, in fact pretty much never. That's not a real team.

The real team is one where they share things with each other completely openly

"A real team is typically three or four people, because the real team in fast-moving companies is one where, when things are going wrong, they share things with each other completely openly. When they have a rotten day, they come in and say, 'I've made a right mess of that, can you help me out, just tell me where you think I should pick it up.'

"Or someone comes in and says, 'I've got this idea, do you think we should do it?' and somebody else will say, 'No, I think that's rubbish actually.' You can have that sort of joint heavy lifting.

There are high levels of interchangeability – if I can't make that meeting, OK, I'll go and pick it up for you. No sweat, no problem. That is a huge advantage to have, but it's unusual.

"The right culture to create is one where there is total transparency. There are no secrets. Everybody knows what everybody else is doing. We all respect each other for what we are doing, but we are able to have an open argument about things, like a family row. I like businesses where people feel able to shout at each other, in a professional way obviously. They are emotional about it and have a go. We may be incredibly aggressive and abrasive, but afterwards we're all friends. We respect each other and we feel better."

We have some awesome arguments; we discuss the undiscussables

Lenovo has a such a fellowship. senior vice-president of human resources Kenneth DiPietro remarks wryly, "We have some awesome arguments; we make it a rule to discuss the undiscussables." Importantly, Bill Amelio and chairman Yang Yuanqing have succeeded in building a vibrant fellowship drawing on people from a wide range of cultures.

Sir John Parker expands on this idea. "In the executive cell, there will be ideally three to four people who collectively drive at pace and with integrity, releasing energy across the whole organization," he says. Ron Havner, Public Storage CEO, thinks that the key thing about his fellowship is that it "promotes more sharing of ideas and issues between fellowship members than in a conventional company management team". Indeed, the most significant danger with a fellowship model is that, in Lord Davies' words, "You have to be careful the top team does not become a cult. In a world of fast change, you continually need new blood and fresh ideas in teams."

A fellowship is a much more effective way to lead a cell business than a more conventional CEO plus strong line manager model for several reasons. First, a cell's leaders need to propagate messages through a dispersed and nonhierarchical organization. Having a group of perfectly aligned executives close to the CEO and core mission allows for a fast-acting viral information flow. Second, fellowship members, by being close to the center, are more empowered to take major decisions, visibly dispersing power right at the top. Finally, entry into the fellowship generates tremendous loyalty and so aids in the retention of top talent.

Being a CEO in a fellowship

Taking the lead remains the role of the CEO. Mitch Garber says, "The true test of a CEO is not when things are going well, but when things are not going well and you have to go off course and ski off piste. It needs real self-belief to change course and make tough, unpopular decisions, but ultimately this is the difference between the success and failure of a leader."

It needs real self-belief to change course and make tough, unpopular decisions

Certainly, businesses should not be governed by majority vote. In that way lies vacillation. However, many CEOs observed how infrequently they take unilateral decisions or override their top teams. Although some situations, such as turnarounds, require strong leadership more than others, most CEOs recognize the value of working in a team.

Rather than robbing the CEO of the initiative or exchanging him or her for a consensus-seeking council, a fellowship model strengthens the CEO significantly. What could have been impossible becomes possible. A CEO in a fellowship is stronger with regard to internal opposition or inertia, as there is a core team of really close advocates within the business. The fellowship can give the CEO valuable support in hard times and the trust they share with him or her can make it easier to face reality in tough spots.

A trusted fellowship can work particularly well during transformation phases. At Tesco, for example, Tim Mason is setting up the Fresh and Easy venture in the US while the rest of the fellowship focuses on the core business.

One danger with fellowships is that they are often forged in periods of super-growth but then their spirit and speed are lost as the business grows and solidifies. However, having a really close team provides the CEO with the chance to be supported through the lows by people with unshakeable conviction in the mission, and to celebrate the highs of success with people with as deep a commitment to the outcome as the leader.

Building a fellowship

Leadership is situational – you should choose a CEO whose leadership type best matches the challenges the business will face in the future. For example, a global missionary is likely to be best placed to revitalize a large global company that has lost its way. However, the cell model works with any situation and with any CEO type and always requires that the CEO be supported by a close-knit fellowship.

The closeness of fellowship members requires a much closer alignment of personal values than most leadership teams manage. The fellowship members have to be very clear on what moves them individually and as a team. They must invest heavily in probing and really understanding the other members' values, so that they can all align their beliefs on how to conduct business and be fully frank and open with each other as disagreements arise. Fellowship members must also respect and value each other's skills so that there can be mutual respect and equality of contribution. Finally, there must be a sense of collective responsibility, so that all fellowship members back the decision of the CEO whatever the previous argument and its intensity.

But, above all, fellowships are built on everyone digging in together. As Mukesh Ambani confirmed: "To build bonding (what you call fellowship) takes three years of going through hell. Everyone wants to go to heaven but you have to die to go to heaven. You have to go through a painful process – that builds ability to do this stuff."

Several CEOs told us that their fellowships do not map to the company's senior management team; some of that team may well be excluded and some more junior executives may be part of the fellowship. The most important questions in selecting members are:

- ❏ Do they have the shared appetite to do something great?
- ❏ Do they have the specific skills you need?
- ❏ Who in the fellowship is outstanding in each skill area?
- ❏ Do all of the fellowship have a deep commitment to the cause and the right values and beliefs?

❏ Is there a natural chemistry – and friendship – between the fellowship members?

The nonexecutive board in a fellowship

Clearly, the board in the future will increasingly have to be prepared to work effectively with executives operating in more tightly knit fellowships. Consequently, as Paul Manduca, former chief executive of Deutsche Asset Management, states: "The nonexecutive boards of tomorrow will have to be highly supportive of these talent teams but still not be afraid of testing strategy and key operational risks. In addition, the boards of fellowship-led companies are more likely to be successful, but they must ensure that the company continues to adapt to changes. It will be their role to check that the fellowship still has the right members to address each phase in the company's development."

In an ideal world, the nonexecutives would be a close-knit team too that would work closely with the executive fellowship and maintain a constructive dialogue about the business. Such a dialogue can allow boards to continue their strong testing and challenge of executive decisions, but also develop a careful, guiding rapport with the leadership team that allows them to reduce the need for heavy direct interventions in the business.

Conclusion

Tomorrow's CEOs will abandon the outmoded command-and-control model that is too inflexible for the modern business environment. Instead, the best businesses will be fueled by an ambition to be the clear number one business in their industry. Inspiring people with a moving aspiration for the type of business they want to be, top CEOs will create a generation of truly globally organized companies.

These new champions will be bold, entrepreneurial, and win in the right way. Built around the world's best talent, they will be empowering, innovative places to work where employees find fulfillment and focus on driving commercial results.

These businesses will be led by close-knit fellowships that contain people with complementary skills who truly pull together. Fellowship members will work together at the heart of the business and their deep relationships will lay the foundations for constructive conflict and stronger performance throughout the company.

10

PREPARING TO LEAD

"If you want to be a CEO, then you must focus on being a great leader."
Richard Baker, former chief executive, Alliance Boots

"I want to learn the ways of the Force and become a Jedi."
Luke Skywalker to Obi-Wan Kenobi, Star Wars

For those of you at the start of your career in the new world of work, the first and most important thing to do if you believe you want to be a CEO is to unpick your motives and understand why. Wanting the title and money, power and status is understandable and not unusual. However, as an audacious life goal, setting your sights on that title alone is probably a recipe for disappointment. Remember that, where the Top Gun fighter pilot school aims for the top 1 percent of pilots, the CEO of a large international business is in the top 0.001 percent of the company, so it's a tough position to go for. If, on the other hand, your aspiration to be a CEO is really an expression of wanting to realize your potential and make a significant difference in business and beyond, then you must recognize that you are not talking about a title – you're talking about a career mission. And critical to its successful fulfillment will be becoming a leader skilled in both business and personal leadership.

To become a complete leader for tomorrow requires an apprenticeship. Learning leadership is like a quest – there's no defined path to success.

In this chapter we provide advice from visionary CEOs on how to start your quest, share views on the career foundations you need to build, and then, for those of you preparing to become CEO soon, we lay out the way to pull up mid-career, check on your progress, and reassess your aspirations. We've discussed how to lead a twenty-first-century company in Chapter 9, but at the end of this chapter we also share thoughts on how to step back from the CEO role and look beyond building an orthodox "plural" career.

Where most conventional career advice is linear, most CEOs we talked to thought that traditional career planning is outdated and that it is better to think of your career as divided into broad phases of leadership development. However, we are well aware of how life tends to upset carefully laid plans, so this chapter is designed to help you roll with the ups and downs.

WHAT DO YOU WANT FROM YOUR CAREER?

Very few people know what they want to do from the outset. Keith Butler-Wheelhouse, former CEO of Smiths Group, was in that camp. He recalls, "I always wanted to be a general manager. I was 19 when Henry Ford II came to the Ford plant I worked at. He asked what we wanted to do in life. I said I wanted to run Ford. I got a lot of ribbing for that from the others, who had been less ambitious in their aim, but Ford respected the question and asked me why. I said I wanted to learn to integrate the facets of the business together. And I spent the following 20 years at Ford training myself in all elements of the business. That education has stood me in great stead."

However, the majority of our CEOs only got a sense of their career mission in their late 20s or 30s. Paul Thompson would hope that you do not want to be CEO of the business you are in at 25. "You should be more of a rebel than that," he says. "Wanting to be the boss shows too much empathy for the establishment." Meanwhile, Eric Daniels says: "I guess I was a late developer. My career's really been a series of lucky accidents. I've done all kinds of jobs. I worked in a grocery store at 15, on a construction site at 18, then a petrol station, a library, and a shop, and I had two stints at a paint factory. When you're working in a paint factory, you cannot imagine what a dirty, dangerous job it is. Work on enough of those jobs and you'll want to make the world better. My 17-year-old son doesn't know the answer to that at the moment. This doesn't bother me."

Over time, your career mission will emerge and become clearer. At Tiger Airways, CEO Tony Davis advises that instead of a fixed plan, "you need a thread to your life". His own career is connected to an early passion for flying; like many boys, including a young Paul Walsh, he wanted to be a pilot in the RAF.

Remember that insight into your career mission need not come just from business experience. Narayana Murthy tells of a formative experience hitchhiking home to Mysore in southern India that decided him on entering business. He reached the city of Nis in what is now Serbia and Montenegro at night and slept on the platform of the train station for two nights running, as he had no local currency. He eventually caught a train into Bulgaria and tried to engage two fellow travelers in conversation. Having struggled with the boy, who spoke neither English nor French, Murthy talked instead to the girl. Somehow angered, the boy called the police. "They threw me into an 8ft by 8ft cell," recalls Murthy. "I had no food or water for another 72 hours and the floors in Bulgaria are very cold in winter. Eventually, after 108 hours without food, they put me in the guard's compartment on a freight train to Istanbul and would only return my passport when I got there. That long, hungry journey gave me time for introspection and I decided to conduct an experiment in entrepreneurship in India."

By the end of your 20s you will know the sort of direction you want to head in. Many of the CEOs we interviewed realized in their late 20s that they were driven by a desire for freedom out of a frustration with poorly managed command-and-control enterprises. For Nick Basing, a serial venturer who has grown several businesses and is former CEO of Paramount Restaurants, a key motivator has always been "feeling restless about missed opportunities. I always got frustrated that lots of opportunities were being missed by the organizations I was in." Paul Thompson adds: "Above all, I hated being told by anyone what to do, even if they were right. For me, being CEO is all about freedom; people who find making big decisions lonely are not cut out to be CEO." Richard Baker was driven through his retail career by "two main driving forces: (1) to not be bossed around and to have the freedom to act; (2) to be economically independent and to be able to walk away from work if I wanted to". He says he "realized early on that the only way not to be bossed around was to be the boss".

The only critical element at the beginning of your career is to be determined to do great things. The truth is that most people are afraid to be bold and to commit to achieving their career mission. So although you don't know how things will turn out, dare to be great. Thras Moraitis has only one regret. "I started and sold several very good businesses as a young man, but for the same effort I could have done great things," he muses. "Aim for great things."

Tan Pheng Hock values passion in young leaders. "Coming from humble beginnings has taught me never to take anything for granted and to treasure every bit I have," he says. "Never be afraid to dream, and to work hard toward that dream. There are no short cuts in life, and no promises. But if you're passionate enough about what you believe in, you can succeed." Of course, as Philip Green says, "the best foundation will be to work with a twenty-first-century global leader – but there aren't many of those around."

If you are committed to undertaking a leadership apprenticeship, five points are fundamental in starting out:

❑ Commit to finding your ultimate career mission and to doing something great.
❑ Commit yourself to excellent leadership and personal development from the outset.
❑ Lay solid foundations, but then move faster and take bigger risks and ignore conventional advice founded in the old world of work.
❑ Find your mentor – work for a great leader.
❑ Don't neglect family and friends and enjoying your 20s.

BUILDING THE RIGHT FOUNDATIONS

To become a CEO for tomorrow you will need a very broad range of experiences. Lord Browne states: "The first few years of a career have to be about investing to understand. Be an apprentice, get your hands dirty, and take risks. It's generally better to do it early. It's a really bad idea to have a rigid life plan. You know nothing early on; you only really get to see what business is all about once you're past 40. Before then, it's about getting loads of experience." Damian Reece, head of business at the Daily and Sunday Telegraph, observes that "the younger generation of CEOs are less conservative, probably because they have been schooled in an internet decade and are naturally, therefore, more ambitious, confident, commercial, aggressive, and 'can do'. Build a career: ignore conventional advice, take more risk at an earlier age, and aim to be a great leader."

Ignore conventional advice, take more risk at an earlier age, and aim to be a great leader

Eric Daniels adds: "If you set your heart on being a chief executive, your chances of being disappointed are very high, so that aspiration is likely a waste of your life. The question is: 'What do you like?' Try a lot of things and figure out what you like during your early life and career.

"Apprenticeships take many forms, but never forget that the objective is to become a leader. You need to discover whether you have got leadership qualities or not and you can only discover that through experience, because leadership is a very personal quality. It can't be taught and you don't know until you've tried to lead."

CEO apprenticeship requires you to have a medium-term goal but not to overplan. Tony Davis thinks that youngsters try to plan their careers too much. "You cannot lay out an objective and a route to it when you're young," he says. "You should be more flexible and take more risks. Broaden your perspectives and experience, change country and industry: that depth of experience marks you out to employers."

But don't read this as counsel for an easy life, as skilling up is a very serious business. "You need to know where you are," says Daniels. "The 20s are the new teens. They're all about discovery about yourself, but they're also about building skills because, if you don't, you're unlikely to be happy down the track."

Life is not a game of chess in which every move can be planned out. The first phase of your career is about the serious business of exploration: exploration of yourself, business, and the wider world. Potential CEOs need to accumulate a broad range of business and personal experiences, build a platform of hard business skills, and learn about themselves early on.

Your parents' advice when choosing a career was almost certainly to get a great education, get a profession, and work for an already well-established and well-known company. That advice is rooted in the old world of work. It remains good advice in the twenty-first century – but only at the very start of your career. The new world of work is where those entering the workforce today will have 13 jobs by the age of 38, as we saw in Chapter 3. More than ever, a great education will be the bedrock of your career. Even today, 59 percent of Fortune 100 CEOs and 45 percent of FTSE100 CEOs have advanced degrees; indeed, only 4 percent of FTSE100 CEOs do not have a degree at all (in 1996 that figure was 37 percent).[60]

Getting experience at a good company at the start gives you a platform to allow you to take more risks and to move quickly later. Not only that, but in the future employers will expect you to move faster and get broader experience than people did in the past. Equally, those same employers will be open to you having done "unconventional" things. Historically in Europe, for example, a failed early-stage business was a CV stain. Increasingly, however, CEOs today see work in new ventures as the experience accelerator it really is.

As importantly, doing "adventurous" things is fun and, in fact, you will underperform against your potential maximum if you get too comfortable. James Bilefield remarks,

The key thing is to keep life fun and not to get bored

"Every time I've moved company, people have thought me mad. I've left successful positions with great prospects for riskier options because I get frustrated if things aren't moving fast. The key thing is to keep life fun and not to get bored. I've been lucky to be able to do that. Get out there and take risks."

Lord Browne agrees: "It's dangerous when a person or a company says that things are so good that they don't want to do anything or change anything; that's the time to check out and do it again." If you're still hesitating, remember a point on which Browne was emphatic: "The risk downside is lower than you think at any point in your life." In most decisions, you are probably over-estimating the personal career risk involved. Thras Moraitis also speaks from experience on this point. "Find a trend, get a foothold, raise capital, and take an expansive view; there's no issue if you blow out early," he says. "I had 13 ventures before Xstrata."

Remember that the financial sums you put at risk early on in your career are tiny compared to your likely earnings later, as Tony Davis learnt. "When I was leaving British Airways at 29 to go to the Middle East, I was really concerned about my pension," he says. "That's now a tiny sum of money for me."

Make your first job a fast stable

Your first job has to be in what Archie Norman calls "a fast stable". He believes that the great leadership brands, companies like Mars and Tesco and many professional services firms, give employees "fast experience. It will be tough at times, but will take you through the hoop. You want leaders to have come through a variety of different situations and been challenged, who have known fail-ure, who have felt the fire."

At the very outset of your career, your main priority has to be to learn the basic technical skills of business as quickly as possible and to find some of your personal limits. And joining a fast stable will probably keep your mum off your back and put money in your pocket.

Get broad experience as fast as possible

A fast stable will also set you up to broaden and collect business and personal leadership experiences and take on calculated risk even more quickly.

Having decided aged 19 that he wanted to run Ford, Keith Butler-Wheelhouse trained himself in all aspects of the business: "manufacturing, product development and engineering, finance and treasury, sales and marketing". He credits a measure of his success as a CEO to having a broad grounding in business.

Similarly, Paul Thompson says: "I was a young man in a hurry. I would not have had the patience to plot a career through a big organization. I wanted to get to the City and do deals and get that excitement and rub shoulders with CEO clients. I got a look at boardroom issues, what it's like to get into tight spots, and saw the sharp commercial end of delivering or not getting promoted or paid. But at 25, I was thinking about getting some grounding. I went to an accounting firm, because I thought, 'Let's get a bit of professional training.' I knew I would not stay five minutes after qualification." Stanley Cheung, managing director of Walt Disney China, has placed "a huge commitment to learn and a desire to lead" at the core of his career.

At both the fast stable and broadening stages, some experiences carry a premium. Arguably, with the high value on flexibility and growth that will be seen in the next 10 years, strategy consulting and global operations consulting firms will be an even stronger background than accounting. Like investment banks, consultancies can give you exposure to CEOs and some of their most important problems as well as broad cross-industry experience very quickly. Professional services firms also put you under pressure to perform from the get-go. You'll find your personal limits pretty quickly.

Mitch Garber agrees: "The professions are a great grounding: accounting firms, consultancies, and investment banks all give you business experience in deals, finance, and people, but also complex problem solving, presentation at board level, and also performing under pressure." It's the route Brent Hoberman took. "In my mind, I always knew I wanted to set up my own business," he says. "But I went into consulting first for a couple of years to give me an experience base. It also gave me the ability to simplify complex problems and build business models. If starting again, I would join a start-up or early-stage consultancy with a focus on business transformation to maximize the experience. In the future, it will also be key for a CEO to have a period in an entrepreneurial high-growth business; it helps you not be afraid to change if things are not working and also to take more commercial risk. There are also operational benefits such as the ability to

The professions are a great grounding

bring urgency and get things done by doing things in parallel rather than in series."

Equally, this is not to say that the great industrial brands like GE and Procter & Gamble will not continue to be training academies for world-beating CEOs. However, the trick will be to judge at what point in your career a move into one of the behemoths makes sense and what to jump out of them for. In a big business, joining – or starting – special projects that broaden you and give you a chance to learn about and profit from wider trends in your industry and the world is a smart way of driving both business growth and your own development.

As you move around, try to get experience of two to three industries, three to four functions within them, and of working under different capital structures, such as for private equity owners or a family office.

Australia Post CEO Ahmed Fahour provides a great example of a twenty-first-century career. An Arabic-speaking Lebanese, he was brought up in Australia and joined Boston Consulting Group there. Having made partner with BCG, he co-founded a private equity firm, iFormation, backed by Goldman Sachs and General Atlantic Partners. A few years later, he was headhunted to run corporate development for Citigroup before being made CEO of Global Alternative Investments in his 30s. After four years, and wanting to raise his family in Australia, Fahour returned there and joined National Australia Bank – where his father was once a cleaner – to help John Stewart with its turnaround. It is clear that the start in BCG's fast stable and a mix of private equity and large corporate experiences have rounded Ahmed out and helped in his fast progression.

Wherever you're working, stay close to the customer, where the money is made, and solve today's problems or build a growth engine for the future.

Go where the growth and future opportunities are going to be

From early on in your career, try to put yourself in some kind of historical context. As Tony Robbins reminds us: "Most people predict tomorrow looking at yesterday, but the great leaders recognize the cyclical nature of the world." You should also recognize the cycles that markets and the economy go through and position yourself to take advantage.

Take Richard Baker. "In my mind, it is clear you have to be in the right industry," he says. "I started as an engineer in the UK motor industry, but figured out that was not going to be a winning industry in the long term. Moving from industry to retail was a huge leap of faith for me, but I knew that there was a shift in power going on in the UK economy. So moving from Asda to Boots was a conscious move into healthcare. Today, the obvious move is into the emerging markets. Rising tides lift all boats; only go into a winning company or a winning sector – you can be as good as you like in a poor environment and it won't do you any good."

Growth industries mean disruption and innovation. As Michael Dell is keen to emphasize, this means that "learning to thrive in an era of constant change is a competitive advantage that every business leader has to embrace. Success comes down to listening – listen to the customer you want to serve and fully understand their needs. Then, and only then, can you offer products and services that are truly differentiated and valued by your customers."

Work globally

Philip Green advises: "You'll need to have a feel for the world in terms of the history and cultures of western countries, but also emerging markets and undiscovered countries, to be an effective global CEO in the future." Frank Brown, dean of Paris-based business school INSEAD, believes that future business executives should make a deliberate effort to become global by spending periods in foreign cultures. "It's about not going from the US or the UK to Australia for a six-month pub crawl," he says, "but going to Tokyo, Beijing, or São Paulo, really experiencing a different culture and trying to get by in a different language. It's about understanding that things there are much, much different. It's critically important that people get that experience early on so they are open to it later on."

Muhtar Kent, president and CEO, The Coca-Cola Company, "needs people who can move seamlessly across borders and cultures and who feel as comfortable working in Mumbai as they do in Atlanta; people who can speak the language of sophisticated modern trade. We're looking for people who are flexible enough to understand the pressures and local cultural nuances associated with being a sole proprietor of a small street-corner bodega or kiosk." Make your career global as early as possible.

Damian Reece agrees. "For UK leaders, one problem is that the FTSE is a bit like the premier league," he says. "It has attracted some of the top management talent from around the world and there is a danger that local talent get crowded out. Also, if you are pursuing a global career, better to be 'schooled' in international experiences earlier rather than later."

Ideally, work for a great leader

As we have seen from Part II, only a limited number of CEOs and senior executives today are true leaders for tomorrow. However, such leaders do exist – leaders who are brilliant at bringing on young talent. In the UK, two good examples are the late Sir John Harvey-Jones and Archie Norman. If you have the opportunity to work for a similar leader today, ideally as part of their fellowship as they transform an industry, then this experience is the best learning you can get. If you do get the chance, hang on tight!

Develop tomorrow's leadership habits

Alongside taking the concrete actions above, you'll be speeded through your apprenticeship if you develop the following habits.

Adopt the mindset of a CEO

Whatever your responsibilities and lack of seniority, you should always seek to adopt the mindset of a CEO. You can think of this at two levels. From the bottom up, assume the mindset of a CEO in your core work activities: deliver first, but take a broader view on how to help the wider business be more successful. From the top down, learn to assess the business from the point of view of the CEO: how is it faring against the elements of the cell described in Chapter 9? Are there gaps that you can develop new projects to fill? For example, if you think carbon footprints are important, is the business carbon neutral? If not, why not set up a task force to make it so?

Develop winning habits, but know how to lose
Many of the CEOs we interviewed had experienced serious failure or very difficult situations at work or in their life at some stage, and almost all of them believed that these were some of their most valuable experiences. In developing your career, never forget that, as Lord Browne puts it, "Everything adds to you: a book read, a business, traveling to somewhere that you fail. Experiences build character and you grow your intelligence, skill, and judgment." Another FTSE 100 CEO added: "It is better to fail early and badly and bank the learning rather than fail big and publicly later on when the stakes are high."

Indeed, when hiring senior executives Ron Havner and Archie Norman actively look for people who have faced really tough times. Havner says: "When I'm hiring I test whether the candidate has faced adversity and failure at work, like going into liquidation, or tough times at home, like a death in the family. Dealing with these troubles and bouncing back breeds inner belief and deep confidence."

Norman adds: "By the time it comes to 35, if it's all gone swimmingly and it's all pulled through and they have been mentored by the chief executive and been on programs, that's fine, but it's a bit of case unproven." When he hires people he wants to know: "What has been the moment that you have stared into the cavern? What did you have to do where you had to confront really difficult people, people you just didn't get along with or you didn't like? You had to work with them and they didn't perform, but how did you do that?" Failure can make you a much better leader.

Be a student of personal development
Try to pick up a coach and a mentor pretty early on. Hone your strengths and work on your weaknesses where you can. For example, is poor energy management what really holds you back? Vitally, integrate what you learn about yourself into your everyday life.

Have a life

Early in your career, you are balancing money with gaining top-drawer experience quickly. But you have to unpack the question of experience and measure it against the elements of tomorrow's leadership that we've discussed in this book: business leadership, personal leadership, and your own needs.

Take investment banking: this provides a fantastic grounding in finance (a critical technical skill), it gives you a good network, and it certainly means that you work in a fast stable. However, it is likely to give you an inadequate grounding in the softer side of personal leadership. Banking can also be grueling. For example, one CEO told us about his son's experience in investment banking. The son only took two days' holiday in two years and once fell asleep during a client board meeting. Shaken by how exhausted he had become, he decided to resign, even though he was highly regarded by the bank. When he revealed his decision, the incredulous boss offered him double and then four times his salary to stay. He still quit. The truth was that although he was becoming wealthy, he hadn't had time to find a partner or buy a house or have any life beyond work.

Many CEOs are like Mitch Garber and make a point of hiring people with life experience outside work. "It's important to have not just strategic and business leadership experiences but a broad enough experience of life," he says. "For me life experience has included my marriage, bringing up my kids, setting up a shop at 14, being a lawyer, being a professional skier, and my interests in food and travel. It is diverse experiences which allow me to talk to and relate to employees at all levels."

There's a lot more to life than work and money. If you can't manage your work–life balance in your 20s, you won't stand a chance later in life as personal and professional obligations become more significant.

Learn to celebrate your successes

The top executives we meet in our day jobs are typically single-minded in the pursuit of their objectives and are often quick to identify the next objective as soon as they have achieved a goal.

Clearly, this ability to prioritize and deliver is a strength to develop early in one's career. Equally, however, Tony Robbins stresses that great leaders also take the time to celebrate their successes, because "if you do not celebrate your successes, then your quality of life will be poor. Don't be superstitious – if you celebrate, you will actually achieve more in life."

Show total commitment, but ruthlessly change role if you're not stretched
Sir Bill Gammell, CEO of Cairn Energy, has a philosophy called "go or grow". "If any part of the business is less than 10 percent of the value, it has got to go unless I can see it growing," he says. "I am always looking to see if I can double our value every three years." A similar mentality will serve you well in developing your career.

A number of CEOs said that it was vital to absorb everything you can from every role before moving on; do not only excel in your job, but observe how the business you're in works and what's going on around you. You must balance your ambition and goals with 1,000 percent commitment to the role in hand and an absolute determination to achieve the goals you set yourself. Variety of experience is no excuse for throwing in the towel. Alexey Mordashov, chief executive of Russian steel company Severstal, says: "Always you'll come up against reality. Then you need to come around again. However, weak people too easily say, 'You can do nothing about this.'" Move on without regret only when you've sucked the experience dry.

Above all, be true to yourself
The biggest risk is to lose sight of your career mission so that you don't fulfill your potential or – worse – you are not true to yourself at work. This can be a lasting disappointment at the end of your life.

Bill Amelio tries always to stay true to his roots. "Having spent the first 21 years of my life in Pittsburgh, I like to think I now have a 'True Grit' spirit. With our blue-collar, no-nonsense style, Pittsburghers are tough-minded people who talk straight and are driven. I am proud of my formative years, and I would encourage CEOs in training to leverage the values and ethics of their individual upbringings to ground themselves. While their professional development may never end, it's their respective early years that will never change. These roots must always be valued and respected.

"Many memories still flood my mind when I visit my dad's shoe-repair shop in Pittsburgh. At 'the shop', as we affectionately call it, he taught me the importance of customer service, quality, and a strong work ethic. Additionally, I watched and learnt as he dealt with a wide variety of customers and customer problems. It's these roots that form the core of the person I am today and, like any effective leader, I'll always try to be true to this core."

Ben Verwaayen highlights the importance of the self-knowledge he sees in his senior teams at BT. "If you look to our top teams, I like to think you'll find much more authentic, different individuals whose personal choices they articulate, that they can put words around, and know why they do things, and therefore they are better in the role that they play," he says. "Authenticity is only possible with confidence because the temptation to be a conformist is enormous." You may feel that your beliefs and values are fully formed on leaving school or university, but you will find that they mature and are reshaped as you experience the world.

In short, be yourself. When push comes to shove, you have to make all your big decisions with your heart; you can't lead if you're acting.

If you follow the advice from our CEOs, you'll be well equipped for the next phase of your career, becoming a leader for tomorrow.

BECOME A LEADER FOR TOMORROW

Having laid the basic foundations, you will naturally start to take on bigger and bigger business responsibilities and greater leadership challenges. As you do so, bear in mind the key experiences that CEOs told us are needed to prepare you to be the CEO of a global company. Heed the advice from Gigi Levy, CEO of online casino 888: "In mid-career, the trick is to look for quantum leaps in experience, not just in middle to top management but also in technical domains, different industries in small to big business, and in public or private equity settings."

There's no doubt that successfully taking responsibility for driving performance and operations in a number of significant profit-and-loss accounts is critical experience for becoming CEO of a major business. Direct accountability for business units fundamental to winning today and in the future, such as a major country like the US or China or a key region like Asia, will be invaluable experience for later. Likewise, successfully taking responsibility for key elements of the company's growth agenda – ideally a mix of acquisitions, partnerships, new ventures, and key game-changing or future-proofing projects – will give you an understanding of how to drive super-growth in the future. As the world becomes more multipolar and business comes to interact with wider constituencies than previously, make sure you've had the opportunity to interface directly with a range of stakeholders such as shareholders, regulatory bodies and politicians, lobbyists, and pressure groups. You also need to be on top of the talent agenda. Clearly, you have not only to take responsibility but also to excel and ensure that your success is sustainable when you move on.

Ideally, in getting these experiences you will find yourself increasingly involved in your business's CEO fellowship and build a role in that fellowship that plays directly to your unique strengths and what you enjoy.

Interestingly, as they collected ever more valuable experiences through this period of blossoming in their career, most CEOs we interviewed found that their world view shifted and became much broader. This prompted many to reflect more deeply than they had previously on their motivations:

❏ Can I be the CEO?
❏ Do I really want to be the CEO?
❏ Should I be here or somewhere else?

The iterative process of action and reflection helped them develop a better sense of what situations and companies they would thrive in if they were to become a CEO.

Reality check
─────────────

Eric Daniels advises: "By your 30s, you need to be managing some considerable part of a firm with people and a profit-and-loss account. This is when you distinguish yourself or don't; it's when you go up or sideways." Many CEOs agreed that the critical part of their career came between about 35 and 45. Lord Browne says that he found that his understanding of the world and his career underwent a massive acceleration from about 40. Likewise, Richard Baker has for a long time believed that "if you're not in the big job by 40 you are gone; a few people make it there before 40 but very few make it there after 40 – there's then a younger generation coming through. I applied for the Boots job in part because I was 40 and thought I had to act."

Indeed, research by Heidrick & Struggles has shown that the average age of FTSE100 CEOs is dropping, so it may be that in the coming years the critical point will be earlier than 40.[61] The inescapable conclusion is that by your mid-30s you need to be actively focused on whether or not you are going to step up to the CEO job and what you need to do to get there. You have to take a mid-career reality check.

You should weigh up the strength of your current position and prospects against leaping into a new role and the risk of that not working out. Assuming that you are on track within your current business, internally you will have a track record of achievements and successes, you will have career momentum in terms of promotions and increased responsibility, you will be senior and ideally in the CEO's fellowship, and you will have some sense of the likelihood of future progression and whether you are on path to becoming CEO. You will also have some degree of lock-in, either financial or emotional, in terms of invested effort and loyalty to people and the company mission. You have to balance these known quantities against new opportunities and their relative attractiveness in terms of scale of responsibilities, degree of promotion compared to your current role, company reputation and the prestige of the new role, your ability to make a huge success of the new venture, the level of remuneration, and the opportunity cost of closing out as yet unavailable moves. These are tricky decisions – not to mention the personal assessment of what is right for your family.

However, if your ambition is to be a great global leader, it is more complicated still. You have to ask whether your current business, and those you are trading it off against, constitute your final target, your Mount Everest, or whether you are actually looking at a Mount Kilimanjaro that will help you further build your capabilities ready for the final assault on Everest. The assets differ but include:

❏ Relevant business and personal leadership skills and experiences that you've been building up over time.
❏ Your responsibilities.
❏ Your reputation in the market.
❏ Your personal network and access to key industry forums and influential opinion formers.

Many CEOs emphasized two further points. First, you should always move if you stop believing in the value and culture of the business you're in, even it's prospering and you're doing well. Second, in most cases, if you're unsure whether to stay it's usually better to move.

You'll probably feel like you're standing on a Snakes and Ladders board looking for the long ladders of momentum and personal asset accumulation, and squinting to see whether the opportunity you jump on is going to turn out to have been a treacherous snake that will set you back. But in a sense, that's the essence of being a CEO. Taking a new leadership role is always a leap of faith. As Paul Thompson says: "The challenge of the CEO is stretching out. If you don't, no one else is going to."

In reality, you should never feel 100 percent confident that you know you can do the next job. If you do, you're not stretching yourself and learning. The risk is always lower than you think at any point in your life.

STEPPING DOWN FROM THE BIG JOB DOESN'T MEAN RETIREMENT!

Retiring as CEO need no longer signal the end of your career. Many retired CEOs we talked to felt like Brent Hoberman: "After you have succeeded in growing a successful business early in your career, then I have found that you move toward trying to find a balance between family/kids time, potentially wanting to invest, and also wanting to share experience and mentor others in a chairman role." Such former CEOs are finding that there are many ways to take a leadership role.

In the past decade, most CEOs have tended to move into a plural career of nonexecutive positions as a way of continuing in business and sharing the benefit of their experience and wisdom. They have then in time replaced their nonexecutive roles with lead director or chairman roles, once they have become experienced nonexecutives. However, off the record many ex-CEOs, while enjoying having more free time, find nonexecutive roles unrewarding from a business point of view (not least because most consider nonexecutive boards to be too heavily focused on corporate governance and not sufficiently value adding or commercial).

In the next decade, CEOs expect stepping back from an executive career to be a more gradual process. Some will move into chairperson roles at their own businesses while remaining hands-on in their approach. You see this already in particular among entrepreneurs: Sir Stelios Haji-Ioannou of easyGroup and Sir Richard Branson at Virgin Group are active chairmen. There are, of course, questions of ensuring good corporate governance by balancing a strong chairperson with strong senior independent directors. Equally clearly, there must be closely defined responsibilities between the new CEO and the heavily involved chairperson to allow a new partnership to develop. Other CEOs will combine chairmanships with pursuing their personal passions in not-for-profit activities or business activist forums such as the World Economic Forum.

If a business has been a roaring success, huge care has to be taken that the loss of a star CEO from the fellowship does not wound the company. As several CEOs and chairmen emphasized to us, imagination has to be used to make sure that momentum is passed to the next generation and continuity of leadership is assured.

The best twenty-first-century leaders will learn from the small group of twentieth-century CEOs who saw themselves as CEOs second and leaders first. They viewed their role as giving back by bringing on the next generation of CEOs; that mission did not finish with the end of their CEO job. Sir John Harvey-Jones was a great example. He had an impact on a large number of organizations after his executive career and mentored a number of today's top leaders.

Never lose sight of the starting point

So even toward the end of your career, don't forget that you set out on an apprenticeship to become a global leader and achieve your mission. You wanted an adventure on the rollercoaster and you wanted to learn how to change the world. Hopefully, you will have. However, as Lord Browne states, "You are always learning. At the age of 55, for example, you could start to learn from people at the start of their lives who have a different mindset and watch the changing values and the changing incentives." Every day of your life is about training.

You need to be able to look back at what you've done and feel both that you've achieved something and that you've had some magic moments through your work. So stay fresh and make room for all those non-work-related ambitions you harbor. Learn to take advantage of the calmer spells in your career so that you're not constantly being hard on yourself, as well as determinedly seizing the key opportunities to grow. You do need to ride the waves of career momentum when they come, but equally you must welcome the lulls as periods to reflect and refresh. Take these opportunities to step back and commit time to family and friends and your wider interests.

As Apple CEO Steve Jobs says: "We don't get a chance to do that many things, and every one should be really excellent. Because this is our life. Life is brief, and then you die, you know? … We've all chosen to do this with our lives. So it'd better be damn good."[62]

11
HEEDING THE CEO HEALTH WARNING

"Leaders need a deep sense of self and how they feel about the world. The very best leaders first start with a sense of being."

Lord Browne, former CEO, BP

"I can't remember the first two boys growing up when I was with my first wife." FTSE100 CEO

"You don't know how fast you're going until you hit the wall."

Narain Karthikeyan, India's first F1 driver

The fantasy comedy *Click* carries an important warning for every global CEO. Adam Sandler plays a loving family man with the modest aspiration of becoming a partner in the firm of architects he works for so that he can spend more time with his picture-perfect wife and children, and their dog. One night, he gets frustrated with his television remote control and decides to get a universal control for all his gadgetry. In the event, he accidentally comes home from the shops with a control for reality that allows him to fast forward through his own life and see how it turns out.

The experience is not pleasant. Sure enough, he gets promoted, but the film charts the future life to which his workaholism is leading. His marriage breaks down and his wife remarries, his weight balloons then shrinks under unpleasant liposuction, his children act in ways he does not approve of at all, he is diagnosed with cancer, is distracted by work in what turns out to be his last conversation with his father, and, eventually, dies of a heart attack.

As Sandler lies dying, he despairs of the choices he's made through his life. Then, with a flash, he wakes to find he's been whisked back from death to the evening he started playing with the universal remote control, and has the opportunity to prevent the future unwinding in the way he's seen. Elated, he leaps into action, rushing to show his affection for his father and his family.

None of us has a time-accelerating remote control, so we cannot be certain how our own life will turn out. However, there is no doubt that CEOs run all the risks parodied in *Click*. For example, one FTSE100 CEO confided to us: "I have been married twice and have four kids and one grandchild. I can't remember the first two boys growing up when I was with my first wife. We separated when they were 8 and 9. I can't remember them when they were young." Another equally senior CEO admitted ruefully: "I didn't see my son grow up; we're only now building a relationship in his late teens."

In fact, not only do the demands of the role often rob CEOs of life's pleasures, they even strip the role of some of the allure that had them chasing the promotion in the first place. As Archie Norman relates: "If you ask chief executives, there is a peculiar phenomenon that very few of them say, 'I have a terrific time, I love doing this.' They're all thinking, 'Oh, another couple of years and then, you know, maybe I'll take a few chairmanships.'"

With workers in developing economies pushing to build a comfortable life for themselves, western concerns about work–life balance might seem to be relics of a past age. Nevertheless, the CEO role can get on top of you, damage your body, mind, and spirit, and ruin your personal relationships, so you owe it to yourself to heed the CEO health warning. Why wait for your deathbed to wish you'd done the right thing? Surely you want to have a satisfying family and personal life? CEOs and their closest advisers tell us that there are three things you need to do to achieve just that:

❑ Drive your agenda, don't let the business drive you.
❑ Build an active support network.
❑ Ensure you are always at your best.

DRIVING YOUR AGENDA

The happiest CEOs we've met are those who have managed either to build strong boundaries between their work and home lives, so that home refreshes them for work and work does not impinge on home; or those who have fully integrated their work and their personal lives and do not see a massive tension between the two.

Steven Crawshaw, former chief executive of bank Bradford & Bingley, falls into the first camp. "I'm firmly of the view that it's possible to have a work–life balance but you need to draw some very clear line," he says. "I have a *cordon sanitaire* between work and home. I don't need my wife to make my business decisions." In the latter camp, Ian Coull's wife has given up a high-powered career to travel around with him while he is CEO of Segro. Paul Thompson is of a similar persuasion, thinking that "fixing firm boundaries is too structured and naive. Life has to be much more interlinked, but you have to be very disciplined about how you manage yourself." While both approaches seem to work, both require tremendous personal discipline.

We know this is hard. There are times when business takes over everything. We've all been there: "We have to close this round of funding next week or we close the business", "I have to do this investor roadshow in Shanghai over our wedding anniversary", and so on. Even when there is no abnormal event, the fact is that when you're looking after a whole company – perhaps hundreds of thousands of people – there's always something that might go wrong or a project that could be improved. Modern technology, far from being a useful tool, can seem to create a treadmill of urgent priorities with no end in sight. Tony Davis knows the feeling only too well: "The train seems to be going faster and faster, and every now and then you need to apply the brakes so that it does not become a runaway train."

But hold on, you're the CEO. You control the agenda. Paul Walker, CEO of Sage, says that you can run a wildly successful company and be in control of all other aspects of your life: "It is possible to organize life in such a way that you can balance private life and business. If you work hard and have the right people around you, you can make it work. If you delegate, put in controls, you can have a good home life."

Make time work for you as well as the business

Sir John Parker is insistent that you are paid to be smart, not tired, so keeping mentally fresh and alert is part of your job. For him, managing your personal life is part of being a complete CEO. "It is totally possible to have a balance and in fact it's essential," he says. "It's totally easy to become stale when you don't have time to sit with family and friends. Treadmills do not make for good leaders and managers; stressed people do not get the best results. What's work–life balance about? It's about managing your time. My father used to say to me that if you cannot manage your time you cannot manage anything. You need to ask yourself: 'What am I doing two weeks from today?'"

Create protected time every week

Harriet Green warns against losing the initiative on a daily basis. She argues that one should not "be too responsive. I've taken to walking to the train from home. It takes 35 minutes, but gives me time when I'm not on the Blackberry and I can think, really think. You must not let the technology control you." Richard Baker says that at Alliance Boots he always managed every week so that he had a thinking day to reflect on events and gain perspective. At New Oriental group, chairman Yu Minhong divides his time into "three equal parts. One third is family time (time with my wife, my kids and on my own). You do need personal time to cool down or else you do not have time for philosophical matters. The second third is spent in our field offices around China. And the final third's at head office."

Know what can refresh you daily

Keith Butler-Wheelhouse refreshed himself while CEO through routines based on exercise and domesticity. "I go to the gym and play tennis frequently," he says. "I'm also a fixer. One of the kids kicked in the swimming pool light over the weekend. I pulled the part out, stripped it down, found the faulty part, and my driver's purchasing it now. I'll spend 20 minutes installing the replacement tonight. It matters to me that I can still do ordinary things – that's important."

Set simple rules that impose structure on your life

Cris Conde thinks that the answer to balance is having bright-line rules. "Twenty years ago, I set two very simple rules for myself: I do not take or make calls in the evening and I take my vacation," he says. "These rules clear time to think and be with my family, and they are all I need. I advise everyone to come up with rules that work for them and apply them carefully."

Be as serious about time "off" as time "on"

At times of peak stress, most of us assure ourselves that we will take time off to destress completely. However, for most people the dips in activity are rarely as deep as the peaks. How many of us are guilty of being chained to the Blackberry by the holiday pool? Therefore, a critical piece of advice from CEOs is to make sure you do take time to let your internal spring uncoil completely.

For Richard Baker: "The most important thing is my family and friends; I take every holiday day I'm entitled to." Brad Mills is even more extreme and has developed a technique of complete isolation. "As for me, I go for two weeks each year of hardcore fishing," he explains. "I leave my wife and kids and don't take anyone with me. You need to recharge your spirituality and you cannot do that easily in an urban environment or working situation. When you are sitting in a stream, and your cellphone doesn't work, and there's absolutely no way that anyone can contact you, your mind roams around for the first few days. Then you get on with it. Fishing is meditation for me."

Know your source

Philip Green marries the physical, the spiritual, and business in how he seeks satisfaction, which boils down to "the 5Fs – Faith, Family, Fitness, Fun, and the Firm where I work. My Christian faith is at the core of who I am and the first three are the bedrock for my own performance and allow me to be at my best in my role." He is one of a small but increasing group of CEOs who are explicit about how their faith underpins their leadership. There are also a growing number of CEOs who draw on spiritual values in leading their businesses – especially in the emerging markets.

BUILDING AN ACTIVE SUPPORT NETWORK

Leadership is lonely. More than half the CEOs we surveyed say so. And most of the rest admit that they would be lonely if they hadn't taken deliberate action to build the support networks they need. Many CEOs draw on a tailored support network in their professional and personal lives.

CEOs do also need to be able to get a perspective on themselves, their colleagues, and the performance of the fellowship as a whole. They draw on three principal elements: their chairperson, external coaches, and their family and friends. Finding the right blend of support – chairman, coaches, mentors, family, and friends – depends on your preferences and needs, but top CEOs were insistent that building and maintaining the right support network is essential and takes careful thought and the investment of quality time.

The chair as sounding board

Unfortunately, in many cases a key role of the chairperson is to sack the CEO if he or she is not performing. Worse, in many cases that's also the chairperson's default position when bad news hits – they are often very concerned to protect their own reputation and personal brand. This is equally often a significant mistake.

However, good chairpeople see themselves as absorbing some of the flack for the CEO.

Certainly, that's the view of BAA chairman Sir Nigel Rudd. "As chair, I see my role as a lightning conductor to take some of the heat when it gets a bit stormy," he says. Paul Adams says that he is fortunate to be able to use his chairman as a sounding board. "If I wanted to chew something over I would go and talk to the chairman because that's his job," he explains. "If his job is not to help the CEO then you've got the wrong CEO, in my view. I tend to go and see him when I'm ruminating on something. He says 'Oh yes' and he listens while I talk. By the time I have finished talking I have come up with the answer. I say 'Thank you very much' and the chairman says 'I haven't done anything'. That's the job of a good chairman." There's no doubt that chairpeople like that can really empower their CEOs.

A coach for gaining perspective

Richard Baker says: "It is extraordinary to think you can be excellent at something without a coach. The notion that Roger Federer would not have several coaches is ridiculous. One of the best things that happened to me was to get a coach. I think it's been massively helpful. When the waves were breaking over me, I got a coach. Within 10 minutes, he'd correctly identified the one thing I needed to do. As a CEO, the idea you can do it on your own is extraordinarily arrogant. I think the coaching industry is a whole industry that has yet to be born; it needs to be developed."

About 40 percent of FTSE100 CEOs have used coaches and an even higher proportion advise their top team to use one.[63] Executive coaches are just like sports coaches: they help you with your technique. As Alan Watkins observes, they typically fall into one of two camps: "The first type, which includes the majority of coaches working with CEOs, operate tactically. They help the CEO consider the tasks he is engaged in and his behavior on key issues. Then there is the second type, a much smaller group of coaches who work more fundamentally and are focused on helping the CEO become a better leader. Their conversations are focused on equipping the leader to lead, inspire, and cope much more effectively with whatever tasks he is facing. The first type of coach focuses on 'doing', the second on 'being'. In reality, the first type is a management coach, the second is a leadership coach." Both are useful depending on the situation you find yourself in.

At Standard Chartered, Lord Davies used a management coach. He recalls: "I got someone who catalogued how I spent my time and went through my diaries and measured my progress on a 360-degree basis. It was brutal, but I am a great believer in courageous conversation. I don't think I agreed with him; I was allowed to argue." Equally, one FTSE100 CEO says of his adviser: "If I called her a coach she would be furious. She's one of the smartest people I've ever met. We talk about leadership. She always comes up with three or four questions and I come away with an action list."

Paul Thompson also values the independent view, counseling, and energy recharge that his coach provides him with, but he is clear that he does not discuss every issue he faces. "It's a lonely job. There's no way you can please all the people all the time and there's no way you can be everyone's friend," he explains. "You have this difficulty of being able to relate to people and like people and still use people well. Everyone wants to be liked, but you have to be able to put all your energy into other people and then you need to get your personal energy from somewhere else. It's quite challenging. My coach has given me the personal energy and maturity to deal with things. It gives me more inner strength and helps me to cope with having to give lots to other people and often getting nothing back, because that's what it's about. But I do not need to talk to someone about all the issues. You need to be able to make decisions yourself."

Many CEOs also have mentors. They tell us that they benefit from having someone experienced outside the business who has their success as the sole objective, and so can provide both robust counsel and a sympathetic ear. Ideally, a mentor has been through the type of role you are currently in, so can truly relate to the pressures and advise you from real personal experience. Ruby McGregor-Smith, CEO of support services business MITIE, says: "As you get more senior in your career, you need someone outside your business who can give you cold clarity of thought. Close colleagues and friends and family cannot give this. And you especially need help at times of change in your career (such as having a family). This is something I wish I'd had."

Indeed, one former CEO of a major financial company took this approach to its logical extreme. "In my later days as sales director, I knew the CEO was going to move on at some stage and I wanted to work out whether I really wanted to be a CEO," he says. "I worked out the pluses and minuses and got my head around it. At the time I thought I had only a 20 percent chance of getting the job, so I went to see a coach and asked him what I needed to do to get that up to a 50 percent chance within a year. Some of the coaches I went to see could not understand this at all, but I found one who really helped me with it.

"Six weeks afterwards, I was appointed as CEO. The board was braver than I thought it would be and the coach was fantastic. It was a question of getting the right discipline. The coach I saw was an ex-CEO who had been through some really bad times as well as some good times. He helped me get it clear in my head and I now encourage my people to go through a similar exercise."

Above all, coaches and mentors are not there to take ultimate responsibility – that's the role of the CEO. So in choosing a coach, it is important to be clear why; it may be that you need a mirror held up to you, or counseling support on a particular technical aspect of your role or leadership. You also need to be very disciplined and discerning about the coach you choose for the task identified. Finally, CEOs agree that you must not rely too much on one coach and, above all, not become dependent.

Family and friends to keep you grounded

There has to be more to your life than your job. Having a happy family is good in itself. However, if you need a cold business reason to justify creating room for a family life, the truth is that spending time with family can get you back to the business refreshed and refocused.

It's very simple for Terry Duddy, CEO of Home Retail Group, owner of UK household names Argos and Homebase. "My support network is my wife, because she's in charge of all the things that are really, really important," he says. "I don't lie in bed worrying about what's going to happen tomorrow. My business is on my mind all day, but the next business day does not arrive until 5 a.m. the next day."

Recognizing the potential conflict between work and home, some CEOs have found ways to integrate their families completely into their professional lives so that the apparent tension dissolves. Gareth Davis says: "I talk a lot to my wife about the business but we only see each other at weekends. Weekends are quite precious and we talk a lot about work. She loves to talk about it."

You need to show your colleagues that you have more to your life than your work, otherwise you look like a deal-junkie or a megalomaniac. Remember that they are probably not going to gain so heavily in personal terms from whatever deal or growth you are currently working on. You must nurture your family relationships for another reason, too: if your long-term happiness becomes entirely bound up in your job, you'll find it very hard to recover at the end of your career.

CEOs told us that there are three tricks that most miss. The first is that the intensity of the effort made during a big push has to be matched by the intensity of the effort after that push; effective recuperation is vital. But, as Alan Watkins states, recuperation is not just a case of putting your feet up: "The antidote to exhaustion is not rest but doing something that makes your heart sing."

The second, and more important, trick is that top CEOs don't compromise on significant personal moments such as births, deaths, and critical childhood successes, which are nonnegotiable – the business has to wait. Your family will judge you on these and your performance will be the foundation of your long-term relationship with family and friends.

Finally, one very successful CEO told us: "However tense it gets, you have to demonstrate to others that it is not your life. It might be the little things – like a text to the kids at the height of the deal. My wife is hugely sympathetic during the tough events, the all-nighters on a deal, and so forth. She understands that I can't run the kids to school at those times. But I need to demonstrate that I keep some time for them still – something to keep the family together and protect me. For example, it might be a call to them while they're on the school run."

Ultimately, as another former FTSE100 CEO observed: "At the end of the day, you have to play like the job's as important as life and death but recognize that it is not life and death, because when it goes wrong (as it sometimes will) you need the safety valve. You also need other things in your life because if you don't, you will not be detached in your thinking, and you have to be detached." Mitch Garber agrees that perspective is vital in good decisions, as well as essential to keeping a balance: "When you are faced with big and difficult life experiences, you must take a deep breath and realize that business experiences are seldom the end of the world. This also allows you to step back and make better decisions."

BEING AT YOUR BEST

Most CEOs have confidence in their business abilities and belief in their own leadership or they would not take on the job. However, most of our interviewees told us that they find it difficult to be at their best day in and day out, while at the same time concluding that the role will become increasingly global and correspondingly harder in the next 10 years. Given this, as we have said we expect that a majority of CEOs will use one or more coaches within a few years.

In addition, in recent years there have been a number of break-throughs in our understanding of the human system, which have significant implications for our ability to improve the performance of global business leaders. These advances have mostly been made in the fields of psychology, neuroscience, peak performance, and neuro-linguistic programming, and by trainers drawn from a range of disciplines working with elite sportspeople. Many of the latest advances have already started to be used to accelerate sporting per-formance, but have yet to be applied widely within the corporate world.

From our interviews, it was clear that there are a number of dif-ferent challenges with which CEOs are grappling and which stop most from being at their best. These issues typically concern energy management, achieving mental clarity, and maintaining emotional stability. However, some CEOs even find themselves questioning their sense of self. The diagram below breaks these challenges down into the four fundamental aspects of peak performance and gives an indication of the most relevant fields of human development that can help CEOs to maximize their performance.

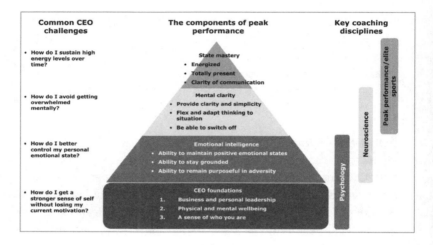

CEO foundations: Do you know who you are?

The truth is that, in Lord Browne's words: "Leaders need to understand themselves and the world around them. This takes time, success, and failures to develop. You need to become more free of your own prejudices so as to listen to others, to reflect, to pick and choose people. With that understanding, you can trust and then you can really achieve." As Mike Roney says: "You have to have strong emotional security. You have to believe in yourself and be able to continue to drive the business without instant feedback." Another senior CEO states: "The most important thing CEOs are paid for is judgment. You have to be centered to do that. It is vital to do personal development so you can be centered in all situations and be more consistent."

To lead effectively, you need to know what you believe in and what you are here to achieve. States Tony Robbins: "When you find a top performer in any field, including CEOs, part of what makes every one of them great is that they are clear on who they are – their true nature. If a person does not have a personal sense of meaning in their life, they will not succeed. No matter how cerebral they are, unless they have a clear mission and outcome, they cannot fulfill themselves." This foundation of self-knowledge is essential to maintaining the drive and focus to win professionally and personally through the ups and downs of a career and life. Unfortunately, as executive coach Peter Hogarth acknowledges, "Few chief executives have done an analysis of what drives them and what success looks like to them."

> If a person does not have a personal sense of meaning in their life, they will not succeed

Ido van der Heijden, a corporate psychologist with 30 years' experience of working with top executives, agrees. "Chief executives face a dilemma: when you climb to that level, you do so at a cost," he says. "To get there, you need to be psychologically well defended, be very ambitious, and may have a pretty big ego. In being top dog, you risk losing some of your human freedom. This lack of freedom can limit and stifle personal development and can lead to uninspired leadership. The challenge is to continually define your sense of meaning and purpose, which is very hard if you are disconnected from the deeper aspects of yourself."

One of the most effective ways of deepening your sense of self is to frame and reframe key life experiences with an expert, drawing on the latest developments in psychology. Doing this helps you recognize crucibles in your personal and professional life when you go through them and actively learn from the experience, and it enables you to formalize your motives and objectives at any point in your life.

This is easier said than done. Van der Heijden observes that frequently people have become very senior because of a powerful psychological circumstance, such as poverty in childhood or a sense of duty to parents who sacrificed a lot to get them their start in life. "Often people are not aware of what drives them. They need someone to encourage them to turn over untouched stones and examine what's underneath them," he says. "I find that often people come to look for this self-examination between 35 and 45. This is the stage in their lives when typically wives and children start to complain that they are not providing the intimacy desired.

"These executives need to rebalance their lives. They come to me fearing they will lose their drive, but in fact they learn that their identity can be far broader than their position of power. We all have programs running in the background and unless one is aware of them one cannot control their effects. To understand them requires an exercise of digging through history, the good bits as well as the more painful experiences. The very qualities that helped you to get to the top may also be the ones that can cause a divorce. To integrate your history gives you more freedom in being able to express yourself in different ways. It can give you the emotional courage needed to lead and inspire."

The very qualities that helped you to get to the top may also be the ones that can cause a divorce

Unfortunately, many chief executives seem resistant to embracing such an approach. Van der Heijden says: "Although a lot of senior executives and teams approach me to work with them, it's rare that a chief executive is willing to submit to the same treatment. My clients may work with me just before the big promotion, then have me work with their team, but, once promoted, sitting CEOs very rarely submit. It's a real challenge for CEOs to realize that emotional courage, self-awareness, and the willingness to examine yourself are qualities that can make the difference between effective and inspired leadership."

If you're not ready to work with someone else to delve into your motivation, try a little reflection on your own. As Deepak Chopra says: "The seeds of your essence are in your heroes; your qualities are in your true friends, sustaining relationships and unique talents." Put on some music that moves you and make a list of your closest friends, magic and tragic moments in life and your career, your mentors and role models and your heroes (from whatever source, be it real life, films, or elsewhere), and push yourself to figure out what it is that you're trying to move toward. Stuck? It might be worth getting a friend or expert confidant to help you think it through.

Do you have high emotional intelligence?

Generally, CEOs assume that there is a certain base level of IQ among all corporate leaders. Most therefore value EQ over IQ as a way of discriminating between great leaders. However, CEOs – albeit with a few notable exceptions – do not have a deep understanding of emotional intelligence and have not invested in developing their own EQ beyond their experience of dealing with the business situations they have encountered.

The human body can experience a vast array of emotions. Daniel Goleman, author of *Destructive Emotions* written in conjunction with the Dalai Lama, documents an estimate by Tibetan Buddhists that they can attain 34,000 distinct emotional states. To put that in context, research undertaken by Cardiac Coherence on CEOs indicates rather worryingly that an average CEO will manage fewer than 15 of these states in a typical 24-hour period.[64] It seems clear that there is much for CEOs to learn about emotions!

Research into this phenomenon and others by neuroscientists like Antonio Damasio[65] has shown that every decision is shaped by your emotions. The measurable and dramatic effect of emotions on decisions and performance means that great CEOs must develop more sophisticated emotional intelligence. They need to understand how their emotions affect their decision making, and their ability to influence and lead others is greatly improved if they can spot emotions in others, both individually and collectively.

The good news is that over the last ten years scientists have started to subject emotions to proper study and a few sophisticated coaches are now able to help leaders increase their awareness, manage their stress and anxiety better, and empathize with others so they can manage their own emotions more effectively.

Tony Robbins' research suggests that human emotional states are driven by positive values, which we move toward, and negative values, which we move away from. In his advanced coaching programs he gives participants the tools to elicit their own values, helps people to understand their subconscious rules, and – having understood them – to reprogram them to create the mental toolkit they need to move ahead as they desire. Bob Quintana, a former senior Robbins trainer and CEO coach, says, "Many top CEOs are driven by the desire for significance and the need to make a difference, but have very demanding rules which don't allow them easily to feel successful or fulfilled. One CEO I work with had subconscious rules that he would only feel successful if he had changed an industry and done something no one had thought possible with a team that's widely recognized in the business world. Not surprisingly, he didn't feel successful, despite having achieved things which most others would judge remarkable."

Developments such as these across science and peak performance coaching will in the coming years be increasingly helpful to CEOs seeking to boost their emotional intelligence.

Do you have sufficient mental clarity?

Many CEOs complain of being mentally overwhelmed for significant periods during their time in the role due to the relentless demands of switching focus continually throughout a day. One moment you're finishing a strategy session, the next minute taking a call requiring a decision on the basis of detailed data, then you're dealing with an unhappy customer straight after. In addition, you are at risk of being thrown a curve ball – the one question from an analyst you weren't expecting, for example. In these situations, it's all too common for the brain to almost shut down; if it does, you're sunk. Taking the analyst as an example, the biological source of the "mind going blank", as it does under pressure sometimes, is well understood and is called "cortical inhibition". The curve ball puts you into a chaotic mindset and effectively reduces mental clarity and creativity, as well as lessening the ability to solve problems and make effective decisions. As ever, your body and your mind are intimately linked.

In short, great CEOs need to have mental clarity on demand. Here again, recent developments have much to offer and there is strong scientific evidence to show that we can train ourselves to generate a coherent signal to the brain and therefore enhance clarity, creativity, and speed of thinking. For example, we're all told to take some deep breaths before a speech to calm and energize ourselves. The latest research shows that in fact there are 12 elements of breathing that can change your physiology, and that each of the 12 elements can be controlled and turned to use in calming and focusing you. Alan Watkins comments: "Many negative emotional states are associated with disordered breathing patterns. There is good evidence to show that rhythmic breathing may explain the health benefits of meditation and rosary prayer."

So how well do you think the majority of our current crop of CEOs do in keeping their brains fully activated today?

Can you sustain peak performance?

Just like being a top athlete, being a CEO requires that you are as close to your best as much of the time as possible. You have to be able to peak for the big points in a match, but also win a grand slam over a season. States Paul Thompson: "You have to be running at – say – 90 percent so that you can go to 120 percent when the big thing hits." So aside from mastering your emotions and clearing your mind, you need to figure out how to increase your energy levels when necessary – and how to relax and recharge when you have the opportunity. Building capacity requires that you push beyond your normal limits but then factor in time for recovery; many people fail to include this recovery time and so find it difficult to build greater capacity.

As we've seen, emotions have a huge impact on performance. Two of the key hormones that drive results are cortisol, the body's main stress hormone, and DHEA, the performance hormone. Cortisol tends to lead to negative emotional states, while DHEA can make you feel better. Alan Watkins has spent 15 years researching the impact on CEOs of these hormones and their associated emotions. Inadequate understanding of their emotional states causes most CEOs to underperform because they spend most of their days in an active catabolic state.

The optimal states for decision making are anabolic. Active anabolic states, such as passion, are critical to performance. In fact, passion is the number 1 predictor for all types of performance, including health.[66] This is the state the CEO would access before motivating an audience, such as at a new product launch. There are, however, times when a relaxed anabolic state will serve the CEO best, when he or she needs to be receptive, calm, and open to others, for example when making layoffs.

In contrast, many CEOs spend most of their time in catabolic states. The active catabolic state is that designed by nature for flight – it's what makes a CEO fluff the analyst's question, when the brain shuts down its higher functions to focus on the simple decision to run away from the modern equivalent of a tiger in the trees. A relaxed catabolic state is not much more use – it's designed for playing dead – and exhibits itself today as apathy, detachment, or inattentiveness.

It's all very well recognizing the state you're in, but the real key is to be able to *change* your state. This is well understood by elite performance coaches, especially in sprinting or contact sports, who have developed methods that allow athletes to move themselves from, for example, a relaxed catabolic state to an active anabolic one.

There is a body of compelling evidence that emotional mastery, mental clarity, and conscious state control can boost executive performance dramatically. At the moment a majority of coaching remains behavioral and situational. However, it is clear that it is only a matter of time before some of the breakthroughs in human performance touched on fleetingly above will be adopted by CEOs who are looking to be at their best and get a edge. This drive will also transform the executive coaching industry as we see it today. Tony Robbins comments: "When people get a taste of personal development, they understand what it feels like to have a sense of mission; a good personal coach can help leaders reinvigorate that insatiable hunger for success in them."

The expectations of personal performance from global CEOs have massively increased. Top CEOs need coaches or coaching teams who can help them always be at their best. The challenge for coaches, then, is not to be narrow specialists but to understand all levels of human performance and to be able to tailor each CEO's coaching intervention to his or specific needs – whatever they may be.

The acid test

Do you need to take action? We'd suggest a quick self-diagnosis:

❑ Are you realizing your career ambitions and enjoying work?
❑ Are you aware of how your emotions affect your decision making?
❑ Are you tuned into others' emotions?
❑ Do you always think clearly?
❑ Are you always able to put yourself into the best state to perform in any situation?
❑ Is your current lifestyle good for your health and wellbeing?
❑ Are you comfortable with the tradeoffs you've made between career, family, friends, and yourself?
❑ Are you truly happy and content with life today and your honest expectations for the future?

Conclusion

Being a CEO is one of the toughest jobs in the world. It requires exceptional levels of determination and resilience, as well as the ability to cope with stress and not let the role totally dominate your life. It's therefore not a healthy ambition for many successful businesspeople.

The best CEOs are passionate, enjoy the job, and recognize that they are privileged to lead. They are not only strong, with deep-rooted self-belief, but also build robust personal and business support networks, supplemented by coaches and mentors as required. The coaching industry is now beginning to step up and provide the expertise on human performance that is required to complement traditional business coaching.

With a great fellowship and the support to ensure that you're performing at your best, this really is the best job in the world!

EPILOGUE:
WHY NOT YOU?

A s a kid, did you dream about how you would change the world? Some of the best global CEOs believe that this will be the decade when you really can. The world has opened up to global markets on a scale not seen for several hundred years and, at the same time, the internet is connecting us all together. In parallel, the reset has focused us all on how corporates need to play a bigger and more responsible role in society.

We do have a small number of fantastic leaders who are heading a new generation of great businesses, which have developed more fluid and innovative cell-like organizations and are bonded together not by one person but by a close fellowship. Many of these businesses have featured in this book and form the start of a new breed of champions which are loved by shareholders, have fanatically loyal customers, are magnets for the top 1 percent of global talent, and are sustainable. In addition, the success of these companies will mean that they go further and start to address the broader social imbalances in society in an innovative way.

However, as we speak these twenty-first-century global leaders are vastly outnumbered; the majority of corporates, especially in the western world, are managed in a twentieth-century fashion. These companies contain legions of trapped people with unfulfilled ambitions and untapped talents. Millions of people only work to live.

Alongside these developments, Generation Y and behind them the so-called dream generation are growing up with fresh aspirations for themselves and the world and striving for a better life than their parents had. These generations will have the mindset and skills to be a vital part of reinvigorating corporates – or they could turn their back on the business world entirely if companies don't change fast.

So, whether you're reading this book in the hurly-burly of Mumbai, listening to a podcast in the Yellow Mountains in China, or accessing us in Second Life from a coffee bar in downtown Detroit, we hope that this book has stirred you to ask yourself: "Why can't I be a CEO?" If you're an existing CEO, we'd like to think we may have encouraged you to set a new standard of leadership for yourself.

Being a CEO carries a serious health warning, but it's not mission impossible. Imagine working with your fellowship to energize everyone in your company to change your markets and customers' lives around the world. What sort of legacy would that leave for you, your family, your company, and the world? Imagine what your leaving party would be like!

Connect with Steve at www.xinfu.com and with Andrew at andrew.cave@telegraph.co.uk and let us know how you get on.

NOTES

1   Business and Social Responsibility Conference, New York, 6 November 2009.
2   Democratic Caucus Retreat, Williamsburg, Virginia, 6 February 2009.
3   Confederation of British Industry Conference, Birmingham, UK, 23 November 2009.
4   "The new (recovery) playbook. Jeff Immelt, Andrea Jung, and other CEOs are ditching the waiting game and writing their own rules for a rebound", Ram Charan, CNNmoney.com, 13 August 2009.
5   "WPP's Sir Martin Sorrell bets on a LUV-shaped recovery as sales decline slows", *Daily Telegraph*, 30 October 2009.
6   "Google's Eric Schmidt on why bankers deserve little sympathy and Obama does", *Daily Telegraph*, 9 January 2010.
7   Democratic Caucus Retreat.
8   "Google's Eric Schmidt", *op. cit.*
9   "Procter & Gamble: Tumble cycle", Jonathan Birchall, *Financial Times*, 17 December 2009.
10 Purchasing price parity (PPP) adjusted GDP, WPP Annual Report 2006, p. 87.
11 "The N-11: More than an Acronym", Goldman Sachs, March 2007.
12 *CorpComms* magazine, July 2007, www.thecrossbordergroup.com/cc_archive/pages/1516/June+2007.stm?article_id=11897.
13 Heidrick & Struggles Breakfast with the Board, 3 December 2007, attended by over 60 CEOs and chairmen.
14 *Mapping Global Talent: Essays and Insights*, Heidrick & Struggles, September 2007, compiled in cooperation with the Economist Intelligence Unit.
15 "Tesco gets more convenient," news.bbc.co.uk, 30 October, 2002.
16 "Tesco acquires Dobbies Garden," Financial Deals Tracker, 22 November 2007.
17 "Tesco moves in on the housing market," *Daily Telegraph*, Nick Britten, 2 July 2007.
18 "Sir Terry Leahy," Andrew Cave, *Daily Telegraph*, 21 November 2005.
19 *Ibid.*
20 http://news.bbc.co.uk/2/hi/business/4436113.stm.
21 *Ibid.*
22 http://search.ft.com/ftArticle?queryText=Alison+Maitland+Sir+terry+leahy&y=4&aje=true&x=6&id=030730000812&ct=0.
23 Business Today, International Conference Keynote, Spring 2009.
24 "The Monday Interview: Mick Davis, Chief executive, Xstrata, Big hitter prepares Xstrata for joining the market's elite," *The Times*, Nigel Cope, 11 March 2002.
25 Unless otherwise noted, quotes in this profile are from a lecture and round-table discussion at Cornell University Department of Applied Economics and Management, 19 October 2007.
26 "Irene Rosenfeld, the big cheese who wants to go to work on a creme egg", Stephen Foley, *Independent*, 13 September 2009.

27 "Irene Rosenfeld, Cadbury's new best friend who dared mess with the Oreo", Chris Blackhurst, *Evening Standard*, 20 January 2010.

28 "About Irene Rosenfeld", www.kraftfoodcompany.com.

29 www.wpp.com/WPP/About/whoweare/History.htm; "The interview: Sir Martin Sorrell, Chief Executive of WPP," Damian Reece, *Independent*, 26 March 2005.

30 WPP Annual Report 2007.

31 www.wpp.com/WPP/About/whoweare/History.htm.

32 "Martin Sorrell: Persistence and determination," *Benjamin's Boardroom*, CNN, 16 December 2005.

33 *Ibid*.

34 *Ibid*.

35 "£30m payout for ex-wife eases misery of divorce," *The Times*, 24 October 2005.

36 "The Sunday interview: Charles Dunstone (the TalkTalk man)," Simon Fluendy, *Mail on Sunday*, 5 November 2006.

37 *Ibid*.

38 www.bp.com/onefeedsection.do?categoryId = 773&contentId = 2002459; Heidrick & Struggles analysis.

39 *Sydney Morning Herald*, 2 May 2007.

40 *Ibid*.

41 *Management Today* Annual Awards.

42 "Sun King of the oil industry," Tobias Buck and David Buchan, *Financial Times*, 12 January 2007 and as updated in conversation with Lord Browne.

43 *Ibid*.

44 *Ibid*.

45 *Ibid*.

46 "BP executive slams strategy," Caroline Muspratt, *Daily Telegraph*, 19 December 2006.

47 www.chemsafety.gov/index.cfm?folder = current_investigations&page = info &INV_ID=52.

48 www.boardex.com.

49 Andrew White, ArabianBusiness.com, 5 December 2009.

50 "Why Barclays banks on this Oxford ascetic," Andrew Davidson, *Sunday Times*, 6 August 2006.

51 Google Founders' Letter and Owners Manual, 2004.

52 Tony Robbins, "Unleash the Power Within," London 2008; interview May 2008.

53 *Tomorrow's Global Company: Challenges and Choices*, Tomorrow's Company Inquiry, 2007.

54 Localization of MNOs panel discussion, China Entrepreneurs Summit, Beijing World Hotel, 6 December 2009.

55 Google Founders' Letter, 2005.

56 *The Master Strategist: Power, Purpose, and Principle*, Ketan Patel, Random House, 2005.

57 Jeannie J Yi and Shawn X Ye, "The Haier Way: The Making of a Chinese Business Leader and a Global Brand".

58 Tom Peters, London, Autumn 2007.

59 Leaders in India Business Forum, moderated by Steve Tappin, Mumbai, October 2009.

60 *Route to the Top: A Transatlantic Comparison of Top Business Leaders*, Dr Elisabeth Marx, Heidrick & Struggles.

61 *Ibid.*

62 Quoted in "The World's Most Admired Companies," *Fortune*, 24 March 2008, page 43.

63 Heidrick & Struggles survey, 2007.

64 Alan Watkins, Cardio-Coherence, based on >1,000 monitoring sessions with senior executives.

65 *The Feeling of What Happens: Body and Emotion in the Making of Consciousness*, Antonio Damasio, Harvest Books, 2000.

66 Alan Watkins.

INDEX